Becoming Carole Lombard

Becoming Carole Lombard

Stardom, Comedy, and Legacy

Olympia Kiriakou

BLOOMSBURY ACADEMIC
NEW YORK • LONDON • OXFORD • NEW DELHI • SYDNEY

BLOOMSBURY ACADEMIC
Bloomsbury Publishing Inc
1385 Broadway, New York, NY 10018, USA
50 Bedford Square, London, WC1B 3DP, UK
29 Earlsfort Terrace, Dublin 2, Ireland

BLOOMSBURY, BLOOMSBURY ACADEMIC and the Diana logo
are trademarks of Bloomsbury Publishing Plc

First published in the United States of America 2020
This paperback edition published in 2021

Copyright © Olympia Kiriakou, 2020

For legal purposes the Acknowledgments on p. x constitute an
extension of this copyright page.

Cover design by Ben Anslow | Cover photograph © Alamy

All rights reserved. No part of this publication may be reproduced or transmitted
in any form or by any means, electronic or mechanical, including photocopying,
recording, or any information storage or retrieval system, without
prior permission in writing from the publishers.

Bloomsbury Publishing Inc does not have any control over, or responsibility for,
any third-party websites referred to or in this book. All internet addresses given
in this book were correct at the time of going to press. The author and publisher
regret any inconvenience caused if addresses have changed or sites have ceased
to exist, but can accept no responsibility for any such changes.

Library of Congress Cataloging-in-Publication Data
Names: Kiriakou, Olympia, author.
Title: Becoming Carole Lombard : stardom, comedy and legacy / Olympia Kiriakou.
Description: New York : Bloomsbury Academic, 2020. |
Includes bibliographical references and index.
Identifiers: LCCN 2019034894 (print) | LCCN 2019034895 (ebook) |
ISBN 9781501350733 (hardback) | ISBN 9781501350740 (epub) |
ISBN 9781501350757 (pdf)
Subjects: LCSH: Lombard, Carole, 1908–1942. |
Motion picture actors and actresses–United States–Biography.
Classification: LCC PN2287.L625 K57 2020 (print) |
LCC PN2287.L625 (ebook) | DDC 791.4302/8092 [B]–dc23
LC record available at https://lccn.loc.gov/2019034894
LC ebook record available at https://lccn.loc.gov/2019034895

ISBN:	HB:	978-1-5013-5073-3
	PB:	978-1-5013-8583-4
	ePDF:	978-1-5013-5075-7
	eBook:	978-1-5013-5074-0

Typeset by Integra Software Services Pvt. Ltd.

To find out more about our authors and books visit www.bloomsbury.com
and sign up for our newsletters.

CONTENTS

List of Figures vi
Acknowledgments x

Introduction: Carole Lombard, the screwball girl? 1

1   Slapstick, body politics, and Sennett Girl Comedies 13

2   Hollywood's best-dressed star, 1929–1934 49

3   The queen of screwball comedy 71

4   "Goodbye Carole 'screwball' Lombard; Hello Mrs. 'Ma' Gable": gender, identity, and the classical Hollywood star couple 135

5   Lombard gets dramatic: melodrama, domesticity, and performance 155

6   "If women ruled the world": Lombard as protofeminist 177

Conclusion: Carole Lombard's legacy, 1942–present 197

Bibliography 209
Index 226

FIGURES

1.1 & 1.2 Lombard frequently played adolescent characters in Sennett's films. She is pictured here as Norma Nurmi in *Run, Girl, Run* (Alfred J. Goulding, 1928). 29

1.3 In this still from *Run, Girl, Run*, Coach Minnie Marmon (Daphne Pollard) pleads with Sunnydale School's track star, Norma Nurmi (Lombard), to give it her all in her final race. This film gave Lombard the chance to show off her athletic prowess. 30

1.4 Carole Lombard's first appearance in *The Campus Vamp* (Harry Edwards, 1928) embodies her character's youthful energy and spirit. 33

1.5 Lombard (right, holding bat) again demonstrates her "natural athleticism" while playing baseball in a scene from *The Campus Vamp*. 35

1.6 *Matchmaking Mamma* (Harry Edwards, 1929) was one of several films produced for Mack Sennett's "Girl Comedies" series. These films were structured to showcase the physical allure of Sennett's "Bathing Beauties." 44

1.7 In shorts like *Matchmaking Mamma*, Mack Sennett used Technicolor film stock to emphasize the visual spectacle of his "Bathing Beauties." 46

2.1 Carole Lombard and William Powell became a real-life couple while making *Man of the World* (Richard Wallace, 1931). The pair were married on June 6, 1931. Although they divorced less than two years later, they remained friends for the rest of Lombard's life. 58

2.2	Carole Lombard is pictured alongside Fredric March in *The Eagle and the Hawk* (Stuart Walker and Mitchell Leisen, 1933). Her character's name, The Beautiful Lady, signifies the extent to which Lombard's star persona in the early 1930s centered around glamour. 63
3.1	In *Twentieth Century* (Howard Hawks, 1934), Oscar Jaffe (John Barrymore, pictured top left) draws chalk lines for ingenue Lily Garland (Lombard, pictured bottom right) during a play rehearsal. This film is considered one of the first screwball comedies. 82
3.2	Lily's feigned outburst reveals her emotional and behavioral similarities with mentor, Oscar. 84
3.3 & 3.4	Lily confronts Oscar over his controlling behavior. These film stills capture how Lombard uses physicality to represent Lily's frustration. 87
3.5 & 3.6	In *Love Before Breakfast* (Walter Lang, 1936) Kay Colby (Lombard) gets a black eye after being punched in a police wagon. Lombard's performance in this film represents the balance between physicality and physical beauty underpinning her star image. 93
3.7	In *My Man Godfrey* (Gregory La Cava, 1936) Lombard plays opposite her ex-husband, William Powell. He agreed to play the title role only if Lombard was cast as the scatterbrained heiress, Irene Bullock. 98
3.8 & 3.9	Lombard uses her body and voice to convey Irene's feigned hysterics. 101
3.10	In what is arguably Lombard's most physically demanding role, Hazel Flagg is punched and kicked by her love interest, Wallace Cook, in *Nothing Sacred* (William Wellman, 1937). This action was deemed inappropriate by the Production Code Administration's head, Joseph Breen, but he ultimately agreed to leave it in the film because it would "cause great difficulty to delete it." 108

3.11 & 3.12	Hazel's feisty personality is on display in these stills from *Nothing Sacred*. This film and, in particular, Lombard's performance, led to a trend in the late 1930s of films that featured female physicality. 110
3.13 & 3.14	Although Hazel is tough and combative, she is also conventionally feminine in appearance. Hazel's contradictions speaks to the complexity of Lombard's own star persona. 117
3.15 & 3.16	Ann (Lombard) and David (Robert Montgomery) Smith play footsie under the breakfast table in *Mr. & Mrs. Smith* (Alfred Hitchcock, 1941). These shots cleverly reveal the couple's mutual sexual attraction and emotional range. 122
3.17	Ann hides her true feelings toward David by pretending to have trouble putting on her skis. 123
3.18	The final shot of crossed skis is a subtle yet evocative confirmation of Ann and David's sexual reconciliation. Filmmakers in the classical Hollywood period often had to rely on visual or dialog innuendo to work around the Production Code's strict moral guidelines. 126
3.19	Carole Lombard radiates an "effulgent dazzle" in her first appearance in *To Be or Not to Be* (Ernst Lubitsch, 1942). 128
3.20	Maria Tura (Lombard) uses her feminine charm and physical beauty to seduce Nazi Alexander Siletsky (Stanley Ridges). 131
4.1	Although they did not become an off-screen couple until 1936, Carole Lombard and second husband Clark Gable's screen chemistry is evident in *No Man of Her Own* (Wesley Ruggles, 1932). 139

4.2	Carole Lombard and Clark Gable's Encino ranch was symbolic of their atypical Hollywood star personas. (Copyright holder unknown.) 146
5.1 & 5.2	Carole Lombard appears as Jane Mason in *Made for Each Other* (John Cromwell, 1939). This was the first of a series of melodramatic roles Lombard played in the late 1930s and early 1940s in an effort to prove that she was not just a comedic actress. 159
5.3 & 5.4	Lombard's performance style in her dramatic films was often understated and introspective, as illustrated in these film stills from *Made for Each Other*. 160
5.5 & 5.6	While audiences were likely more familiar with Lombard's high energy, full body screwball performance style, in dramatic roles like Julie Eden in *In Name Only* (John Cromwell, 1939), she conveys restrained emotion through her face and voice. 164
5.7 & 5.8	In *Vigil in the Night* (George Stevens, 1940) Lombard plays an English nurse named Anne Lee, who faces a smallpox epidemic in her underfunded hospital. This is arguably Lombard's most unglamorous and complex role, allowing her to demonstrate her performative versatility. 170
6.1	In this June 1937 *Photoplay* article, Carole Lombard offers her "rules" for women to be successful at work and home. These types of publicity materials worked in tandem with her screen image to reinforce her independent star persona. (Copyright holder unknown.) 182

ACKNOWLEDGMENTS

I would first like to express my gratitude to Gerald Sim, whose mentorship and friendship over the past decade has guided me to this point. His "Film Appreciation" was the first film course I had ever taken, and I enjoyed it so much that I decided to switch my major to film studies. During my four years at Florida Atlantic University, I was inspired by Gerald's pedagogy, sense of humor, and commitment to athleisure. In the time since, I have looked to Gerald for advice, and I am grateful for his continued support and encouragement.

This book would not exist without the support of Ginette Vincendeau and Tom Brown. Our conversations often allowed me to think about my project from new perspectives, and I always felt inspired by their astute guidance, passion, and patience. I'd also like to thank the exceptional faculty at FAU's School of Communication and Multimedia Studies and the Cinema Studies Institute at the University of Toronto. My courses with Stephen Charbonneau and Chris Robé have had a lasting impact on my love for film history and archival research. I would also like to acknowledge Chris Scodari, Mike Budd, Charlie Keil, Corinn Columpar, Nic Sammond, Angelica Fenner, Meghan Sutherland, and James Cahill, whose feedback on my research and writing allowed me to become a better film scholar. Christine Geraghty and Tamar Jeffers McDonald offered invaluable feedback and suggestions, particularly regarding the fan magazine resources I used throughout this book. Great thanks to my editor, Katie Gallof, for her enthusiasm in the book, and to the anonymous peer reviewers whose comments significantly improved this project.

I had the pleasure of discussing Lombard with some fantastic historians. Christina Lane graciously pointed me in the direction of some Lombard scholarship. Robert Matzen helped tremendously with verifying the date of Lombard's car accident, and reworking the timeline of her early career. Thank you to Vincent Paterno of Carole & Co. and Meredith of Dear Mr. Gable, whose websites served as invaluable reference points for my archival research.

I'm also grateful to the archivists and librarians in the archive collections that were integral to this book. Thanks to the staff at the Motion Picture and Television Reading Room at the Library of Congress, and to Sarah

Currant and Ian O'Sullivan the BFI Reuben Library. Mark Quigley at the UCLA Film and Television Archive helped with Lombard's silent films, and I appreciate his assistance in locating some of her hard-to-find shorts.

My friends in Toronto, Florida, and London cheered me on when the thought of revisions seemed too much to bear—thanks for the endless food breaks and Real Housewives gossip. To Baba and Dedo, for their continued support from Havergal to King's. To Anthony, for keeping everything in perspective. My dad, Peter, visited me in London and always pushed me to step out of my comfort zone. The most significant influence in my passion for old Hollywood is my mom, Anita. She first introduced me to *Gone With the Wind* when I was a child, and despite my initial protests that the film was too long, she insisted that one day I would come to appreciate it; by the time I was a teenager, I realized she was right. This and other times spent watching old Hollywood movies cultivated in me a deep interest in stardom and performance, and she encouraged me to turn this interest into my career.

Introduction

Carole Lombard, the screwball girl?

> *She gets up too early, plays tennis too hard, wastes time and feeling on trifles and drinks Coca-Colas the way Samuel Johnson used to drink tea. She is a scribbler on telephone pads, inhibited nail-nibbler, toe-scuffler, pillow-grabber, head-and-elbow scratcher and chain cigarette smoker. When Carole Lombard talks, her conversation, often brilliant, is punctuated by screeches, laughs, growls, gesticulations and the expletive of a sailor'parrot.*[1]

Noel F. Busch's observation in the October 17, 1938 issue of *Life* magazine encapsulates the prevailing conception of Carole Lombard's star persona and her relationship with screwball comedy. Over the past eighty years, similar observations have contextualized Lombard's star and screen personas in relation to the screwball genre. There has been limited engagement with Lombard's non-screwball films, signaling both an incomplete discourse about Lombard's screwball connections and a misunderstanding of Lombard's stardom, film performances, and career as a whole. While Lombard did achieve her greatest success in screwball comedy, she also worked extensively in other genres and had a star persona that evolved significantly in name,[2] image and style. Lombard was more than just a screwball comedian: she was also a performer in varying genres, a popular media figure whose personal

---

[1] Noel F. Busch, "A Loud Cheer for The Screwball Girl," *Life*, October 17, 1938, 48–50.
[2] Lombard was born Jane Alice Peters, and in the early 1930s briefly went by 'Carol' Lombard.

and professional life developed in phases within the Hollywood studio system, one half of two different star couples,[3] and a public personality who intervened in the cultural and political landscape of the 1930s and 1940s.

Busch's quotation is a productive starting point since it is one of the most frequently cited observations about Lombard. It has been widely disseminated in retrospective assessments of Lombard,[4] likely because it summarizes the ineffable qualities attributed to her star persona that are tough to pinpoint in writing. He invokes aural and kinetic imagery in his description, paralleling Lombard's energetic, physically active and modern screwball heroines like Lily Garland from *Twentieth Century* (Howard Hawks, 1934), Irene Bullock from *My Man Godfrey* (Gregory LaCava, 1936), and Hazel Flagg from *Nothing Sacred* (William Wellman, 1937). His words all but bring Lombard to life, a sign of just how integral sound and physicality are to her screwball persona, and to screwball comedy more generally.[5]

Later in his article, Busch offers insight into the social impact of Lombard's zany screwball star persona. Gesturing to the United States's tempestuous political and economic climate in the late 1930s, he claims that she represents "a quality that is currently more precious to the U.S. public ... utter undependability."[6] Lombard embodied the dynamic, vigorous, and impulsive prewar innocence of screwball comedy. Yet at the same time, her impish personality offered American audiences a distraction from the country's uncertain future; her screen persona brought them into fantastic worlds where the economic bleakness of the Depression was shrouded by humor and happy endings. Off screen, Lombard personified 1930s progressive American femininity. Throughout the decade she was a vocal supporter of President Franklin Delano Roosevelt's New Deal economic reform programs, and was also a visible figure in contemporaneous sociopolitical debates about women's rights in the workplace, increased representation of women in politics,[7] and financial independence as a

---

[3] She was first married to William Powell (1931–1933), then to Clark Gable (1939–1942).

[4] For example, see: "Carole Lombard," *Dear Mr. Gable*, accessed November 17, 2015, http://dearmrgable.com/?page_id=3216; Robert Matzen, *Carole Lombard: A bio-bibliography* (Westport: Greenwood Press, 1988), 26; Wes D. Gehring, *Carole Lombard: The Hoosier Tornado* (Indianapolis: Indiana Historical Society Press, 2003), 173.

[5] Jane M. Greene, "A Proper Dash of Spice: Screwball Comedy and the Production Code," *Journal of Film and Video* 63, no. 3 (Fall 2011): 48. See also: Alex Clayton, *The Body in Hollywood Slapstick* (Jefferson, NC: McFarland & Company, Inc., 2007), 138; Tina Olsin Lent, "Romantic Love and Friendship: "The Redefinition of Gender Relations in Screwball Comedy," in *Classical Hollywood Comedy*, eds. Kristine Brunovska Karnick and Henry Jenkins (New York: Routledge, 1995), 328.

[6] Busch, 48.

[7] Ronald Colman, Cary Grant, Carole Lombard, Groucho Marx, Lawrence Tibbett, "The Circle," NBC-Red, Hollywood, CA: January 22, 1939.

solution to gender inequality.[8] Although her star persona itself was often framed by patriarchal discourse, particularly during her marriages to Hollywood stars William Powell and Clark Gable, Lombard nonetheless transcended the gender boundaries of the 1930s through her headstrong and independent nature, and her progressive politics should be viewed within the context of the volatile domestic and international economic, social, and political climate.[9]

Busch's quotation is but one of several dozen interpretations of Carole Lombard's stardom, and he frames her star image as an extension of her on-screen persona as if the two were one and the same. The image he paints of Lombard was a common one found in contemporaneous popular media. Consider a sampling of similar descriptions from fan magazine articles written between 1937 and 1939, the years in which Lombard was at the height of her screwball fame:

She's harum-scarum, she dances in the park at 3 a.m., she dotes on practical jokes, she hates pink, and she's so impulsive she almost lives behind the eight-ball.[10]

Candid! Why it's the very stuff she's made of. Painfully frank all her life, conscientiously brutal, especially where she herself is concerned ...[11]

Screwy? Insane? Balmy? — Okay, then, make the most of it. I simply can't help it. I'm going to tell you about Carole Lombard's home life, and that's all there is to it. You can take it or leave it. All I've got to say is this—when it comes to the business of getting the most downright, sheer fun out of this usually drab business of living, then I hand all prizes unreservedly to Carole Lombard.[12]

Carole stares life smack in the face and laughs ... We walked over to her bungalow, Carole and I. At least, I walked. Carole got there by executing a few spirals and curves and a leap upon her scooter-bike which stands in front of her bungalow handy for her excursions around the lot ... She is "almost forever" laughing, is Carole. She is like something wound up at high tension. But as high tension is her natural métier it is natural.[13]

---

[8]George Madden, "Hollywood is Ruled by Women," *Movie Mirror*, 1934, 46–47.
[9]For example, in her "If Women Ruled" segment from NBC's short-lived program *The Circle*, Lombard encouraged the idea of women entering in national and international politics, and argued they would be more reasonable, non-combative, and level-headed than the male leaders of the Allied war effort. Please see: Ronald Colman, Cary Grant, Carole Lombard, Groucho Marx, Lawrence Tibbett, "The Circle," NBC-Red, Hollywood, CA: January 22, 1939.
[10]Marian Rhea, "Lombard Unlimited," *Radio Mirror*, April 1939, 18.
[11]Katharine Hartley, "What's Become of the Good Scout?" *Modern Screen* (August 1938), 86.
[12]Harry Lang, "The Utterly Balmy Home Life of Carole Lombard," *Motion Picture* (February 1937), 36.
[13]Gladys Hall, "Lombard – As She Sees Herself," *Motion Picture* (November 1938), 35.

Though varied in approach, these quotations mirror Busch's assessment of Lombard's star persona, and the magazine articles from which these statements originate draw symbiotic connections between her "reel" and "real" identities. It is not my intention to assess whether she was as "screwy" as these columnists deemed her to be; I have no way of knowing Lombard's "authentic" self, nor does that line of inquiry get to the heart of understanding "Carole Lombard" as a constructed star image. Rather, I am interested in the way these observations have been amalgamated to form her public identity, and the construction of her star persona rather than the "truth" of said discourse.

In death, popular media sources have uniformly stressed the significance of screwball comedy to Lombard's star persona. Consider the major posthumously released biographies: Larry Swindell's *Screwball: The Life Story of Carole Lombard* (1975), Wes Gehring's *Carole Lombard: The Hoosier Tornado* (2003), Robert Matzen's *Fireball: Carole Lombard and the Mystery of Flight 3* (2014), and Michelle Morgan's *Carole Lombard: Twentieth-Century Star* (2016). Although each writer adopts diverging methodologies and addresses Lombard in different contexts,[14] all of the titles use words or phrases that place an emphasis on the screwball qualities of Lombard's star persona.[15] Likewise, the biopic *Gable and Lombard* (Sidney J. Furie, 1976) goes to great lengths to validate Lombard's screwball reputation. Besides the film's historical and chronological inaccuracies, *Gable and Lombard* offers a one-dimensional portrayal of Lombard that is based primarily upon her screwball image. Her character—played by Jill Clayburgh—comes across as wildly unstable, an impression made clear by the film's opening scene when she arrives at a posh Hollywood party in an ambulance wearing a hospital gown. Lombard did, allegedly, arrive at the party in this fashion[16] but without the proper historical context— the so-called "Nervous Breakdown Party" was given by Jock Whitney on February 7, 1936 in honor of screenwriter Donald Ogden Stewart's wife having just been released from a sanitarium[17]—her bizarre entrance makes no sense other than to confirm her "authentic" screwball proclivities.

---

[14]Morgan's book is a popular biography, and focuses heavily on Lombard's childhood, private life, and her relationships with husbands William Powell and Clark Gable. By contrast, Gehring's book was published by the Indiana Historical Society Press, and emphasizes Lombard's "Hoosier" origins. Finally, Matzen's book includes biographical information but mainly offers a meticulously detailed chronological account of the events leading up to and immediately following the January 16, 1942 crash of TWA flight 3.

[15]Michelle Morgan's subtitle "Twentieth-Century Star" primarily alludes to Lombard's modernity, however it could also be interpreted as a reference to the actress's first screwball comedy, *Twentieth Century* (Howard Hawks, 1934).

[16]Gehring, 131.

[17]Leo Townsend, "Good News," *Modern Screen*, March 1936, 13. See also: Matzen, 96.

Rethinking Lombard's stardom

The book's title, *Becoming Carole Lombard: Stardom, Comedy, and Legacy*, gestures to the cultural, industrial, and ideological factors involved in building Lombard's star persona. My aim is to challenge the prevailing discourse about Carole Lombard as a star restricted to the realm of screwball comedy, but I also hope to demonstrate how she is a productive case study to probe other topics in film studies. Understanding the dimensions of Lombard's star persona speaks to the mutually constitutive relationship between a star and their screen image. Of this phenomenon, Barry King writes, "the persona is in itself a character, but one that transcends placement or containment in a particular narrative and exists in cinematic rather than filmic time and space."[18] Stars exist in "cinematic" rather than "filmic" time and space, which suggests that the star's image both arises from and preempts their individual performances. The changing status of Lombard's stardom from the mid1930s to today exposes the potentially negative consequences of such a tight relationship between star, character, and genre, because her work in screwball comedy has eclipsed any variances in her career and public image. The star-character symbiosis that is central to discussions about Hollywood stardom is useful in analyses of Lombard's screwball films, but it also has the adverse effect of making her stardom appear one-dimensional.

Paul McDonald argues that single-stars [had] "dual capacity as labour and capital," and stars like Lombard were identities manufactured by the Hollywood studios and publicity outlets. But they also became a "form of capital inasmuch as his or her own image can be used to create advantage in the market for films and secure profits."[19] Lombard's stardom is not unusual in the sense that her image was also constructed, and throughout this book I outline the immense and often highly publicized efforts that went into transforming Jane Alice Peters into Carole Lombard. From 1921 to 1942—the year of her first film and the year of her death, respectively—Lombard's stardom took on many forms: from a slapstick player to a glamour girl, then to a screwball comedienne and in the last years of her life, before her untimely death, to a contented housewife—or at least someone happy to present this image. The sheer fact that her persona underwent such drastic changes in just over two decades confirms the ephemerality of her screwball identity.

Finally, while I argue that Carole Lombard is more than just a screwball comedienne, it is also important to acknowledge the impact her stardom has had on subsequent female comedians, the continued influence screwball

---

[18] Barry King, "Articulating Stardom," in *Star Texts: Image and Performance in Film and Television*, ed. Jeremy Butler (Detroit: Wayne State University Press, 1991), 147.
[19] Paul McDonald, *The Star System: Hollywood's Production of Popular Identities* (New York: Wallflower Press, 2000), 13.

comedy plays on Lombard's star persona, and the legacy of her stardom more broadly. This book therefore explores the mystery of stardom and legacy more generally, and uses Lombard as a case study to probe the question of why some stars remain popular while others do not.

The single-star method and textual analysis

Despite Carole Lombard's immense success, box-office bankability, and impact on the progressive feminist politics of the 1930s and early 1940s, historical and theoretical works about her are sparse.[20] As the first book-length study about Lombard, my research will trace the evolution of her star persona and film performances as they intersect with the industrial and cultural politics of the classical Hollywood period. While some may fear that single-star studies can be limited in their scope, Lisa Downing and Sue Harris note that, in fact, this approach "allows for a careful analysis of the way in which a given star text signifies in a number of contexts."[21] Such a rationale makes sense: stars do not simply exist in a vacuum, but are products of a complex industrial system with ideological and cultural implications. The single-star method offers scholars the opportunity to address wider topics in film and media studies through the lens of one star; they are therefore the primary but not singular focus of the scholarship. A multifaceted star like Carole Lombard can become a vehicle to interrogate larger ideas about independent stardom in the classical Hollywood period, feminist ideology, body politics in the 1930s, the star couple, and performance in slapstick and screwball comedy.

In light of the absence of scholarly writing on Lombard's non-screwball films, as well as limited attention to the contours of her comic performance style, it is out of necessity that this book relies significantly on textual analysis. For a variety of reasons including limited accessibility and overall academic neglect, most of the films that I discuss—particularly Lombard's silent comedies and her dramatic films—have been under-studied by biographers and historians. This book will therefore be the first to offer an extended analysis of Lombard's ever-changing star persona and of her film performances across genres and in different performative contexts.

---

[20]For scholarship about Lombard, see: Robert Matzen's *Fireball: Carole Lombard and the Mystery of Flight 3* (2017); Michelle Morgan's *Carole Lombard: Twentieth Century Star* (2017); Michael Hammond's "Good Fellowship: Carole Lombard and Clark Gable," in *First Comes Love: Power Couples Celebrity Kinship and Cultural Politics* (2015); Emily Carman's *Introduction to Independent Stardom: Freelance Women in the Hollywood Studio System* (2015).

[21]Lisa Downing and Sue Harris, *From Perversion to Purity: the stardom of Catherine Deneuve* (Manchester: Manchester University Press, 2007), 8.

The book's methodology also brings together a range of archival research including trade papers, newspapers, studio contracts, and fan magazines. My strong reliance on Hollywood fan magazines as cultural, ideological, and material arbiters of stardom in 1930s and prewar Hollywood brings up the question of how to critically engage with these sources, particularly in light of what Mark Glancy describes as historians' "lingering suspicions of their neutrality and transparency."[22] Given the history of the fan magazine and its role in cultivating stardom in the classical Hollywood period, this suspicion is entirely justified.

By the mid 1930s there were growing concerns from the Production Code Administration (PCA) that pressure from the Hollywood studios' publicity departments led fan magazine editors and writers to "create false impressions in the minds of the public" about Hollywood stars through "inaccuracies, misrepresentation and exaggerations."[23] In response, on August 15, 1934 fifteen magazine editors signed a pledge to publish "clean, constructive and honest material." Additionally, the Studio Publicity Directors Committee arm of the Association of Motion Picture Producers devised a "whitelist" that contained the names of "fifty approved scribes who could be counted on to write tastefully"[24] and who would, in return, be "allowed access to the studio and stars."[25]

The first mass-produced fan magazine was *Motion Picture News Story*, which began in 1911 as a monthly publication "devoted primarily to 'fictionalizing' current films into story form and illustrating them with publicity stills."[26] By 1914, there were "fewer, and shorter, stories ... and many more photographs and articles about stars"; by 1916, the word "story" was dropped from the title.[27] Fan magazines like the newly renamed *Motion Picture Magazine, Photoplay,* and *Screenland* shifted their focus to stories and gossip about Hollywood stars that would allegedly give readers "inside information"[28] in order to create "awareness of stars in the run-up to new releases and, just as importantly, to maintain this awareness in the gaps between film appearances."[29] Tamar Jeffers McDonald writes

---

[22]Mark Glancy, "*Picturegoer*: The Fan Magazine and Popular Film Culture in Britain During the Second World War," *Historical Journal of Film, Radio and Television* Vol. 31, No. 4 (December 2011): 455.

[23]Mary Desjardins, "'Fan Magazine Trouble': The AMPP, Studio Publicity Directors, and the Hollywood Press, 1945–1952," *Film History* Vol. 26, No. 3 (2014): 33.

[24]Ibid, 51.

[25]Desjardins, 33.

[26]Adrienne McLean, "'New Films in Story Form': Movie Story Magazine and Spectatorship," *Cinema Journal* 42, no. 3 (Spring 2003): 3.

[27]Ibid.

[28]Glancy, 457.

[29]Tamar Jeffers McDonald, *Doris Day Confidential: Hollywood, Sex and Stardom* (New York: Palgrave Macmillan, 2013), 35.

that the fan magazines "sought to entice readers to see the latest films of their favorite stars, but also served as a means of keeping in touch with them, maintaining a relationship, when the movies were over."[30] The fan magazines cultivated these relationships by promoting an "interactive culture" with their readers through fan mail and correspondence, contests, and self-improvement advice columns that would "transform spectators *of* celebrity culture into participators *in* celebrity culture" (italics original).[31] In doing so, they "endowed readers with a sense that they had a direct impact" on the film industry and the stars "through their participation in or refusal of certain aspects of consumer culture."[32]

The overwhelming percentage of fan magazine readers in the 1930s and early 1940s were middle-class women, and through a focus on "matters relating to fashion, entertaining, and home decorating"[33] the magazines "offered women a variety of ways" to become invested in the movies and stars featured in them, and to "negotiate their own identities beyond their everyday, lived experiences."[34] Fan magazine stories and glamorous covers featuring Hollywood stars were "windows" to the average female reader's "future self, hinting that she will attain these ideal visions" by being an active consumer.[35] So, for example, when a star like Carole Lombard offered advice on how to plan a party[36] or how a woman can succeed in the business world[37] in separate issues of *Photoplay*, the articles were meant to be "glimpses" into Lombard's personal life. Critically, too, they functioned as aspirational "how-to" guides which female readers could use to improve their own lives.[38]

The Hollywood fan magazines' other important and intrinsically related relationship was with the Hollywood studios. Anthony Slide describes it as "incestuous," built upon "trust and mutual necessity."[39] The studios needed the fan magazines "as a collective mouthpiece," while the magazines relied on the "publicity photographs and access to the stars and to the filmmaking

---

[30]Ibid.

[31]Marsha Orgeron, "'You Are Invited to Participate': Interactive Fandom in the Age of the Movie Magazine," *Journal of Film and Video* 61, no. 3 (Fall 2009): 4.

[32]Ibid, 7.

[33]Glancy, 457.

[34]Orgeron, 8.

[35]Ellen McCraken, *Decoding Women's Magazines: From Mademoiselle to Ms.* (London: MacMillan Press, 1993), 13.

[36]Julie Lang Hunt, "How Carole Lombard Plans A Party," *Photoplay*, February 1935, 47.

[37]Hart Seymore, "Carole Lombard tells: How I Live By A Man's Code," *Photoplay*, June 1937, 12.

[38]Richard Ohmann, Selling Culture: Magazines, Markets, and Class at the Turn of the Century (London: Verso, 1996), 220.

[39]Anthony Slide, *Inside the Hollywood Fan Magazine: A History of Star Makers, Fabricators, and Gossip Mongers* (Jackson: University Press of Mississippi, 2010), 7.

process," without which they would have "nothing to offer."[40] The studio publicity departments' roles in this relationship were to control and shape the public discourse about their rosters of stars.[41] They worked with the magazines to release curated stories that would reinforce a star's persona, so much so that by the mid 1930s, "virtually all fan magazines were submitting stories for studio approval prior to publication."[42]

Fan magazines are invaluable resources because they provide us with snapshots of how studios molded public discourse to promote and cultivate a star's public persona, as well as the relationship between a star's off-screen image and their film roles. Nevertheless, the consolidation of information about Hollywood stars into the hands of a few powerful individuals necessitates that we read fan magazines and other popular sources with a critically detached eye. With each story we must ask what type of information was being disseminated and why; by doing so, we can begin to understand that what was written largely aimed to preserve and promote a star's studio-engineered persona. Although magazine studies is not a new area in film scholarship, this book's focus on Lombard's stardom is part of an ongoing discussion about the levels of industrialized studio labor and publicity mediation that are involved in producing and sustaining a cohesive star figure. It is therefore important to document the symbiotic relationship between Lombard's on-screen roles and the carefully crafted discourse about her evolving star persona, and how these sources promulgated ideological, moral, and cultural positions about femininity in 1930s and early 1940s America.

Chapter breakdown

This book aims to explain Lombard's historiographical value as a star and performer beyond screwball comedy. It asks the question: in light of Carole Lombard's transformative star persona and work in diverse genres, what is it about Lombard that made her such a perfect fit for screwball comedy, and in what ways have her screwball associations impacted her career and star persona? Additionally, this book explores how Lombard's stardom intersects with a multitude of areas concerning the ideological and cultural implications of female comedy, genre, star couples, and independent stardom, proving her value to various realms within film studies. It progresses chronologically, beginning with her formative years in Hollywood as one of slapstick comedy pioneer Mack Sennett's Bathing Beauties, to her work as

---

[40]Ibid.
[41]Desjardins, 38.
[42]Slide, 8.

a contract star at Paramount Pictures, to her later years as a freelance artist and budding film producer and, finally, to an analysis of her posthumous stardom over the nearly eighty years since her death.

Chapter 1 focuses on Lombard's career between 1921 and 1929, beginning with Lombard's first film roles through to her two-year tenure with Mack Sennett. In total, Lombard made eighteen one- and two-reel comedies between 1927 and 1929 while working at the Keystone Film Company.[43] This is the first book-length study to offer extended analyses of Lombard's slapstick films, focusing on the juxtaposition between her "feminine" sex appeal and her "masculine" athleticism in her physical comedy performances. This chapter also situates Lombard's slapstick performances against wider industrial and production contexts.

Chapter 2 picks up where the previous chapter ends, exploring Lombard's early sound-era star persona and film roles between 1929 and 1934. Using a case study of Lombard's so-called "Orchid Lady" persona, I explain the multifaceted nature of her stardom beyond screwball comedy. During this period, Lombard performed in a variety of film genres including horror and melodrama, and her accompanying star persona embodied an air of chic refinement that was, in many ways, the antithesis of both her slapstick and screwball identities. I argue against the oft-repeated idea that there is an inherent connection between her slapstick and screwball periods, and seek to understand the ways in which this false claim was reproduced by the Hollywood studios' publicity departments and supported by the popular media in the latter part of the decade, despite historical evidence to the contrary.

Chapter 3 unpacks the details of Lombard's performance style and stardom as it relates to screwball comedy. Building upon the previous chapter's discussion of the female body politics in the silent era, through formal analyses of Lombard's body and voice in five screwball comedy films I examine the demarcation between her conventional feminine beauty and rough-and-tumble physicality. The films I analyze gesture to Lombard's coexistent off-screen star persona, which also centers around her body. Through my focus on female physicality, I situate Lombard's screwball performances against entrenched cultural assumptions about the fragile female body. On a pedagogical level, this chapter's focus on Lombard's physical comedy challenges the established screwball canon and the scholarly portrayal of female physicality in classical Hollywood comedies. For example, scholars such as Stanley Cavell and Alex Clayton both point to Katharine Hepburn's character, Susan Vance, in *Bringing Up Baby* (Howard Hawks, 1938) as an outlier when discussing the relative lack of female physical comedy performance in screwball films. Although

---

[43]Larry Swindell, *Screwball: The Life of Carole Lombard* (New York: William Morrow & Company, 1975), 305.

Bringing Up Baby is a seminal film for comedy scholarship, and while it and Hepburn herself are useful examples to illustrate the possibilities of female physical comedy, it would be productive to widen the scholarly pool to include other stars and films. During her lifetime, Carole Lombard was—and still is today—more closely associated with physical comedy than Katharine Hepburn or any other screwball actress, and should, in my view, take a more prominent position in the comedy corpus.

Chapter 4 addresses Carole Lombard's shifting star persona during her courtship and marriage to top Hollywood star, Clark Gable. During the mid 1930s Lombard's star persona was often situated in discourses that emphasized her independence and unconventional—for its time—progressive gender politics, however, when she married Gable in March 1939, there seemed to be a tension between her single independent identity and her newfound status as a happily domesticated wife. Through formal analyses of fan magazine and popular press discourse I explore how, by the late 1930s, Carole Lombard's star persona was in a state of flux, caught between her screwball and marital identities. While these sides do not necessarily have to be at odds, in Lombard's case, portraying her as a wife and aspiring mother confirmed Hollywood's investment in conservative marital ideology. The chapter presents Lombard's marriage to Gable as a case study to extend the discourse about the levels of industrialized studio labor and publicity mediation that are involved in producing and sustaining a cohesive star figure. I consider how her persona was used, in different ways, by the Hollywood studios to promulgate ideological, moral, and social positions about femininity in 1930s and early 1940s American culture.

By 1939, Lombard was a freelance star, which gave her more control over the types of roles she played and enabled her to articulate the conditions of her labor within the Hollywood studio system. Eager to demonstrate her versatility as an actress, Lombard announced publicly that she would be taking a break from screwball comedy; for the next two years, she appeared in four successive melodramas in which she played women defined by their domesticity.

Chapter 5 argues that Lombard's shift to melodrama worked symbiotically to merge her on- and off-screen personae and strengthened the marital and domestic traits associated with her post 1939 star image. Through an analysis of Lombard's melodrama, this chapter aims to carve out the parameters of melodramatic film acting, places Lombard's dramatic performances in direct contrast to those from her screwball comedies in order to demonstrate the diversity of Lombard's performance style. While Lombard's screwball performances are body-centric and lie primarily in her malleability and ease with physicality, this chapter makes the case that in her dramatic films, she channels her performance inward and reflects her characters' subtle emotional variances through her face and in her voice.

Lombard's screwball persona was also shaped by her personal politics. She was a progressive Democrat and vocal supporter of President Franklin Roosevelt's New Deal social and cultural programs. She also was a proponent of women's rights, advocating for increased representation of women in business and politics.

Chapter 6 explores Carole Lombard's social activism and gender politics and their effects on her independent star persona. I define her as a proto-feminist, someone with a feminist perspective but without a larger movement in which to couch her politics—her views on gender were quite radical for their time, and mirrored those which have come to be associated with the second-wave feminist movement of the 1960s and 1970s. There is an obvious ideological contradiction in Lombard's proto-feminism, largely due to the trappings of traditional femininity and glamour that were essential for a Hollywood actress, and the extent to which her stardom was contained by the cultural framework and ideological apparatus of the Hollywood studio system. This chapter situates Lombard's proto-feminism against the shifting framework of her Hollywood labor, and unpacks the layers of her progressivism in relation to both the gender roles in the 1930s and 1940s and the conservative ideology perpetuated by the Hollywood studios.

This book uncovers the contours of Carole Lombard's stardom and film career in order to make the case that screwball comedy was a significant, but not singular influence on her star persona, and that this association has hindered comprehensive popular and scholarly engagement with her stardom. It seeks to dispel the prevailing conception about Lombard as a performer and star restricted to the realm of screwball comedy to show that, in reality, she was more than just "the Screwball Girl."

1

Slapstick, body politics, and Sennett Girl Comedies

By the time Carole Lombard made her first screwball comedy in 1934, she had already been working steadily in Hollywood for over a decade. Lombard's formative years in Hollywood are critical to a broader understanding of her career, but unfortunately many sources simply treat them as a precursor to her later screwball stardom. As it stands today, however, little if any substantial analysis exists that solely focuses on Lombard's performances in either her silent comedies or early sound films, and those that do tend to use her slapstick comedies to draw parallels to her screwball persona.[1] With hindsight it is easy to fall into the trap of reading her silent films as benchmarks against her later success. Comparisons will inevitably be drawn, and admittedly they are beneficial when trying to establish a cohesive discourse about Lombard's on-screen persona.

This period in Lombard's career has, at least in an academic context, been under-studied. Recent academic scholarship by the likes of Emily Carman, Michael Hammond, and Christina Lane has made great progress in "correcting" the overall Lombard record, but there is still much left to uncover, particularly as it relates to her silent comedies with Mack Sennett. It is necessary to treat her early career and film performances on their own terms relatively free from the weight of hindsight knowledge, and to consider Lombard's body of early work in relation to her stardom at the related temporal juncture. Only then will a fuller, historically conscious understanding of Lombard's star persona and performance style be possible.

This chapter focuses on the period between 1908 and 1929, examining Lombard's early career and her two-year tenure as a Sennett Bathing Beauty.

---

[1] Wes Gehring, *Carole Lombard: The Hoosier Tornado*. Indianapolis: Indiana Historical Society Press, 2003, 53.

If the chronological boundaries seem exceptionally large, the unfortunate reality is that many of her pre-1927 films no longer survive. The analyses in this chapter are therefore the result of limited access to many of Lombard's early pictures. The first section focuses on her early years in Hollywood and the films she made up to 1927. The task of reviewing this body of work is especially tough because in what few films survive, Lombard either has a minor part, is barely identifiable, or appears in scenes that have been cut out of the final release print. This makes a substantial analysis nearly impossible. I will therefore draw mainly from biographical information and contemporary reviews—when available—to construct a chronology of her childhood and first years in Hollywood, which can provide some contextual and temporal grounding to map out her ascension to stardom.

The second section examines Lombard's silent comedies that she made while under contract to Sennett from 1927 to 1929. My textual analysis is based upon original research conducted at the Motion Picture and Television Reading Room at the Library of Congress in June 2011, and at the UCLA Film and Television Archive in April 2015. Lombard made eighteen one- and two-reel comedies for Sennett over a two-year period, in which she played both supporting and lead roles. The films included in this chapter—and the titles in which Lombard has a role large enough for an analysis[2]—are: *Smith's Pony* (Alfred J. Goulding, 1927), *The Girl from Everywhere* (Edward F. Cline, 1927), *Run, Girl, Run* (Alfred J. Goulding, 1928), *The Campus Vamp* (Harry Edwards, 1928), *The Campus Carmen* (Alfred J. Goulding, 1928), the first reel of *The Swim Princess* (Alfred J. Goulding, 1928),[3] and *Matchmaking Mamma* (Harry Edwards, 1929). I will devote special attention to her body in her physical comedy performances and, in particular, the habitual juxtaposition between her feminine sex appeal and her conventionally masculine athleticism. This is not an exhaustive look at Lombard's work with Sennett, but this chapter is the first scholarly text to offer an extended and detailed analysis of her silent film performance style.

Childhood and early Hollywood years

From an early age, Carole Lombard—born Jane Alice Peters—excelled in sports and enjoyed swimming, boxing, and playing baseball with the boys in her upper class Fort Wayne, Indiana neighborhood.[4] She

---

[2] I also watched *Don't Get Jealous* (Phil Whitman, 1929) at UCLA. I have chosen to exclude it from this chapter because Lombard appears in only one short scene and has one line.
[3] The second reel of *The Swim Princess* was not included in the print I viewed at the UCLA Film and Television Archives.
[4] Betty Boone, "What About Carole Lombard?" *Screenland*, June 1931, 83.

was described as a tomboy who gave up all "feminine interests,"[5] who instead preferred to tag along with her older brothers Fred Jr. and Stuart, and their friends.[6] In news articles from the 1930s, Lombard's often-cited tomboy qualities were used by the fan magazines to decode her mastery of physical comedy[7] and the curious balance between her "masculine deliberation" and feminine appearance, something *Screenland* columnist Betty Boone once described as "amazing in someone so blonde, so blue-eyed, and so fragile."[8] Her love of sports also prompted her entry into the movies.[9] By the spring of 1921, twelve-year-old Lombard had moved to Los Angeles with her mother, Elizabeth (Bess), and two brothers, and was playing baseball in the street one day with some boy friends. Silent film director Allan Dwan happened to be in the neighborhood and observed the children, and was fascinated by Lombard's natural athleticism. In an interview with Peter Bogdanovich from the 1960s, Dwan recalls Lombard as "a cute looking tomboy ... out there knocking the hell out of the other kids, playing better baseball than they were."[10] He was looking to cast the "tomboy kid sister"[11] of leading man, Monte Blue, for his film *The Perfect Crime*. Dwan asked her if she would like to be in his picture, and both she and Bess immediately accepted.[12] Unfortunately the film is now lost, but several stills exist showing Lombard sitting with Blue in what appears to be a private study. Dwan remembers that she "ate [the part] up"[13] during her two-day shoot, and Lombard allegedly decided "it was something she wanted to do again."[14] Despite her private aspirations, she did not make another film again until 1925, and her remaining childhood years were spent away from the Hollywood studios.[15]

In the spring of 1924, fifteen-year-old Lombard was a sophomore track star at Fairfax High School in Hollywood.[16] Her natural athletic skill once again resulted in a brush with stardom: she caught the eye of Charlie Chaplin's talent representative, who was scouting young actresses for Vitagraph Studios'

---

[5]"Carole Lombard: Is She Man-Proof Now?" *True Confessions*, August 1934, 18.
[6]Larry Swindell, *Screwball: The Life of Carole Lombard*. New York: William Morrow & Company, Inc., 1975), 20.
[7]For examples, see: *Carole Lombard's Life Story*, 1942, 8; "A Loud Cheer for the Screwball Girl," 50; Frederick Russell, "The Life Story of Carole Lombard – part one," *Film Pictorial*, June 27, 1936, 11.
[8]Boone, 83.
[9]Gehring, 27.
[10]Peter Bogdanovich, *Who the Devil Made It* (New York: Ballantine Books, 1997), 83.
[11]Swindell, 31.
[12]Ibid.
[13]Bogdanovich, 83.
[14]Swindell, 32.
[15]Gehring, 31.
[16]Swindell, 37.

picture, *The Gold Rush* (1925).[17] Her screen test did not result in a contract with Vitagraph,[18] but the studio did encourage a name change. Biographer Wes Gehring explains the studio allegedly "liked the Peters family name, but the moniker of Jane struck them as too dull."[19] Lombard remembered the popular tennis player Carol Peterson and suggested that her new name be Carol Peters.[20] There is much speculation about when exactly Lombard began spelling her first name with an "e." In later years, she was said to have explained, "I just picked up Carole because I liked it. At first I dropped the 'e', but I tacked it on later for good measure. My first idea was to name myself Carrolle. There's a flossy one ... Then I thought of Carrulle. Isn't it won-der-ful. Carrulle Lombard! But I got sane in time."[21] Lombard historian Vincent Paterno contends that she "began her official movie career as Carole Lombard in 1925," and used both "Carole" and "Carol" intermittently before eventually dropping the "e" when she signed with Pathé on October 6, 1928.[22] Historical documents corroborate Paterno's timeline: in one of the earliest news articles about Lombard from the February 4, 1925 edition of *Los Angeles Times*, her name is spelled "Carole Lombard."[23]

After the Chaplin screen test Lombard faced yet another false start, this time with the Mary Pickford melodrama, *Little Annie Rooney* (William Beaudine, 1925). A Pickford associate had originally promised her a small role, but according to both Swindell and Gehring, Pickford considered her "competitively too pretty" for the role.[24] Bess was eager to help her daughter make headway in the movies and was put in touch with the influential gossip columnist, Louella Parsons, by Vitagraph producer, Al Lichtman.[25] Parsons contacted Fox Films production chief, Winfield Sheehan, on Lombard's behalf because he owed her a personal favor. Lombard received an appointment at Fox,[26] and was immediately signed as a contract player for seventy-five dollars a week.[27] With two actors already under contract with the last name Peters, Fox requested another name change.[28]

---

[17]Gehring, 39.
[18]Ibid, 43.
[19]Ibid, 43.
[20]Swindell, 39.
[21]James Street, "Two Happy People—Part 1," *Movie and Radio Guide*, May 1940, page unknown.
[22]Vincent Paterno, "Prepare for a Sennett September," *Carole and Co.*, July 15, 2012, accessed August 25, 2015, http://carole-and-co.livejournal.com/527662.html. See also: Swindell, 69.
[23]"Society Girl Goes Into Drama," *Los Angeles Times*, February 4, 1925, A9.
[24]Swindell, 40. See also: Gehring, 44.
[25]Swindell, 40.
[26]Ibid.
[27]Kyle Chrichton, "Fun in Flickers," *Colliers,* February 24, 1940, 11.
[28]Gehring, 46.

She and Bess settled on Lombard, chosen in honor of their family friends Harry and Etta Lombard.[29]

Fox assigned Lombard to a series of "lucrative low-budget westerns" including *Gold and the Girl* (Edmund Mortimer, 1925), *Durand of the Badlands* (Lynn Reynolds, 1925), and *Hearts and Spurs* (W.S. Van Dyke, 1925)[30] all opposite Western star Buck Jones. In their review of the latter film, *Variety* described her as "attractive looking ... but for expressiveness she might just as well have been labeled 'for decorative purposes only.'"[31] Lombard then starred with Tom Mix in *Dick Turpin* (John G. Blystone, 1925), but her scenes were cut out of the final release print.[32] In 1936 Lombard allegedly reflected, "All I had to do was simper prettily at the hero and scream with terror while he battled with the villain."[33] Nevertheless, these roles gave her on-camera experience and a chance to establish herself among the roster of contract players. Her next Fox production was in the drama *Marriage in Transit* (Roy William Neill, 1925), in which she plays "a mature married woman" opposite Edmund Lowe."[34] It was originally titled *The Best Man,* and was ultimately a vehicle to showcase Lowe's talents.[35]

Around this time Lombard was gaining publicity, and was included in a *Los Angeles Times* advertisement highlighting some of the screen's most promising new starlets.[36] She then appeared in Fox's *The Road to Glory,* which was released in February, 1926 and directed by her future *Twentieth Century* director, Howard Hawks. Despite Lombard's exposure in Fox's films, she was dropped from her contract, but soon landed a new contract with slapstick comedy pioneer, Mack Sennett in 1927.[37] The precise date of Lombard's contract is unknown, but a full-page advertisement for Sennett's fall lineup from the August 19, 1927 issue of *Motion Picture News* includes a photo that includes Lombard and several of Sennett's "Bathing Beauties." This advertisement confirms that Lombard was working with Sennett as early as the summer of 1927.

Even with her new contract with Sennett, the future of Lombard's career was far more uncertain than biographers have previously thought. In Lombard's spare time she had begun dancing at the Cocoanut Grove, a Hollywood nightclub that was popular among young starlets like Joan

---

[29]Swindell, 41. See also: Gehring, 46.
[30]Gehring, 46.
[31]*Variety*, July 15, 1925, 35.
[32]Swindell, 42.
[33]Frederick Russell, "The Life Story of Carole Lombard – part two," *Film Pictorial*, July 4, 1936, 17.
[34]Swindell, 45.
[35]Gehring, 48.
[36]"How Do You Like These Newcomers?" *Los Angeles Times*, March 25, 1925, C4.
[37]"Kaleidoscope!" *Los Angeles Times*, September 18, 1927, page unknown.

Crawford and Douglas Fairbanks Jr. On September 19, 1927[38] Lombard was out on a date with sixteen-year-old Harry Cooper, who was also a frequent patron of the nightclub.[39] The couple were driving along Santa Monica Boulevard when, "through [Cooper's] negligence," they crashed into another car.[40] A shard of glass cut a large gash in Lombard's face from her nose and across her left cheek to her eye.[41] She was rushed to the hospital and underwent a four-hour surgery that included fourteen stitches without any anesthesia, due to the medical belief that muscle relaxers would cause further facial scarring.[42] She also underwent extensive plastic surgery to minimize the appearance of the scars,[43] though they remained visible on film and in publicity photos for the rest of her life.

To date, it has been difficult for historians to pinpoint the precise date of the automobile accident, and some have it dated in 1926.[44] This may seem like an inconsequential detail, but it is important to reiterate that the accident was a devastating setback to Lombard's career ambitions. Discovering that the accident, in fact, occurred in 1927 reconfigures the career timeline that has been put forth in previous biographies. As early as 1975, Larry Swindell claimed that Fox paid for the basic hospital expenses but not the surgeries, and when Lombard was released she was informed that her contract had been cancelled due to a clause that stated that players must take full "responsibility for their physical being."[45] The story of Lombard's termination has been repeated in other biographies,[46] but by the time of the actual date of the accident in the fall of 1927 Lombard was already under contract to Sennett, making Swindell's theory about Fox's contract termination improbable. In October 1927 she and Bess Peters sued Cooper

---

[38]In my correspondence with Lombard biographer, Robert Matzen, he informed me of a newspaper article that confirms the date as September 19, 1927. See: "Former Fort Wayne Star Asks $35,000 Damages," *Garrett Clipper*, October 31, 1927, 3. However, an article from the October 13, 1927 edition of the *Los Angeles Times* lists the accident happening in 1926. Though biographers such as Michelle Morgan have used the latter article as evidence to support the 1926 theory, I am doubtful of its accuracy, primarily because of the vague date and abundance of incorrect factual details. For instance, Lombard's age is wrongly listed as seventeen; in October 1927 she would have been eighteen. See: "Actress Demands Damages for Cut," *Los Angeles Times*, October 13, 1927, A9.

[39]Swindell, 50. See also: "Former Fort Wayne Star Asks $35,000 Damages," 3.

[40]Ibid.

[41]Gehring, 49.

[42]Marian Rhea, "Lombard Unlimited." *Radio Mirror* Vol. 11, No. 6 April 1939, 19.

[43]Gehring, 50.

[44]Vincent Paterno, "Her Scar, Up Close and Personal," *Carole & Co.* March 31, 2013, accessed July 30, 2015, http://carole-and-co.livejournal.com/589765.html. See also: Gehring, 230; Michelle Morgan, *Carole Lombard: Twentieth-Century Star* (Gloucestershire: The History Press, 2016), 35.

[45]Swindell, 52.

[46]Gehring, 48.

and his parents for $35,000 in damages,[47] arguing under sworn testimony that "the scar greatly detracts from her appearance before the camera."[48] The case was eventually settled out of court and Lombard received $3,000.[49]

In the lawsuit, Lombard—who is identified as Miss Jane Peters—complained that "where she formerly was able to earn a salary of $300 monthly as a Sennett girl, she is now unable to obtain employment of any kind."[50] This statement reinforces the chronological inaccuracy of the 1926 theory, since Lombard was already working with Sennett at the time of her accident. My correspondence with historian Robert Matzen verifies the general feeling at the time that Lombard's career was over because of the severity of her injuries.[51] The language of the article gives us a sense of how dire Lombard felt her situation was in the weeks following the accident, as she claims "the damage is in the form of two deep scars on her cheek, which she asserts have permanently defaced her beauty and completely shattered her screen ambitions." Coincidentally, Lombard's first Sennett film, *Smith's Pony*, was released on September 18, 1927, just a day before the accident.[52] Lombard was therefore justified in her feeling that her future was in jeopardy, for she was in the early stages of her career and still had much to prove in terms of her acting abilities.

Fortunately, the accident did not put an end to Lombard's film career. It was through a combination of luck and circumstance that she was under contract to a director whose filmmaking style was informal and lacking in what Matzen describes as "languid close-ups."[53] Sennett's style of fast-paced comedy and quick cuts worked to Lombard's advantage because it took the focus away from her face and on to her body. Matzen also explained that after the accident, Sennett tried to bolster her career by giving her lucrative roles and ample publicity.[54] One such attempt was a new nickname, "Carole of the Curves,"[55] which was subsequently used by Pathé—who at the time had a distribution deal with Sennett—in publicity photos of Lombard.[56] This nickname simultaneously drew audiences' focus away from her facial scars and worked harmoniously with the physicality and female sensuality that were emblematic of Lombard's performances in Sennett's "Girl Comedies."

---

[47]"Former Fort Wayne Star Asks $35,000 Damages," *Garrett Clipper*, October 31, 1927, 3.
[48]"Actress demands damages for cut," *Los Angeles Times*, October 13, 1927, A9.
[49]"Suit Over Scar on Girl Settled," *Los Angeles Times*, October 15, 1927, 21.
[50]"Former Fort Wayne Star Asks $35,000 Damages," 3.
[51]Robert Matzen, e-mail to author, July 7, 2016.
[52]Paterno, "Carole in Early 'Times,' part 3."
[53]Robert Matzen, e-mail to author, July 7, 2016.
[54]Ibid.
[55]"How Sylvia Changed 'Carole of the Curves' to Svelte Carole Lombard!," *Photoplay*, April 1933, 50–51.
[56]Madame Sylvia, "Fat? Thin? You Can Be Just Right!" *Modern Screen*, April 1935, 92.

Slapstick comedy (1927–1929)

It is rare to read a biographical account or publicity news item about Carole Lombard without some mention of her tenure with Mack Sennett's Keystone Film Company. Even in the 1930s when Lombard's star persona was synonymous with screwball comedy she was still described as the "ex-Sennett girl"[57] who had an "apprenticeship in the Mack Sennett Seminary of Hurtling Pies and Non-Swimming Bathing Beauties."[58] Lombard began her two-year, $300[59] per month contract in 1927, and while under his tutelage completed eighteen one and two-reel comedies, frequently as one of "Sennett's Bathing Beauties." Gehring argues that Lombard was initially hesitant to sign with Sennett, believing that short films would be "a comedown from her previous feature film work."[60] However, I question this theory simply because Lombard had just recently been released from her contract with Fox. In light of the fact that she had not yet established herself in Hollywood and had no other contract options to choose from, it is unlikely that Lombard would be so dismissive of Sennett's offer. Instead, she saw the contract as a promising opportunity, having realized that several famous film actresses like Gloria Swanson, Phyllis Haver, Marie Prevost, and Bebe Daniels all began their careers at Keystone; she allegedly later reflected that she "wouldn't trade that experience for anything."[61]

Comparisons between Lombard's slapstick and screwball work are largely inevitable, as both comic modes rely on the performer's awareness of their body. Tom Gunning calls it a "sense of grace, perfection and freedom" from mechanical inflexibility, an idea ascribed most famously to French philosopher Henri Bergson and his theory regarding the social and ideological functions of laughter.[62] Noel Busch's 1938 *Life* article notes that Lombard "spent two years being hit in the face by pies, tripped, dunked, chased, and generally maltreated,"[63] but does so in fairly vague terms, and ultimately falls short of offering readers any substantial indication of the nuances of her silent performance style. To date, no thorough analysis of Lombard's silent film

---

[57] "Carol Lombard," *Picture Play*, 1930, page unknown.
[58] "What About Carole Lombard," 83.
[59] The amount Lombard made per week while working for Sennett varies depending upon the source. In her court testimony, Lombard's claims she was making $300. Sennett himself says it was $400, while Larry Swindell puts the number at $500. See: Mack Sennett and Cameron Shipp, *King of Comedy* (Lincoln: iUniverse.com, Inc., 2000), 174; Swindell, 64.
[60] Gehring, 53.
[61] "The Life Story of Carole Lombard, part two," 17.
[62] Tom Gunning, "Mechanisms of Laughter: The Devices of Slapstick," in *Slapstick Comedy*, eds. Tom Paulus and Rob King (New York: Routledge, 2010), 148. See also: Henri Bergson, *Laughter: An Essay on the Meaning of the Comic*, trans. Cloudesley Brereton and Fred Rothwell (Los Angeles: Green Integer, 1999).
[63] Noel F. Busch, "A Loud Cheer for the Screwball Girl." *Life*. Oct 17, 1938, 63.

performances exists. Therefore, what follows are close textual analyses of seven of Lombard's Sennett comedies. I will offer substantial descriptions of Lombard's performances, with a particular focus on her body as a signifier of both athleticism and provocative female sexuality.

Smith's Pony (*Alfred J. Goulding, 1927*)

Although Lombard's stardom was in its infancy in early 1927, as the year progressed she was receiving steady press coverage in industry newspapers. In both the June 24 and August 28 issues of *Film Daily*, she was listed as one of several starlets that were to be featured in Mack Sennett's roster of "Bathing Beauties."[64] These news items suggest that Lombard's name carried a degree of weight as a supporting player, and that she was becoming a marketable star. One of her first projects with Sennett was the short entitled *Smith's Pony*, directed by vaudevillian actor-turned-director, Alfred J. Goulding. It was released on September 18, 1927 as part of the "Smith family" series that Sennett began producing in 1925[65] which he conceived as "a series of comedies depicting the average American family … who just naturally manage to get themselves into one predicament after another."[66] Sennett had previously attempted a family series in 1920, but the "Smith" version was his first with the same actors playing the same characters in each film. He cast popular slapstick comedians Raymond McKee and Ruth Hiatt as Mr. and Mrs. Smith, respectively, with child star Mary Ann Jackson as their mischievous daughter, Bubbles, and Sennett's own dog, Teddy III, as Captain.[67] Unlike Sennett's stand-alone films, whose humor derives primarily from his characters' pratfalls and larger-than-life performances, in this series he was banking on audiences' "identification with the family's all-too-familiar foibles" and reoccurring character types.[68] Although the Smiths' antics are arguably more exaggerated than those of the typical American family, the series' relatability stems from the way in which each films speaks to average familial experiences like unruly children, work, vacation, and spousal jealousy. The Smith series was a huge success with audiences, and over the course of four years Sennett made over two dozen films in the franchise.[69]

---

[64]"Sennett Plans More Bathing Beauties," *Film Daily*, June 24, 1927, page unknown. See also: "Sennett Selects Beauties," *Film Daily*, August 28, 1927, page unknown.
[65]Brent E. Walker, Mack Sennett's Fun Factory: A History and Filmography of His Studio and His Keystone and Mack Sennett Comedies, with Biographies of Players and Personnel (Jefferson: McFarland and Co., 2010), 160.
[66]Ibid.
[67]Ibid, 162.
[68]Ibid, 160.
[69]Kalton C. Lahue, *Mack Sennett's Keystone: The Man, the Myth, and the Comedies* (New York: A.S. Barnes, 1971), 222.

Smith's Pony features Lombard along with McKee, Hiatt, and Jackson in their reoccurring roles.[70] Lombard—who is listed in the credits as "Carol"—plays Lillian Saunders, a "riding teacher and dealer in Shetland ponies" from San Francisco. Jimmy Smith (McKee) and his wife, Mabel (Hiatt), are visiting from Los Angeles with their daughter, Bubbles (Jackson). After taking in some of the sights including a trip to Chinatown, the Smiths attend a local horse show. Bubbles becomes fixated on one of Lillian's ponies—also named Lillian—and pleads with her father to buy it. Jimmy loves to spoil Bubbles and agrees to buy the pony, but does not want to tell Mabel until they return home. Mabel overhears Jimmy's bargaining with Lillian and mistakenly thinks the pair are planning on running away together.

The family sails home to Los Angeles but unbeknownst to Mabel, Lillian and the pony are also on board the ship. Jimmy receives a note from Lillian that reads, "Come down to the lower deck and look after Lillian. She's lonesome." Mabel notices Jimmy trying to hide the note, and storms out of their cabin. Meanwhile, Jimmy goes to visit Lillian the pony, and tucks her into bed. Returning back to his room, Mabel asks Jimmy who Lillian is and he answers, "A pony." We then see a shot of Lillian picking up the phone to dial. The film cuts back to the Smith's room where Mabel answers her phone, and it cuts again to an intertitle, "Hello—this is Lillian." Outraged, Mabel hangs up, turns to Jimmy and says, "Your horse called up!" Jimmy rushes back to Lillian's cabin to check on the pony, with Mabel trailing inconspicuously behind him. Waiting outside the closed cabin door, Mabel overhears Jimmy talking baby talk to the pony, who she mistakes as Lillian the woman. He says, "What big brown eyes you have! Come sit on Papa's lap! You mustn't bite Papa!" Fed up with her husband's behavior, Mabel flings open the door only to discover Jimmy embracing Lillian the pony. Although it is not a film one would immediately associate with Mack Sennett's authorial style, the plot of *Smith's Pony* shows how the he could "derive big laughs from a succession of funny situations without resorting to slapstick."[71] The comedy derives from misinterpretation and spousal jealousy—both traits that are common in the Smith family series.

Lombard may only play a supporting role, but her performance as the other woman is key to sustaining the narrative action. Lombard's physical appearance is on display from the first scene in order to establish the motive behind Mabel's jealousy. We first meet Lillian at the horse track, where she is shown in long tracking shot riding on a large black horse. She wears a white hat with a medium brim, a gray tailored riding jacket, white button down blouse, and riding pants, all of which accentuates her toned and slim athletic figure. The long-take tracking shot shows Lillian holding the reins with

---

[70] Ibid, 162.
[71] Walker, 164.

both hands in an assured grip, and she sits atop the horse with a straight back. The shot solidifies Lombard's real-life athleticism and confidence as a horsewoman.

When Lombard's horse completes the jump, the tracking shot cuts to a point of view shot from Jimmy's perspective. The same shot is then shown in binocular shaped silhouette meant to represent Jimmy's point of view, and the footage is in slow motion. Lombard is atop the horse galloping down the track, and the combination of the slow motion and silhouette outline foregrounds her physical form. Jimmy stares through his binoculars for several seconds, then Mabel—who is sitting to his left—notices and furrows her brows to indicate her disgust. In the initial tracking shot the long shot camera angle and movement draws our attention to Lombard's athletic ability; her physicality is on display, but is not overtly sexual. When that same tracking shot is used along with the silhouette, and the film cuts to Jimmy looking through the binoculars, the focus on her physicality turns to her allure.

The binocular silhouette transforms her into an object of desire for Jimmy and exemplifies a process that Laura Mulvey identifies as the scopophilic male gaze.[72] Jimmy takes on the active role of the "looker," and uses his binoculars to ogle Lillian's body and admire her athletic prowess. His gaze is intensified by the fact that she is unaware of his presence; she becomes emblematic of Mulvey's "to-be-looked-at-ness," a term which signifies female sexual objectification. Mulvey writes that women in the cinema are a "sexual object," that which "holds the look, plays to and signifies male desire."[73] But Jimmy's gaze is disrupted—not by Lillian, but by Mabel—and it is precisely his not-so-secret glances that set up the Smiths' subsequent series of misfortunes. The combination of Lillian galloping and the preceding shot of Jimmy looking turns the focus away from her riding skill to her physical allure. Her body is on display for Jimmy and the theater audience, intensified by the slow motion movement and the silhouette framing.

The Girl from Everywhere (*Edward F. Cline, 1927*)

Lombard's next film was the behind-the-scenes comedy short, *The Girl from Everywhere*. Filmed from June to August 1927 and released on December 11, 1927, this was the first installment in the newly conceived "Sennett Girl Comedies" series, and was designed primarily as a star vehicle for Daphne

---

[72]Laura Mulvey, "Visual Pleasure and Narrative Cinema," *Screen* Vol. 16, No. 3 (1975): 8–9.
[73]Ibid, 11.

Pollard, who had just signed a three month, $350 per week plus options contract with Sennett.[74] The "Sennett Girl Comedies" were also structured to "show off his newest batch of bathing girls" including Carmelita Geraghty, Anita Barnes and, of course, Carole Lombard. According to Sennett historian Brent Walker, these films would "take advantage of the new increased Sennett budgets" that were due, in part, to his newly formed Motion Picture Capital Corporation, which gave him the ability to secure outside investors.[75] The "Sennett Girl Comedies" had substantial budgets anywhere between $25,000 and $32,000, and each film included a Technicolor sequence that showed off the girls' figures. Technicolor became so important to the look of the "Sennett Girl" series that Sennett began developing his own Technicolor film stock, which he later renamed "Sennett Color."[76]

The film begins with an intertitle that asks, "Where does the Bathing Girl come from?" emblazoned overtop a silhouette of an unnamed girl diving into the ocean from a rocky perch. The shot cuts to a close-up of the girl's legs standing atop the rocks, then fades to a shot of a horse's legs. It cuts again to a medium shot of Lombard sitting on what is presumably the same horse. She wears a sporty costume consisting of beige riding pants, a white button down shirt, and a newspaper boy hat that sits tilted on her head. Lombard smiles shyly as she pets the horse before it fades to black. The remaining scenes take place on a film set. Director Bill Ashcraft sits alongside his crew as they instruct starlet, Hilda Hay, to dance. Lombard is seated among the group wearing a black vest with a white trim, black shorts, and a black feathery hat—an outfit that is duplicated in the film's exhibition posters. She dances in rhythm to Hay's movements with her crossed legs in full view of the camera. Her character has no name in the credits, has virtually no dialog and is insignificant to the narrative action, all of which reaffirm the gratuitous images of her body in the opening shot.

The rest of the film concerns the hijinks of a homely-looking actress named Madame Zwinga (Pollard). She is a megalomaniac who eats and drinks incessantly on set, which prompts Ashcraft to remark, "No wonder there was a food shortage in Europe. If she acts like she eats, I'm made!" Lombard is visible among the group of onlookers in reaction shots, and she watches Madame Zwinga with a forced smile that signals her character's feigned amusement. She appears more concerned with fanning herself with an oversized black feather, which she does intermittently throughout the scene. A lion from the neighboring "Flaming Mamas" short wanders into Ashcraft's studio and havoc breaks loose on set. The last half of the film details the chaos on set as the cast and crew run amuck to avoid the prowling lion.

---

[74]Walker, 174.
[75]Ibid.
[76]Ibid.

The majority of the short's plot is irrelevant to the question posed by the opening intertitle, and the plot is disjointed due to the inconsistency between the two halves. We never get an answer to the question of where the "Bathing Girl" originates, other than a vague "Everywhere" from the title. Instead, it appears that the short is largely an exercise in physical comedy performance. It contains a combination of slapstick and insult-based humor mostly targeted at Zwinga, that is typical of Sennett's comic style. Lombard plays the title "Bathing Girl," whose sensual body and youthful attractiveness are the sole reasons for her appearance in the short. Slapstick comedy scholar and Mack Sennett historian Rob King explains that Sennett had "tired of the Bathing Beauty promotions by the spring of 1927"[77] and longed for "more dignified publicity." However, Lombard's role epitomizes his commitment to the "Beauties" commercial spectacle and viability.

Sennett first introduced audiences to his "Bathing Beauties" in 1915[78] in his Triangle-Keystone shorts "as a way to extricate his product from Triangle's dwindling fortunes" and to "boost exhibitor loyalty to Keystone during this troubled period."[79] By the late 1910s the "Bathing Beauties" had become "icons of modern femininity" by exploiting female sexuality and middle-class leisure. They reflected the insidious transformation of "female behavior into commercial spectacle" that "relegated women's modernity into the realm of beauty and fashion ads."[80] The "Beauties" brought fashion to life through movement and color;[81] and were symbolic of the burgeoning fashion and beauty industries that manufactured products for mass consumption. In his study of Hollywood and the fashion industry, Charles Eckert writes "If one walked into New York's largest department stores toward the end of 1929, one could find abundant evidence of the penetration of Hollywood fashions …"[82] Sennett's "Beauties" personified the allure of female consumption and targeted the cinema's diverse gender and class audience in a way that reflected the convergence of consumer culture and mass media. They tied the Victorian concept of the "New Woman," popularized by Henry James in the 1880s as a symbol of "female independence,"[83] to consumerism,

---

[77]Rob King, *The Fun Factory: The Keystone Film Company and the Emergence of Mass Culture* (Los Angeles: University of California Press, 2009), 244.
[78]Hilde D'Haeyere, "Splashes of Fun and Beauty: Mack Sennett's Bathing Beauties," in *Slapstick Comedy*, eds. Tom Paulus and Rob King (New York: Routledge, 2010), 208.
[79]King, 210.
[80]Ibid, 211.
[81]Mack Sennett often used two-strip Technicolor to film the "Bathing Beauty" sequences.
[82]Charles Eckert, "The Carole Lombard in Macy's Window," in *Movies and Mass Culture*, ed. John Belton (London: The Altlone Press, 1999), 103.
[83]Victoria Coulson, *Henry James, Women and Realism* (Cambridge: Cambridge University Press, 2007), 2.

thereby suturing the agency women may have achieved through their newfound economic independence to commodity exchange.[84]

Sennett promoted female consumerism in his films through the exploitation of the "Beauties" appearance and their apparel, and used them as a "counterpoint to the violent slapstick, not as participants in it."[85] In contrast to the frantic pace of his slapstick sequences, Sennett and his directors constructed the "Beauties" allure through various camera and editing techniques including slow motion, stable framing, and unobtrusive editing.[86] This is evident in Lombard's binocular silhouette in *Smith's Pony*, as the shots are included for no other reason than to sexualize her body and call attention to her conventionally feminine physical appearance. Although this is not the case in all of her Sennett comedies, her role in *The Girl from Everywhere* is emblematic of the "Bathing Beauties" ornamental purpose. In the scene described above, Lombard says nothing and has virtually no relevance to the story other than to be an attractive distraction from the ensuing chaos. We can assume this is her function because she is the only "Beauty" sitting amongst several men who make up the film crew; her place within the group is altogether unnecessary to the plot and unlikely in such a context.

The ability to perform physical comedy in this short is curiously coded along gender lines, which is an anomaly in Mack Sennett's typically egalitarian slapstick oeuvre. Unlike Pollard, who runs havoc around the set and whose on-screen act is largely dependent on overly theatrical grand body gestures, Lombard's character connotes demure gentility. Pollard's comedy is predicated on physical and performance excess; her homely appearance, short stature, and her character's gluttony code her as being unladylike. Comedy scholar Alex Clayton argues that physical comedy is traditionally performed by male comedians like Buster Keaton, Charlie Chaplin and Laurel and Hardy, and that this imbalance has led to the notion that "the dominant ideal of feminine beauty ... seems fundamentally at odds with the clumsiness, contortions, and spectacular activity that characterizes the slapstick body."[87] This short seems to reinforce the gendered slapstick divide; neither the character nor the appearance of the actress are portrayed as feminine. And while Pollard comes across more asexual than conventionally masculine, the absence of any clearly identifiable tropes of femininity in her appearance and outlandish demeanor justifies her physical comedy performance. By contrast, Lombard's appearance and her character's lack

---

[84]King, 213.
[85]D'Haeyere, 210.
[86]Ibid, 210.
[87]Alex Clayton, *The Body in Hollywood Slapstick Comedy*. Jefferson, NC: McFarland & Company, Inc., 2007), 146.

of agency is contextualized as the feminine "counterpoint" to Madame Zwinga's over-the-top slapstick, and as such her character remains calm and largely immobile amidst the on-screen chaos.

Although Lombard had a relatively inconsequential role in the film, her prominent position on the film's poster and her second billing indicate that her status was rising among Sennett's acting troupe. Larry Swindell suggests that despite her solid performances in Sennett's shorts, the public continued to identify her image only as the anonymous "pretty one."[88] However, news articles published around the release of *Smith's Pony*, as well as advertisements in industry newspapers challenge Swindell's assertion and confirm that Lombard was, in fact, becoming a recognizable performer. Four months before *The Girl from Everywhere*'s national release and one month after Lombard's devastating car accident, she was featured alongside other Sennett actors in a full-page color advertisement in the October 23 issue of *Film Daily* promoting "Mack Sennett's Mighty Array of Funmakers 1927–1928." Lombard's name is spelled "Carolle"[89]—an indication that her star persona was still a work-in-progress), and she is shown wearing a white dress and feathery headdress similar to the one worn in *The Girl from Everywhere*. It should be noted that Lombard is not included among the group of "Bathing Beauties" at the bottom left corner of the poster, but at the center toward the top in between the years 1927 and 1928. In what could be described as a Renaissance perspective, Lombard's placement in the advertisement draws our eyes directly to her figure, a visual cue that confirms her rising prominence among Sennett's roster of talent.

The fact that Lombard is singled out by name and is featured in such a distinguishable place suggests that she was becoming a picture personality. Richard deCordova notes that picture personalities are defined primarily according to the regularity in which they appear in films and extraneous publicity. Unlike the picture star, whose fame rests on the audience's dual knowledge of the performer's personal lives and professional work, the picture personality's recognizability "was produced and maintained largely by the cinema itself; it did not depend so much on outside referent."[90] Although *The Girl from Everywhere* was only Lombard's second Sennett film, it is clear that, in combination with her previous film roles and publicity appearances, Lombard was known by name and not just "the pretty one." This advertisement partially reflects Sennett's promise to give her publicity in the wake of her car accident, but it also suggests that he considered Lombard as a lucrative investment and someone with the potential to become a viable comic actress.

---

[88]Swindell, 60.
[89]Even though her name is spelled "Carole" in *The Girl from Everywhere*'s promotional posters.
[90]Richard DeCordova, *Picture Personalities: the emergence of the star system in America* (Champaign: University of Illinois Press, 2001), 51.

Run, Girl, Run (*Alfred J. Goulding, 1928*)

Lombard's best documented and widely accessible[91] slapstick comedy is in the title role of the collegiate short, *Run, Girl, Run*. It was the third installment in the "Sennett Girl Comedies" series and was released on January 15, 1928. It also marked Lombard's first time as a Sennett lead,[92] an indication that she was being considered a nominal star.[93] She plays Norma Nurmi,[94] the celebrated track star at the all-female Sunnydale School. Like the other pupils at Sunnydale, Norma is boy-crazy and concentrates on "the three Rs—Romeos, Roadsters and Roller-Skates." Under the strict watch of coach Minnie Marmon (Daphne Pollard), described as "a one-cylinder model with an underslung chassis," the team is set to compete against rival school, Primpmore, at their annual track meet. Determined to get her team to win the meet, coach Marmon issues strict bedtime orders to all of the girls. Norma ignores Marmon's rules and tries to sneak out to meet her boyfriend, a "military student specializing in heartillery." As she tiptoes down the hall of her dormitory, Norma is caught by Marmon and brought into the coach's bedroom. Norma signals to her boyfriend—who is outside of the dormitory—to wait for her, and she and coach Marmon get into bed. Norma pretends to have fallen asleep, and in order to trick Marmon into thinking she is still in bed, she and her boyfriend—who has in the meantime come into the room—place a fake rubber hand in her coach's hand and quietly escape out the window.

At the meet the next day, Norma and her team are losing to Primpmore; nobody on the team seems to be paying attention to their events. Norma is more interested in powdering her face with makeup, while the team's fat girl—played by Lombard's best friend, Madalynne Field—is out of shape and gets distracted by a sideline stand selling griddle cakes.[95] Before the final track event, Marmon pleads with Norma to run as fast as she can. In a display of athletic confidence for the benefit of her boyfriend sitting in the stands, Norma breezes past her competitors and wins the race.

Run, Girl, Run was arguably the most physically demanding short to date in Lombard's career. Her character is physically agile, feminine and attractive, and is a precursor to the "beautiful comic" heroines that she often played in her sound comedies. Most of Norma's actions center

---

[91] As of this writing, it is available on YouTube.
[92] Swindell, 63.
[93] Gehring, 55.
[94] The name "Norma Nurmi" was a nod to Finnish track star Paavlo Nurmi—nicknamed the "Flying Finn"—one of the most celebrated long-distance runners of the early twentieth century.
[95] A reoccurring stereotype in many Sennett shorts is the fat character. Played by both male and female actors, this character's body frequently becomes the site of spectacular ridicule and comic relief. For examples, see *For the Love of Mabel* (1913), *Tillie's Punctured Romance* (1914), and *Fat Wives for Thin* (1930).

THE SENNETT GIRL COMEDIES

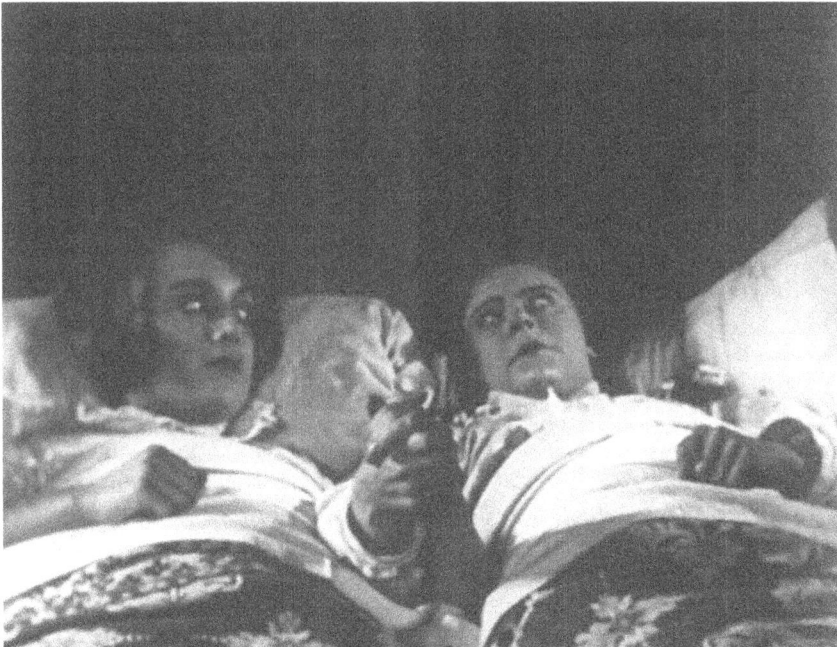

FIGURES 1.1 & 1.2 *Lombard frequently played adolescent characters in Sennett's films. She is pictured here as Norma Nurmi in* Run, Girl, Run *(Alfred J. Goulding, 1928)*.

FIGURE 1.3 In this still from Run, Girl, Run, *Coach Minnie Marmon (Daphne Pollard) pleads with Sunnydale School's track star, Norma Nurmi (Lombard), to give it her all in her final race. This film gave Lombard the chance to show off her athletic prowess.*

around the combination of her effortless athletic skill and her flirtatious, adolescent femininity. She displays Norma's athletic virtuosity with the help of accelerated motion shots, framing, and tracking camera movements. In her final track event, Norma is kneeling at the starting line when Coach Marmon comes over to give her a pep talk. Framed in a medium shot with Marmon, Norma gives the coach a self-assured nod and mouths the word "yeah," as if to say "I can win the race." As the race gets underway, a long tracking shot follows Norma around the track as she effortlessly jumps other hurdles in a display of Lombard's real-life athleticism.

The scene also illustrates Sennett's habitual reliance on in-camera and editing techniques to heighten his characters' spectacular performances. Camera techniques like slow and fast motion were indicative of the Keystone Film Company's "new slapstick style" that "centered upon the super stunt in which the camera is the chief performer."[96] Citing a memo by *Photoplay*

---

[96]Rob King, "'Uproarious Inventions:' The Keystone Film Company, Modernity, and The Art of the Motor," in *Slapstick Comedy*, eds. Tom Paulus and Rob King (New York: Routledge, 2010), 114.

writer Alfred Cohen, Rob King writes that Keystone's "chief policy ... was to thrill 'em as well as make 'em laugh."[97] The studio concentrated on displays of technical virtuosity in order to meet the "emotional needs of diverse film-goers," in which "technological spectacle possessed a mass basis." Keystone "addressed the interests of a technocratic society" by appealing to the interests of different classes of the audience.[98] Sennett's audience would have been conscious of his camera techniques, but the fascination lay in the mystery of how the visual spectacle was achieved.[99] In Norma's running shots he accelerates the film speed to make her look as if she is moving at an incredibly fast pace. The machine-like movement of Lombard's body indicates that the camera has clearly been over-cranked to accelerate the film speed, and her legs move at such a repetitive and rhythmic pace that they become blurred.

The scene's spectacle is twofold, deriving from the technology itself and from Lombard as a figure of athleticism and femininity. Throughout, Lombard transgresses the boundary between masculine and feminine spectacle. On a cultural level, Norma represents the flapper figure of the period: she is "boyish, playful, and rebellious"[100] and liberated. The flapper was the embodiment of sexual freedom and a challenge to traditional morality,[101] and Norma embodies the adolescent version through her focus on romance and disregard for school rules. She is also presented as sexually desirable, and her athleticism—typically coded as a masculine trait—is not made to undermine her conventional femininity. In terms of performance, the sheer speed at which Norma moves calls attention to the spectacular nature of the sequence and the camera tricks that accentuate her body's speed. We are aware that it is impossible for her to run with such intensity and vigor, yet it is mesmerizing to watch a human body—a female one at that—move with breakneck precision. Lombard's performance pushes beyond gender and yet her movement remains both believable and contextually relevant due to Sennett's habitual application of camera trickery onto his diegetic worlds. The scene and others like it are indebted to Sennett's fascination with modernity and technological competence.

The camera techniques and framing accentuate Norma's athletic skill, while her costume constantly reminds us of her womanhood. She wears running attire consisting of black high-cut shorts, and a pale varsity tank

---

[97] Ibid.
[98] Ibid, 122.
[99] Ibid, 119.
[100] Jane Batkin, Identity in Animation: A Journey into Self, Difference, Culture and the Body (London: Routledge, 2017), 14.
[101] Stephen Sharot, "The 'New Woman,' star personas, and cross-class romance films in 1920s America," in *Journal of Gender Studies* Vol. 19 (2010), 74.

top with the letter "S"—for Sunnydale—emblazoned on the chest. The top is revealing of her breasts, and paired with the evident absence of a bra, is yet another reminder of her femininity. Norma's appearance is coded along stereotypical gender lines through her overt display of sexuality. But she is also a symbol of a new type of woman reminiscent of the 1920s flappers: she is flirtatious and confident, headstrong, and rebellious. Like *The Girl from Everywhere,* this short highlights the incongruity of Norma and Marmon's appearances and reinforces gender stereotypes to distinguish the two female leads.

However distinct the contrast between the two women, their differences also signal a potential queer reading through an appeal to the female gaze. We get a sense of this through the all-female school setting in this and Lombard's other Sennett shorts, and also through the scene in which Marmon and Norma share a bed. Although the intended effect of the scene was comic, there nonetheless remains a play to a female gaze in spite of *Run, Girl, Run*'s overwhelmingly heterosexual slant. This point becomes compounded when we consider Marmon's androgynous physical appearance. Pollard was stocky and stood at only 4 feet, 9 inches, considerably shorter than Lombard's toned 5 foot, 5 inch frame. Marmon dresses conservatively in a thick turtleneck and baggy bloomer-style pants. Her hair is hidden underneath a large white hat that conceals any hint of clearly coded femininity from her matronly and desexualized appearance. She embodies the prim and proper "schoolmarm" image that her name implies, while Norma is the epitome of youthful femininity. Norma's costume keeps her tethered to more conventional gender lines, one in which sex appeal and physicality remain key tenets of her performance. And while the film clearly defines Norma as being heterosexual, her interactions with Marmon—and Marmon's presence in the film more generally—allow for such alternative readings of the film's presentation of sexuality.

The Campus Vamp (*Harry Edwards, 1928*)

Carole Lombard's small but powerful role in *The Campus Vamp* provides us with yet another clue as to why film scholars and biographers are quick to draw comparisons between her slapstick and screwball comedy personae. In broader terms, it speaks to the importance Sennett's "Girls" had on the "modern female culture."[102] She plays "Carole," a fun-loving and carefree collegiate who is more interested in her social life than her schoolwork. The film is separated into two largely unrelated halves, the first about the relationship between a socially awkward schoolgirl named Sally (Sally

---

[102]King, 242.

Eilers), and her boyfriend Matty (Matty Kemp). Sally's dorm mother, Dora (Daphne Pollard), and her boyfriend Barney Benson (Johnny Burke), try to teach her how to be flirtatious in order to keep Matty away from Carole. Lombard plays the eponymous vamp who, unlike Sally, possesses an effortless confidence with the boys. At their school dance, Carole quickly sets her sights on Matty, and ends up kissing him in front of Sally. Shortly thereafter the film cuts rather abruptly to a "Sennett Girls" beach baseball game filmed in Technicolor.[103] The scene features Lombard, Eilers, and the other girls playing baseball. Like *Run, Girl, Run* the short relies on a combination of slow motion, framing, and long shots to accentuate the physical attributes, sex appeal and commercialism of Sennett's "Girl Comedies."

Lombard's first scene is indicative of the way scholars have retroactively drawn connections between her screwball and slapstick films. She enters the scene driving in a car full of collegiate boys. She wears a light colored beret, a black and white patterned sweater, and a geometrically patterned

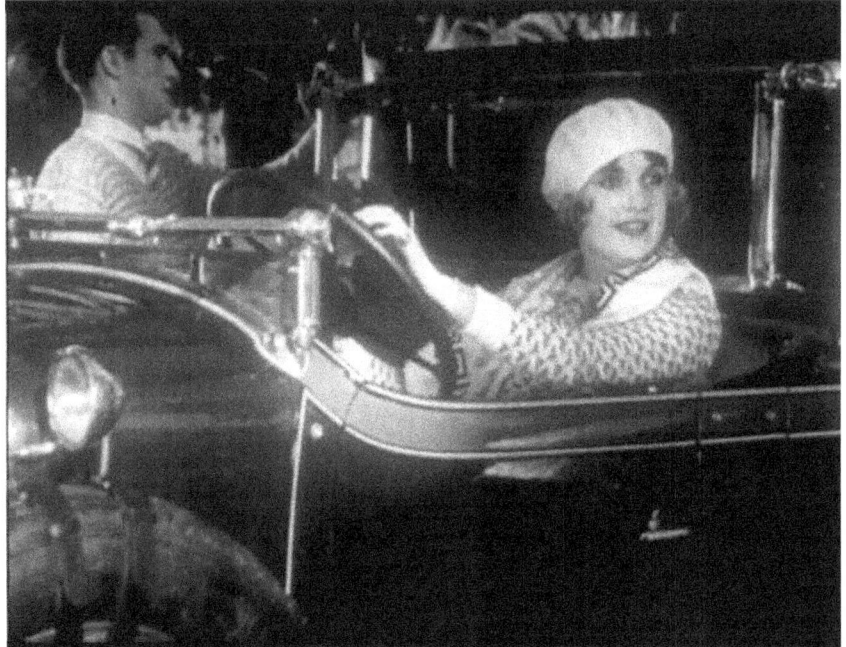

FIGURE 1.4 *Carole Lombard's first appearance in The Campus Vamp (Harry Edwards, 1928) embodies her character's youthful energy and spirit.*

---

[103]Richard Barrios, *A Song in the Dark: The Birth of the Musical Film* (Oxford: Oxford University Press, 2010), 119.

shawl draped over her shoulders. The natural sunshine radiates off of her sparkling blonde hair that, when photographed using black and white film stock, appears an effervescent shade of platinum blonde.

As the camera tracks along the driver's side of the car, we see Lombard in medium shot yelling and waving her arms in the air in merriment. She momentarily takes her hands off the steering wheel to giggle and clap with glee. Lombard's giddiness and body movements mirror the speed of her car, offering a visual complement that once again speaks to the modernist fascination with technology. Like the *Run, Girl, Run* scene, Sennett has accelerated the film speed, resulting in the car's rapid descent down the school driveway. But whereas in the *Run, Girl, Run* example her fast movements highlighted her athletic prowess, in this scene it foregrounds her character's abundant energy and conveys Lombard's seemingly unrehearsed and fluid performance style.

Historians have often identified Lombard's "natural" acting quality in order to draw parallels between her early slapstick and screwball performances. Of her slapstick tenure, Wes Gehring writes that Sennett "endowed her with the practical comedy suggestion of 'just be yourself,' a lesson reiterated again later by both Hawks and La Cava."[104] He notes the similarities between Lombard's slapstick performances with those from *Twentieth Century* and *My Man Godfrey*—directed by Howard Hawks and Gregory La Cava respectively—and ultimately attributes her knack for "natural" performances to her early work with Sennett. Similarly, in a 1937 *Life* review of Lombard's film, *True Confession* (Wesley Ruggles, 1937), the author describes how Lombard "can lay some claim to have started the current craze for slapstick farce." It continues "Miss Lombard has been doing the same sort of comedy, on and off screen, for the better part of her 29 years."[105] This author conflates screwball and slapstick, even going so far as to erroneously use the latter genre title to describe the former.[106] The Gehring passage is from a contemporary source while the *Life* quote is of the period, but in different ways they draw unfounded connections between Lombard's slapstick and screwball work. While neither mention *The Campus Vamp* by name, the scene I have described is one of many examples that would appeal to this retrospective application of her screwball personality to her earlier, unrelated work in slapstick comedy.

The film's second half addresses Lombard's physical agility, as well as the combination of consumerism and spectacle behind Sennett's "Girl Comedies." Sennett once again employs camera techniques like slow and fast motion to draw attention to the women's bodies. Carole is at bat wearing

---

[104] Gehring, 58.
[105] "Movie of the Week: *True Confession*," *Life*, December 13, 1937, 70.
[106] "Screwball comedy" was a term used in the industry by 1936, and Lombard had already been informally crowned "The Queen of Screwball Comedy" in 1937.

FIGURE 1.5 *Lombard (right, holding bat) again demonstrates her "natural athleticism" while playing baseball in a scene from* The Campus Vamp.

a black one-piece suit, complete with a collar and buttons. She wears a red and white scarf wrapped like a turban around her head, and white ankle socks with dark sandals.

Framed in a medium shot, she hoists the bat behind her right shoulder ready to hit the baseball. Scattered even further in the distance are other "Sennett Girls" cheering on the teams. The film cuts to a reverse shot of Sally, the pitcher, who is standing several feet from the shoreline. She cranks her right arm in preparation to throw the ball, and as she does, we cut back to the shot of Carole, who hits the ball with her bat. She tosses the bat to the ground, and the camera begins to track alongside her as she runs around the bases. With the sunlight shining down on her to reveal her shimmering blonde hair, she sprints back toward home plate. It appears that Sennett has accelerated the speed of the film because her running seems unusually fast. However, this is done subtly and is only identifiable after several close viewings of the scene.

Carole's hit sends the ball flying into the ocean, and intercut with shots of her running the bases is a long shot of an unidentified girl running into the breaking waves to catch the ball. The film cuts back again to a medium-long shot of Lombard, this time in slow motion as her character dives into home plate. She jumps into her dive and as she does, lifts her arms in front of her as if she is plunging into a pool of water. In slow motion we see her land chest first into the sand, her legs flung into the air as the sand creates a dust cloud around her face. Carole's successful run alludes to her real-life childhood history playing baseball, and in keeping with Sennett's mantra of "just be yourself," it is possible that he was aware of her fondness for the sport. In that way, Lombard's "real-life" brings some verisimilitude to her "reel-life."

Rob King writes that Sennett believed his "Beauties" fascinated both male and female spectators by "crossing lines defined by gender and sexuality."[107] There is a blatant appeal to the male gaze; the slow motion and color film stock used in the Lombard sequence "authorized [the men] to gaze guiltlessly on the bodies of young women who, Sennett's publicity team reassured them, were "healthy" and "wholesome," girls whose poses lacked "any suggestion of offensive."[108] According to King, female interest with the "Beauties" was "at a far deeper level," specifically their ties to consumerism and as aspiration models representing the modern female.[109] The commercial incentive behind the "Bathing Beauties" is well documented, and as Sennett himself explained, they were initially conceived as a marketing gimmick to garner publicity for his studio and films.[110] As mentioned earlier, Sennett frequently used color film stock like two-strip Technicolor to advertise new trends in beauty and fashion.[111] Lombard and the other actresses from *The Campus Vamp* were therefore both performers and fashion models. Their presence exposes the way commercial filmmaking in the 1920s was used by advertisers to reach the masses and, in particular, the large demographic of female consumers.[112]

The "Beauties" were also models in another sense of the word. King writes that they appealed to "young women's own desires for self-transformation," and were often considered "role models who mediated modern gender ideals for a consumer society."[113] They would frequently be featured in magazines offering advice on fashion, lifestyle, and beauty.[114] Women were thus encouraged to look at the "Beauties" as symbolic of contemporary style and female modernity. But King's analysis ignores the appeal to a more voyeuristic and sexualized female gaze, one not entirely related to consumerism and leisure. Like *Run, Girl, Run, The Campus Vamp* indulges the female gaze through the all-girl school setting, as well as the habitual use of slow motion and languid long shots of the "Beauties'" youthful and athletic bodies.

---

[107] King, 242.
[108] Ibid.
[109] Ibid.
[110] Mack Sennett, *King of Comedy* (Lincoln: iUniverse, 2000), 167.
[111] D'Haeyere, 222.
[112] Ibid, 223.
[113] King, 242.
[114] Ibid.

The Campus Carmen (*Alfred J. Goulding, 1928*)

Lombard followed *Run, Girl, Run* and *The Campus Vamp* with yet another film in the "Sennett Girl Comedies" series, *The Campus Carmen*. She plays second lead to Daphne Pollard and Johnny Burke, a sign that she was rising in the ranks of Sennett's troupe and making a name for herself among the other Sennett Girls. Through an analysis of Lombard's costume and performance in the film's opening pillow fight and the final theatrical sequences, I will demonstrate how her character both conforms to and transgresses gender boundaries. Unlike Lombard's previous shorts where her characters are clearly coded as being traditionally "feminine," her character's sexualized male soldier costume and sword fight in the latter half of the film actively addresses the gender ambiguity underpinning the film's narrative. Lombard plays Carole, a college girl at Sunnydale School, and she and her classmates are putting on a production of Bizet's *Carmen*. We are first introduced to Carole in the girl's dormitory on the eve of their opening night. The introductory intertitle reads "Some of the girls slept in dormitories—but most of 'em wore pajamas." The intertitle fades to a wide shot of the dormitory bedroom, where dozens of girls are having a pillow fight. The film cuts to a closer medium shot, and we see Lombard in the middle of the group. She wears a light colored silk robe and a ribbon in her dirty blonde hair, which falls just below her jaw line. Her robe hangs open to reveal a matching silk romper. Lombard smiles excitedly to convey that her character is immersed in the pillow fight, and she repeatedly picks up pillows and throws them at nearby students. The juxtaposition between her costume and her enthusiasm for the pillow fight makes it is impossible to describe her as entirely girl or woman, for her actions and eager participation in the game do not match the sensual maturity of her appearance.

After the introductory shot of Lombard, it cuts to a medium shot of Fanny (Madalynne Field), who is described as "nature's gift to the candy industry," sitting on her bed eating a box of chocolate, then cuts back to a close-up of Carole whirling a pillow with her right hand over her head. She concentrates on her target with eager determination; her gaze is focused on Fanny—just out of frame. She lets go of the pillow and as she does, the film cuts back to Fanny, who gets hit in the face. As the pillow drops to the ground, we see that chocolate is smeared all around Fanny's mouth and she looks as if she is about to burst into tears. The film cuts to a dialog intertitle that reads "Nobody can hit me in the refreshment period—and live." Fanny stuffs her pillowcase with shoes and whirls it above her head in a circular motion. We cut again to a long shot of the girls with Lombard in the foreground. Fanny's pillow flies into the frame from the top right of the screen, and hits Carole in the face. Lombard conveys the momentum of the impact by falling back onto Carole's bed, and finally flipping into backward somersault onto the ground.

Like her other Sennett shorts, *The Campus Carmen* introduces us to the idea of Lombard as the paradoxical beautiful comic. But as much as this sequence demonstrates physical comedy, I would argue that her physicality is clearly marked according to conventional ideas of femininity. In her study of female comedians in early twentieth-century films, Kristen Anderson Wagner argues that "comediennes at this time were highly visible examples of women defying expectations regarding ladylike behavior and proper femininity."[115] Slapstick challenged gender roles by offering male and female comics relatively equal opportunity to partake in physical comedy.[116] Anderson Wagner explains that "the inherently aggressive nature of comedy is also diametrically opposed to the cultural ideal of femininity ... with its emphasis on submissiveness, deference, and passivity."[117] I agree with her assessment, although the pillow fight scene confirms the potential boundaries of female gender transgression. While the scene appears to show women "acting out" and defying gender expectations, upon further examination it upholds gender norms by portraying the "Beauties" through an objectified and juvenile lens.

At first glance one could argue that the sheer fact that the girls hurl objects at each other and become victims of pranks "crosses social boundaries into unacceptable behavior."[118] However, we must consider the limits of this physical comedy performance. Their costumes and locale tether them to a domesticated and infantilized milieu. They are in a shared dormitory monitored by the dorm matron, Tillie Toober (Daphne Pollard), whose job is to maintain order among the girls and to keep them confined to their rooms. When she hears them getting rowdy, she barges into their room and gets hit in the face by a pillow. This is a clear example of unladylike female behavior and even an act of rebellion against authority (Tillie), but the diegetic space and method of their rebellion confirms the limits of the students' transgressions. Additionally, we cannot ignore the gentle and childish nature of the pillow fight itself. Alex Clayton writes that women are often marginalized in slapstick due to "the severe range of expectations that traditionally govern the female body in patriarchal society."[119] In general, Lombard challenges Clayton's assertion by using

---

[115] Kristen Anderson Wagner, "Have Women a Sense of Humor?": Comedy and Femininity in Early Twentieth-Century Film," *The Velvet Light Trap* Number 68 (Fall 2011), 35.
[116] Ibid, 36.
[117] Ibid, 37.
[118] Ibid, 35.
[119] Clayton, 146.

her body as the center of her comic performances. In a different way than Lombard's demure character in *The Girl from Everywhere,* the first half of *The Campus Carmen* demonstrates how she and the other girls conform to patriarchal society's "range of expectations." The pillow fight itself is juvenile, and pillows are hardly objects that cause any severe bodily harm. The only time that it becomes a potentially dangerous object is when Lombard gets hit with Fanny's shoe-filled pillow. That said, it is important to consider that in contrast to her later screwball heroines who have the pleasure of performing slapstick pranks, here Lombard's character is the unassuming victim, the one who suffers the fate of getting hit by a shoe-filled pillow. Her reaction further confirms the limits of that moment of transgression: she lays on the floor and flails her legs in the air. It is a declaration of defeat, a confirmation of her character's atypical female fragility.

The potential for transgression becomes clearer during the girls' theatrical performance. Since there are no boys enrolled at the Sunnydale School, the girls are required to play both the male and female acting roles. This opens up a space for a queer reading of the gender reversal role-playing, particularly through the lead characters' costumes and mannerisms. Fanny plays the eponymous Carmen, however unlike Bizet's character, her version is uncoordinated, overweight, and unladylike. She is dressed in a ruffled Spanish style dress and wide brimmed sunhat, which superficially mark her as feminine. However, Fanny's actions on and off stage do not meet the expectations of seductive femininity required of the role of Carmen. She struggles to climb up the ladder to the on-stage balcony due to her weight, and breaks the bottom rungs. As she climbs up the ladder on her knees the camera shoots her from a slight low angle, which exaggerates the plumpness of her bare legs. Once on the balcony—which is on the verge of crashing to the ground due to the pressure of Fanny's weight—she puffs away at a long cigar and spits throughout her opening song. The repeated references to Fanny's weight and her brash "masculine" mannerisms on and off the stage function to desexualize and de-feminize her body.

Conversely, Lombard plays a male Spanish soldier whose costume reveals explicitly the feminine curves of her body. She wears tight black shorts, black knee-high boots, and a fitted, sleeveless, and backless military vest that emphasizes the curves of her breasts. While her physical appearance is clearly coded along conventional gender lines in the first half, the film consciously plays with her gender during the latter half. She plays a male character and is wearing a "masculine" costume, yet the style and fit are revealing and sexually provocative. The erotic undertones of their costumes are further compounded by Carole's sword fight with Tillie, who plays Carmen's love interest, Don Jose. Lombard and Pollard stagger around the stage with long metal swords drawn above their heads, the obvious phallic symbol reinforcing the sexual innuendo of their relationship and the gender ambiguity of both characters. In contrast to the other women in the play, Tillie wears a baggy torero costume and an oversized fake mustache. Although bullfighters typically represent virility, machismo, and strength, Pollard's short and stocky, asexual physique, and uncoordinated sword fight with Carole adds yet another comic element to the play on gender. The muddy representations of masculinity and femininity in this scene highlight the gender inversion running throughout the short film. The opening and closing scenes offer several different interpretations of femininity through the characters Carole, Fanny, and Tillie, and in different ways, each is portrayed in a comic light. In doing so, one could argue that the film rejects a unilateral definition of femininity, and more broadly acknowledges the performative nature of female identity.

The Swim Princess (*Alfred J. Goulding, 1928*)

Unfortunately, the print of *The Swim Princess* that I watched at UCLA did not include the second reel. The first reel features Lombard performing what I would consider to be the most physically demanding comedy routine of the silent comedies included in this chapter. The film was co-written by James J. Tynan and Frank Capra—both uncredited[120]—and released on February 26, 1928. It features Carole Lombard in a leading role along with Daphne Pollard and vaudeville actor turned Sennett player, Andy Clyde. From what I understand of the plot, the events once again concern the collegiate activities of the Sunnydale School, this time following the personality clash between the swimming coach, Sally Forthe (Daphne Pollard), and her star swimmer, Trudy (Lombard). According to the opening intertitle, swimming was such a popular sport at Sunnydale that "even the goldfish wore one piece suits." The team gears up for their annual meet against the Rainbow School. Sally is in charge of keeping the girls in line, but she fails to notice a sneaky school reporter, Gordon Ginsberg (Andy Clyde), putting a bottle of gin inside a hollowed out camera while the team waits for their train at a station. An intertitle introduces him as "one tank that has never seen war service." This description sets up Ginsberg's excessive drinking habits for what I assume to be his consequential role in the second half of the film—however, he remains absent from the remainder of the first reel.

After we are introduced to Ginsberg, the film cuts to a long shot of a man and a woman standing with their backs to the camera, leaning on the side

---

[120] Joseph McBride, *Frank Capra: The Catastrophe of Success* (Jackson: The University Press of Mississippi, 1992), 183.

of a convertible several feet away from the train. The unidentified woman shakes her head, and the film cuts to a close-up of her face; the mystery woman is, in fact, Lombard. This type of introduction is typical of a "big reveal" that one would associate with a major star's first appearance in a film. This shot further challenges Larry Swindell's claim—cited earlier—that Lombard was known merely as "the pretty one," for although Lombard was not yet a household name, such an introduction makes sense given her status as a Sennett picture personality.

From the opposite side of the car, the film cuts to a close-up of Trudy who says something to her boyfriend, Jim (Jim Hallett). Lombard smiles coyly to indicate Trudy's flirtatious nature. The accompanying intertitle reads, "Trudy, Sunnydale's champion swimmer, was pretty enough to attract attention without a bathing suit." Through this introduction, we understand her character to be the typically rebellious and effortlessly athletic collegiate girl that Lombard often played in Sennett films. The film cuts to a reverse close-up of Jim who pleads "If you really loved me, you'd let me drive you to the meet." The scene then breaks the 180 degree rule and cuts to the front of the car, giving us a full view of their bodies. In long shot, we see Lombard fiddle with Jim's vest button in a playful manner that again hints at Trudy's flirtatious personality. The couple kiss, and as they are in the midst of their embrace Sally sneaks up behind them and sticks her head between theirs. Lombard slinks her body down to sit on the side board of the car, tilts her head back and rolls her eyes to convey Trudy's annoyance and adolescent embarrassment.

The next scene takes place inside the train. In a close-up, Trudy turns her head away from the camera to look out of the window. In the distance, we see Jim speeding off in his car alongside the train. He motions to Trudy with a wave to come to the train door, and the film cuts to an even closer shot of her face. She winks and moves her hand in a hitchhiking motion toward her back. Another cut takes us to a long shot of Trudy running down the aisle of the train compartment toward the door, before cutting again to an overhead tracking shot of the back of Jim's car cruising down the road parallel to the train compartment door. In the same tracking shot, we see her stick out her leg trying to "catch" the car with her foot. In a marvelous display of physicality, Lombard touches the side of the car with her left foot while the two vehicles are in motion. For a significantly long and uninterrupted tracking shot she is shown suspended between the train and car.

Sennett often used trick photography techniques that were first developed in French comedies, but his scenes appeared more realistic because of the professional automobile drivers, aviators, and "bumpmen"[121] that were

---

[121]An early name for stuntmen.

hired to execute the stunts.[122] Sennett also gave his actors the opportunity to perform their own stunts. For example, in 1914 Sennett hired Walter Brookins—who flew with the Wright brothers—as Keystone's official aviator, and he later trained Mabel Normand to fly.[123] Normand performed many of her own stunts including diving off a cliff in *The Squaw's Love* (D.W. Griffith, 1911), racing in *Mabel at the Wheel* (Mabel Normand and Mack Sennett, 1914), and flying in *A Dash Through the Clouds* (Mack Sennett, 1912), the latter noted as being the first film that features a woman in flight.[124] Unfortunately, production information of Lombard's Sennett films is meager, however, given Sennett's production practices it is highly likely that no trick photography was used to achieve Lombard's stunt. The fact that this scene was filmed outdoors on actual moving vehicles adds a deeper layer of awe-inspiring danger to Lombard's performance.

In this sequence, Lombard's malleable body once again becomes intertwined with technology in a way that is reminiscent of what Tom Gunning calls the 1920s aesthetic and political "romance with modernity," which teetered between the Russian Constructivists' vision of the "utopian possibilities of the machine man" and "the pliant automation" conceived by industrialists Henry Ford and Frederick W. Taylor.[125] Lombard is the human link between both vehicles: the image of her straddling the train and car evokes the style of one of silent cinema's most well-known modernist comics, Buster Keaton, whose performances in such films as *The Navigator* (Donald Crisp and Buster Keaton, 1924) and *The General* (Clyde Bruckman and Buster Keaton, 1926) capture his bodily "identification" with machines and the "demands of systematic environments."[126] Keaton frequently "achieved his gags with a sort of automatism" that critics saw as a reflection of the "non consciousness of the machine."[127] In *The Swim Princess,* Trudy makes a successful jump into Jim's car, and as they speed away from the train the couple waves at the camera, breaking the fourth wall in a concluding display of spectacular physical skill. Although Lombard's stunt in this scene is nowhere near as elaborate as some of Keaton's most memorable gags, it

---

[122]Walker, 34.

[123]Ibid.

[124]Timothy Dean Leffner, *Mabel Normand: The Life and Career of a Hollywood Madcap* (Jefferson, NC: McFarland & Co., Inc., 2016), 35.

[125]Tom Gunning, "Buster Keaton, or the Work of Comedy in the Age of Mechanical Reproduction," in *Hollywood Comedians, the Film Reader*, ed. Frank Krutnik (London: Routledge, 2003), 76.

[126]Ibid, 74–75.

[127]Ibid, 75.

is similarly dependent on "anthropomorphizing the inanimate" through extended physical contact with the train and car.[128]

Unlike *The Campus Carmen,* here Lombard refutes the patriarchal assumption that women's bodies are "too fragile, too precious" for physical comedy,[129] because the spectacle lies in the impressive dexterity of her nimble body. As in *Smith's Pony, Run, Girl, Run* and *The Campus Vamp,* in this film she again plays the star athlete. It is interesting to document the pattern of Lombard's Sennett heroines, as they all possess a natural athletic ability but are also all headstrong, feminine glamour girls. The need to display physical comedy in such films largely dictates the abundance of sports, and in light of Sennett's mantra, "Just be yourself," Lombard's roles in these shorts as the "star athlete" are, at least partially, a result of him tapping into her strength as a physical performer. We cannot overlook the fact that Lombard's athletic skill is never called into question and made into the butt of a joke. Instead, she routinely performs each sport—riding, track, baseball, and presumably swimming—with ease and, as I have argued earlier, with the help of camera techniques like slow and fast motion, the audience is meant to marvel at her athletic proficiency.

The Swim Princess is no exception, the train stunt being what I consider the pinnacle of her physical comedy achievement in this early period of her career. Like her earlier films, Lombard's comic performance invites our gaze and asks us to consider the magnitude of her physical triumph. Alex Clayton writes that "the brutal force of a slapstick pratfall has the capacity to reawaken us to the fundamental physicality of the world, and hence to its detail: to its textures and rhythms, to relationships elemental and vivid, to the momentary triumphs and failures of human endeavor."[130] Lombard's train stunt does just that: the movement of both vehicles awakens us to the physicality of her performance. When watching the scene, the spectator cannot help but notice the concrete details throughout the frame—the gravel on the road that became blurred by the tracking camera, the wind rustling Lombard's dress, the sunshine beating down on her leg—all "real" visual elements that bring the stunt to life. Clayton further explains that "physical comedy involves itself in a forceful declaration of the body."[131] This entire scene is predicated on the sheer malleability of Lombard's body. There is a "forceful declaration" of her body in the stunt since its physical interaction with the moving vehicles creates the scene's suspense. As Lombard dangles between the train and car, we wonder how the stunt was achieved and whether or not she will complete her jump successfully. It is less of a "comic" physical moment but rather one that encourages audience to revel in Lombard's display of choreographed mastery.

---

[128]Ibid.
[129]Clayton, 148.
[130]Ibid, 12.
[131]Ibid, 128.

Matchmaking Mamma (*Harry Edwards, 1929*)

One of Lombard's last films with Keystone Film Company is *Matchmaking Mamma,* which was released on March 31, 1929. It tells the story of Mrs. McNitt (Daphne Pollard) and her quest for herself and her daughter, Phyllis (Lombard), to become paragons of society. Mrs. McNitt wants Phyllis to marry Larry Lodge (Matty Kemp), the son of a well-to-do family. She hires a drama coach named Clifford Figfield (Irving Bacon) to direct a charity pageant starring the young couple. However, Larry falls in love with Phyllis's stepsister, Sally (Sally Eilers). Mrs. McNitt tries to keep Sally away from Larry by telling her he is a helpless flirt who is engaged to Phyllis. Unfortunately Phyllis is more interested in Clifford, which leaves Sally and Larry's love to blossom relatively uninterrupted.

Lombard's role is surprisingly minor, especially considering that the short was completed toward the end of her two-year contract. The narrative action is bookended by two-strip Technicolor scenes and in both, Lombard reprises her "Sennett Girl" role. Like *The Campus Vamp*, the scenes

FIGURE 1.6 Matchmaking Mamma *(Harry Edwards, 1929) was one of several films produced for Mack Sennett's "Girl Comedies" series. These films were structured to showcase the physical allure of Sennett's "Bathing Beauties."*

showcase the narratively disparate, ornamental purpose of the bathing girls. The first time they appear is at the film's opening in an unrelated scene at the beach. The beauties stand in a line waving pom-poms at the camera, breaking the fourth wall in such a way that calls attention to their "extrafictional" spectacular function.[132] Emblazoned in white type over the image are the words "Sennett Girls." Lombard stands in the middle of the frame atop a rock, which suggests that she is the "star" of the group. She is wearing a black one-piece suit with green detailing, and a red and white scarf wrapped around her head. The shot immediately fades to black and the story begins.

The second Technicolor scene is significant because of the combination of both diegetic and non-diegetic spectacles, and the way in which Lombard and the other actresses address the spectator's fetishistic gaze. In a medium shot, we see a man who we think is Larry enter the left of the frame dressed in a Sheik's garb that is reminiscent of silent screen idol Rudolph Valentino, and a mask to conceal his identity. As Larry moves around the frame Phyllis follows him. Lombard shuffles quickly on her knees to show that Phyllis is pleading for Larry's affection. An intertitle reads, "Come on Larry—you're supposed to kiss me here!" In the same shot, Phyllis grabs Larry's hands and places them on the lower part of her back, in an effort to make their love scene appear authentic. She wraps her arms around his neck, and waits for him to kiss her. Lombard purses her lips childishly to convey Phyllis's annoyance at Larry, then leans toward him and kisses him passionately.

The scene then cuts to a medium shot of Mrs. McNitt, her friend, and Sally sitting in chairs applauding at the scene. Larry falls backward to the ground, seemingly overtaken by passion. Lombard stands beside him facing the camera and curtseying timidly to show Phyllis's feigned modesty; despite what her body language implies, her kiss confirms that Phyllis is no shy schoolgirl. Her smile disappears from her face, and Phyllis makes a surprised grimace. We cut to a close-up of an equally surprised looking Clifford, who disguised himself in Larry's costume.

Much like the color sequence in *The Campus Vamp*, the two Technicolor scenes in *Matchmaking Mamma* are primarily included for the purpose of creating a visual spectacle and to acknowledge the presence of the audience in a vaudevillian mode of performance. In his study of comedian comedy, Steve Seidman reminds us that in comparison to narrative films and traditional theater, where the "function of acting" is to "become a character within the context of a coherent, contoured fictional situation," a performer's success in vaudeville lay in "exhibiting the self in such a way as to induce

---

[132]Steve Seidman, "Performance, Enunciation, and Self-reference in Hollywood's Comedian Comedy," in *Hollywood Comedians, the Film Reader*, ed. Frank Krutnik (London: Routledge, 2003), 21.

FIGURE 1.7 *In shorts like* Matchmaking Mamma, *Mack Sennett used Technicolor film stock to emphasize the visual spectacle of his "Bathing Beauties."*

an immediate response ... from the audience."[133] Unlike the color scene in *The Campus Vamp* that appealed to the male and female gaze without ever acknowledging the audience, these sequences engage the spectator by way of direct address, which Seidman describes as the "functional equivalent of the vaudeville 'aside.'"[134] These moments are significant because the actor briefly "removes themselves from the fiction" to convey additional information— by way of an expression, gesture, or, in the case of sound comedies, dialog— to their audience.[135] Specifically, the direct address in *Matchmaking Mamma* indulges what John Ellis calls the spectator's fetishistic gaze. He writes that this type of scene "tries to abolish the gulf" between the spectator and actor on screen, and that it "implies the direct acknowledgment and participation of the object viewed."[136] Whereas the scopophilic gaze maintains a distance between the spectator and the thing being viewed, the fetishistic gaze openly

---

[133] Ibid, 22.
[134] Ibid, 24.
[135] Ibid.
[136] John Ellis, *Visible Fictions: Cinema, Television, Video* (New York: Routledge, 1982), 43.

acknowledges the spectator's look. Part of the pleasure associated with this type of look is that the person or object on display has given their consent to being watched.

Ellis's term is productive insofar as it captures the spectacular nature of *Matchmaking Mamma*'s color sequences and the ornamental function of Lombard and the "Sennett Girls." In both scenes the "Sennett Girls" look into the camera, confirming their role as objects to be looked at. Their smiles and waves to the camera break the fourth wall, "abolishing the gulf" that separates them from the cinema audience. When Phyllis acts in her pageant scene with "Larry" (Clifford), she is consciously playing for two audiences: the one in the diegetic world and the film audience in the movie theater. Each time she addresses the camera, she steps out of her role as Phyllis back into Lombard the actress, which alludes to the layers of identity at play in this performance. But it appears that only Phyllis and the other girls are aware of the camera, for none of the other characters ever break the fourth wall. In his close-up after being kissed, Clifford's gaze remains focused off camera in the direction of Mrs. McNitt and her friends. His embarrassment is made clear to the film's audience by way of close-up framing, but Irving Bacon gives no indication that his character is acting for the benefit of the camera. By contrast, when the shot immediately cuts from Clifford's close-up to Phyllis's curtsey she directs her actions toward the camera, not the diegetic audience sitting just out of frame. Larry, Clifford, and Mrs. McNitt remain enveloped by the diegetic world, whereas Phyllis and the "Sennett Girls" can transcend the boundaries of the frame and, to a certain extent, their objectification by way of their direct address. Lombard's direct address is not necessarily an erasure of objectification, but rather a complicit knowingness—a cinematic wink, if you will—of her status as a spectacular object.

Conclusion

The films included in this chapter are by no means a complete list of Lombard's work with Sennett, but this is the first scholarly textual analysis of her performances in slapstick comedy. I have gone into some detail because Lombard's slapstick comedies should not be overlooked: they are imperative to the overall understanding of her star persona, and to the ways her performance style evolved from silent to sound cinema. These films offer us clues into the origins of the Lombard heroine: her looks, her movements, her interactions with other characters and the space around her.

One of the conclusions I have drawn after my initial viewing of these shorts is that contrary to popular opinion, Lombard is not consistently physical in all of her roles. In some shorts like *Matchmaking Mamma*, there is no substantive physical element to her performance. In others like *The Swim Princess* and *Run, Girl, Run*, rough-and-tumble physicality is the backbone of her performances. However, a consistent theme that runs throughout these shorts is the spectacular function of Lombard's body: whether signifying her athleticism or her feminine sensuality, it is often turned into a site of visual spectacle. In different scenarios her slapstick body juxtaposes her natural athleticism with her femininity, creating in Lombard the image of the beautiful and physically agile comic. Her roles also reflected slapstick comedy's ties with consumer culture and gender. Finally, through Sennett's habitual employment of camera techniques like fast and slow motion, the focus on her body also crystalized the role of cinema as a modern technological medium.

Most of this chapter has focused on Lombard's performances, however, she was also making some headway off screen. Although the breadth of publicity material available about Lombard during this period is meager, snippets from newspapers and industry trade papers indicate that she was starting to make a name for herself within the industry. In addition to the Sennett shorts, in 1928 Lombard acted in five feature films for Pathé including *Show Folks* (Paul L. Stein) and *Power* (Howard Higgin).[137] For her performance in the former film, *Picture Play* magazine described her as "a very pretty blonde ... worth watching."[138] Her promising performances in these features led to a "small but entertaining part as a waitress being hustled by a bootlegger" in *Ned McCobb's Daughter* (William J. Cowen, 1928).[139] Lombard again received positive reviews including one from a critic for *Film Spectator* who noted "Carole Lombard repeats the good impression she made on me in *Show Folks*."[140] Although Lombard had not yet achieved stardom, her tenure with Sennett's troupe proved advantageous not only in terms of publicity, but also as a platform to gain experience in front of the camera. As Lombard transitioned away from slapstick in 1929, her star persona began to transform significantly.

---

[137]Gehring, 62. I had the chance to view a print of *Show Folks* at the Library of Congress, however Lombard's role is too minor to warrant any substantial analysis. *Power* is in the public domain and is available to purchase as a bootleg copy. Like *Show Folks*, Lombard's role is quite small.
[138]"Review of *Show Folks* (Pathé)," *Picture Play*, March 1929, page unknown.
[139]Gehring, 62.
[140]"Review of *Ned McCobb's Daughter* (Pathé)," *Film Spectator*, November 10, 1928, page unknown.

2

Hollywood's best-dressed star, 1929–1934

In the years I have spent researching Carole Lombard, I have often come across observations that draw connections between her slapstick and screwball comedies. Given the prevalence of physical comedy in both the slapstick and screwball genres, the link between Lombard's two comic personae is, to a certain extent, justifiable. This line of thinking also speaks to the way the Hollywood studios groomed their stars' public personas. In Lombard's case, publicity outlets of the period frequently alluded to her work in slapstick as a way to contextualize her allegedly natural screwball persona. However, there is no historical evidence to connect these two phases of her public image and career, and such a theory ignores the nearly five years between Lombard's last slapstick comedy and first screwball film. This chapter therefore aims to correct the oft-repeated assertion that after leaving Mack Sennett's troupe in 1929, Carole Lombard was on a path toward screwball stardom.

In reality, the early 1930s was a period of great change for Lombard's personal and professional life. In late 1928 she made the brief transition from Mack Sennett's company back to Fox for a one picture deal, then again to Pathé,[1] who handled the domestic and international distribution of Sennett's shorts. In 1930 she left Pathé and signed with Paramount Studios,[2] where she remained under contract until 1937. At Paramount's behest Lombard acted in a variety of genres including western, thriller, comedy, dance films and melodrama, in an effort to find a screen persona that would resonate with film audiences. Lombard made twenty-three films between her last Sennett short and her first screwball film, *Twentieth Century* (Howard

---

[1] Robert Matzen, *Fireball: Carole Lombard and the Mystery of Flight 3* (Pittsburgh: GoodKnight Books, 2014), 31.
[2] Gehring, 74.

Hawks, 1934), and only about half of those titles are comedies. Like many of her Hollywood contemporaries, many of these films were the result of "loan out deals" orchestrated by Paramount with other studios, which Emily Carman explains proved that Lombard was a "box-office commodity, and inadvertently led her to take ownership of her career" in the late 1930s for more challenging and lucrative professional opportunities.[3] In fact, by the end of her career, Lombard had made at least one film at all eight of the top Hollywood studios, most of which had been completed during this under-studied post slapstick phase.

Not long after signing her long-term contract with Paramount, the studio set about to build up Lombard's star persona. In the late 1920s and early 1930s Paramount had successfully marketed both Kay Francis and Marlene Dietrich in the glamour tradition. By 1932 Lombard was two years into her long-term contract, but the studio had not yet found her niche with film audiences. With no clear direction to her career and a largely undefined star persona, she became their latest ingenue whose image was molded using the same formula.[4] Thus, between 1932 and early 1935 she was known as one of Hollywood's glamour girls, a persona that was grounded in sophistication and high fashion and was, by nature, the opposite of her more famous earthy and vibrant screwball persona. In keeping with her new image, Lombard was crowned "Hollywood's best dressed star" by several fan magazines, and was featured in articles offering fashion and beauty advice to female readers.[5] She carried her clotheshorse title even after she began making screwball comedies, a fact that confirms she was not immediately groomed for screwball stardom. She also starred in films that reinforced her glamorous star persona like *Man of the World* (Richard Wallace, 1931), *White Woman* (Stuart Walker, 1933), *Bolero* (Wesley Ruggles, 1934), and *No More Orchids* (Walter Lang, 1932). I will address the trajectory of Lombard's glamour girl image later on in this chapter, and consider the effects it had on her film roles and stardom.

Although one could justifiably argue that Lombard is not an exceptional star in terms of this transformative period of her public image, it is worthy of renewed study because its omission—or, at least, the marginalization—has sustained a discourse about Lombard's "natural" comedic inclinations that is both incomplete and unsubstantiated, given the interweaving cultural and industrial mechanisms involved in producing and sustaining a cohesive star figure. More broadly, these popular sources ignore both the technological and stylistic differences between slapstick and screwball comedy subgenres, and

---

[3] Emily Carman, *Independent Stardom: Freelance Women in the Hollywood Studio System* (Austin: University of Texas Press, 2016), 27.
[4] Gehring, 101.
[5] Dorothy Kugler, "How Carole Lombard Became the Best-Dressed Star," *Movie Classic*, May 1935, 28.

the specific social and ideological preconditions regarding female agency and independence in the 1930s from which Lombard's daffy "screwball girl" persona could emerge. If we consider the breadth of genres Lombard acted in between 1929 and 1934, it becomes clear that she was not on a singular path toward comedy. Lombard grew into her screwball fame after a nearly five-year period of trial and error, and only after she made *Twentieth Century* in 1934 did she begin to be seriously considered as a viable comic actress, but even that transition was slow at best.[6] This point touches upon one of the broader goals of this book, which is to show that Lombard's performance style and star persona should also be addressed outside of a screwball context.

The incongruity between Lombard's glamour girl and "Screwball Girl" personae and the frequency with which she was loaned out to other studios suggest that neither Pathé nor Paramount recognized any obvious financial or ideological incentives to promote her star persona around comedy. I contend that Lombard's star persona did not follow a linear progression from slapstick to screwball; it was not the inevitable next step to her slapstick tenure. Rather, it took several years, different genres, and multiple tweaks to Lombard's star persona to arrive at a formula that resonated with her public. It is therefore useful to first address the historiographical problem with linking slapstick and screwball comedy and why Lombard's persona did not immediately become associated with the latter comic mode.

Reassessing the evidence

Physical comedy is a feature of slapstick and screwball, and there is an obvious temptation to draw parallels between the subgenres. As I have demonstrated in my analyses of the Mack Sennett shorts, physicality was frequently part of Lombard's slapstick comedy repertoire, and it later became a defining trait for her screwball heroines. Nevertheless, we cannot ignore the fundamental stylistic, thematic, and sociohistorical differences. At the most basic level, slapstick focuses on body-driven comedy, modernity, consumerism, and cause–effect gags[7] in an effort to appeal to a wide range of class tastes that the cinema targeted as a medium designed for mass audiences. There was a sense of sexual freedom in slapstick comedies of the 1920s, partially a result of less reticent views toward sexuality and relaxed censorship oversight

---

[6] *Twentieth Century* was not identified as a screwball comedy upon its initial release. Such a designation was applied retroactively once the genre's formal and thematic traits were better defined. For a more detailed discussion of the origins of screwball comedy, see chapter 3.
[7] See: Donald Crafton, "Pie and Chase: Gag, Spectacle, and Narrative in Slapstick Comedy," and Tom Gunning, "Crazy Machines in the Garden of Forking Paths: Mischief Gags and the Origins of American Film Comedy," in *Classical Hollywood Comedy*, eds. Kristine Brunovska Karnick and Henry Jenkins (New York: Routledge, 1995), 87–105.

throughout the United States,[8] a "burgeoning youth culture,"[9] and the sexual and sociopolitical liberation of the "New Woman."[10] Screwball,[11] on the other hand, was born out of the economic malaise of the Great Depression and industry-wide censorship regulations. The delicate balance of physical comedy and subtle, witty dialog reflected the sexual repression of its characters—physical comedy being an allusion to sex[12]—and the morally conservative guidelines of the Production Code.[13] Each subgenre has its own style and tone, both of which are determined by their unique industrial, ideological, aesthetic, technological, and economic conditions. To suggest that Lombard simply made the leap from slapstick to screwball ignores the historical, formal and contextual specificity of each comic mode, and the range of genres she appeared in between these phases of her career.

We cannot take Lombard's screwball success for granted simply because of her early years making slapstick films. The types of arguments I have frequently come across make rather bold and unfounded associative links. Take, for example, the following list of quotations from Lombard biographies, genre studies scholarship, and contemporaneous media sources:

> Blonde, beautiful, and spirited, Carole Lombard was, and still is to some, the finest satiricalcomedienne the screen has ever known, the embodiment of screwball comedy, the queen of the genre ... A stint with Mack Sennett, the acknowledged "king of comedy" during the silent era, taught her the impeccable timing which was at the heart of her comedic genius.[14]
>
> Carole Lombard's past as a Mack Sennett girl was known to just about every movie fan; years later, that slapstick experience would pay off when Lombard became a legend of screwball comedy.[15]
>
> *True Confession* is a "screwball farce," and Carole Lombard can lay some claim to having started the current craze for slapstick farces ... During her late teens she trained for comedy by dodging custard pies for Mack Sennett.[16]

---

[8] Joshua Zeitz, *Flapper: A Madcap Story of Sex, Style, Celebrity and the Women Who Made America Modern* (New York: Three Rivers Press, 2006), 23.
[9] Lucy Fischer, "Introduction: Movies of the 1920s," in *American Cinema of the 1920s: Themes and Variations*, ed. Lucy Fischer (New Brunswick: Rutgers University Press, 2009), 6.
[10] Ibid.
[11] A more detailed explanation of screwball can be found in chapter 3.
[12] *Romantic Comedy: Boy Meets Girl Meets Genre*, 30.
[13] Jane M. Greene, "A Proper Dash of Spice: Screwball Comedy and the Production Code." *Journal of Film and Video* Vol. 63, No. 3 (Fall 2011), 48.
[14] Doris Milberg, *The Art of the Screwball Comedy: Madcap Entertainment from the 1930s to Today* (Jefferson: McFarland & Co., Inc., 2013), 8.
[15] Vincent Paterno, "'Motion Picture,' May 1932: They also served for Sennett," *Carole and Co.*, May 27, 2013, accessed October 6, 2015, http://carole-and-co.livejournal.com/604533.html.
[16] "Movie of the Week: *True Confession*."

All in all, Lombard's signing with Sennett had been a positive experience, providing a comedy apprenticeship and proving to Hollywood that Lombard had a future in film despite her accident ... The Sennett period had greatly contributed to reducing the power of the unknown in Lombard's life.[17]

The Sennett slapstick legacy later became synonymous with Lombard's screwball comedies.[18]

The crowning irony was that Jean Arthur, Carole Lombard, and Myrna Loy could all trace their movie experience [in screwball comedy] back half a dozen years before talkies gained their final dominance.[19]

Had she gone on to playing conventional heroines, Lombard's career would almost certainly have petered out with the beginning of talkies. At Sennett's, however, she spent two years being hit in the face by pies, tripped, dunked, chased, and generally maltreated ... she had acquired a magnificent sense of comedy timing which, when Sennett farce was sublimated into screwball comedy, became her greatest asset.[20]

Each puts forth roughly the same argument, namely that Lombard's work in slapstick comedy was an "asset" to her screwball success, and that slapstick was a stepping stone to inevitable screwball fame. Lombard's "apprenticeship" with Sennett is described in educational terms and the Keystone Film Company was her de facto school where, as one source notes, she "trained for comedy by dodging custard pies." The persistent references to teaching, learning and, as the last quote claims, the acquisition of comedic timing imply that Lombard signed with Sennett for the purpose of becoming a comic actress. But as I have argued earlier, her success with Sennett was not a deliberate goal but rather the circumstantial result of her automobile accident, the professional setbacks it caused her, and the subsequent buildup Sennett gave her in the following months.

The last quote is especially troublesome because it paints a doomed scenario that, ironically, was not too dissimilar to Lombard's post slapstick career path. Writing in 1938 when Lombard was at the peak of her screwball fame, *Life* reporter Noel F. Busch hypothesizes that had she gone on to play "conventional heroines," she would not have been able to achieve stardom. He argues that Lombard used her Sennett education to her advantage when slapstick "sublimated" into screwball comedy. There are a number of problems with this statement, the least of which being that it ignores the historical and technological progression of comedy between the introduction of sound in

---

[17] Gehring, 59.
[18] Ibid, 53.
[19] Swindell, 188.
[20] Busch, 63.

American films in 1929 and the beginning of screwball in 1934, particularly the succession of pre-Code romantic comedies such as *The Greeks Had a Word For Them* (Lowell Sherman, 1932) and *She Had To Say Yes* (George Amy and Busby Berkeley, 1933) and their well established theatrical antecedents.[21] Additionally, it skims over the developments in sound and voice recording technology during the early 1930s that made screwball comedy's verbal banter possible.[22] The idea that Lombard's career would have "petered out" had she begun playing "conventional heroines" suggests that she lacked acting talent beyond comedy. On a broader level, however, it could also demonstrate the lengths media outlets like *Life* took—on behalf of the Hollywood studios' publicity departments—in trying to merge her "reel" and "real" personalities into a cohesive star figure. By that logic, Busch validates her screwball identity as being an "authentic" extension of her real-life screwball persona.

Busch's opinion does not take into account the actual trajectory of her post slapstick career. Despite being a Sennett picture personality, by 1929 Lombard was not yet a "star" in the same sense of the word as she was in 1938, so the risk of "petering out" was not as dire as Busch claims it to have been. And while he fails to define "conventional heroines," her roles immediately after signing with Pathé were in run-of-the-mill genre films like *Big News* (Gregory La Cava, 1929) and *The Racketeer* (Howard Higgin, 1929). She was briefly cast as the lead in Cecil B. DeMille's *Dynamite* (1929), but was replaced after the production was delayed and the producers of *High Voltage* (Howard Higgin, 1929) requested her for their film.[23] Larry Swindell writes that by the end of 1929 Lombard was "employable" and "could get work," but had no tangible contractual security,[24] nor did she have any "certainty on what was to be done with her in the ways of subsequent picture assignments."[25] Lombard's stardom was still in its infancy; her future in Hollywood was promising, but greatly uncertain.

William Powell and a stab at sophistication

To understand just how underdeveloped Lombard's star persona was in the early 1930s, we need not look further than the spectrum of roles that she played between 1930 and 1934 and her short-lived glamour girl persona.

---

[21] Charles Musser, "Divorce, DeMille and the Comedy of Remarriage," in *Classical Hollywood Comedy*, eds. Kristine Brunkova Karnick and Henry Jenkins (New York: Routledge, 1995), 282. See also: Billy Budd Vermilion, "The Remarriage plot in the 1910s," *Film History*, Vol. 13 (2001), 363.
[22] Gehring, 6.
[23] Grace Kingsley, "Actress Returns to Pathé," *Los Angeles Times*, January 22, 1929, A10.
[24] Ibid, 85.
[25] Ibid, 94.

In late 1929, Pathé Studios was taken over by political patriarch Joseph Kennedy in an effort to turn around the studio's dwindling finances.[26] Kennedy decided not to renew Lombard's contract, citing "the bad economy" as grounds for her termination. Robert Matzen writes that the reason was that Pathé had just signed a contract with Constance Bennett who, in the summer of 1929 had just returned to the United States to "resume her career" after a divorce from her second husband, millionaire shipping and railroad heir, Philip Morgan Plant.[27] Due to an alleged clause in Bennett's contract that stated the studio was obligated to "to divest itself of other, similar blondes,"[28] Lombard and a few other starlets were released from their contract. Considering that stars were deemed as financial investments for the Hollywood studios,[29] it seems unlikely that, regardless of her bankability or familial reputation, one actress like Bennett could have such influence in a multinational company like Pathé. I tend to believe that Lombard's termination was, in fact, a financial decision to cut costs and not because the studio simply caved in to Bennett's outrageous and subjective contractual demands.

In the spring of 1930 Lombard signed with Paramount and appeared as second lead in the romantic comedy, *Fast and Loose* (Fred C. Newmeyer, 1930), written by Preston Sturges and co-starring Miriam Hopkins and Frank Morgan. Lombard plays a chorus girl named Alice, who is dating Bertie Lenox (Henry Wadsworth), the son of a prominent Long Island banking family. Fearing for their son's future and their family's reputation, Bertie's parents try to break up the relationship which causes tension in the once tight-knit family unit. Filmed in the summer of 1930 at Paramount's New York studio[30] and released on November 8, 1930, it was labeled by one critic as a "good audience farce" with "competent acting." The same critic predicted the film's failure because it lacks "an effective cast of players known to the regular customer."[31] It was a box office flop and made only $52,100 in the first weeks after its release.[32] *Fast and Loose* is most notable for the legend surrounding the spelling of Lombard's first name. According to some sources, prior to *Fast and Loose*'s release Lombard had been known

---

[26]Cari Beauchamp, "The Mogul in Mr. Kennedy," *Vanity Fair*, April 2002, accessed October 9, 2015, http://www.vanityfair.com/news/2002/04/joekennedy200204.

[27]Brian Kellow, *The Bennetts: An Acting Family* (Lexington: The University Press of Kentucky, 2004), 126–127.

[28] Matzen, 31.

[29] P. David Marshall, "The Cinematic Apparatus and the Construction of the Film Celebrity," in *The Film Cultures Reader*, ed. Graeme Turner (New York: Routledge, 2002), 231.

[30] "Coming and Going," *The Film Daily*, June 24, 1930, page unknown.

[31] "Fast and Loose," *The Film Daily*, November 30, 1930, page unknown.

[32] "$94700 for 'Lightnin', Roxy; 'Morocco' and 'Blue Angel' Only Other Standout Films on B'way," *Variety*, December 10, 1930, 9.

in the press and in film credits as "Carol" Lombard,[33] but after Paramount's publicity department made a typographical error in the film's credits, she became known as "Carole" Lombard.[34] Earlier in this chapter I confirmed that there is evidence that shows she spelled her name with an "*e*" as early as 1925. The widespread circulation of this legend points to the constructed nature of her image, since the spelling of her name was but one of many details that transformed Jane Alice Peters into Carole Lombard. It also reveals the instability of her star persona during the early 1930s: consistent spelling would be extremely important in order to establish her star persona, because her name was essentially her "brand," a means of identification. This is yet another example that refutes the claim that Lombard made a swift ascent from slapstick comedy to screwball superstardom.

In Lombard's next two pictures she starred alongside her first husband, William Powell. Together they made two romantic pre-Code dramas *Ladies Man* (Lothar Mendes, 1931) and *Man of the World* (Richard Wallace, 1931); in the latter Lombard was again brought in as a replacement for Miriam Hopkins.[35] Tracking the parallel careers of Powell and Lombard reveals that around the time they wed, their individual star personae were both in the midst of significant transformations. Prior to 1930, Powell was best known for his villainous and sinister characters like Boldini in *Beau Geste* (Herbert Brenon, 1926) and Clan Dillon in *Nevada* (John Waters, 1927). Powell biographer Roger Bryant writes "Paramount in 1930 and 1931 moved Powell towards the sophisticate persona that would become familiar in future years," typified by his reoccurring Nick Charles role in the hybrid screwball-detective drama *Thin Man* series.[36] Off screen, Powell was part of a social circle of stars that the gossip press deemed Hollywood sophisticates, including Ronald Colman, Richard Barthelmess, and Warner Baxter. He had recently divorced from his wife of fifteen years, Eileen Wilson Powell, with whom he had his only child, William Jr. Around this time fan magazines played up his "divorced bachelor image" to complement his new debonair screen persona, a tactic that included an article about his secret apartment which was described as a "trysting place," that he rented under the pseudonym "Mr. Thorne."[37] The press also went to great lengths to merge Powell's on- and off-screen images, featuring him in nationally syndicated profile stories that described him as a "meticulous and neat ... extremely

---

[33] As evidenced by an article released in conjunction with *Fast and Loose*'s premiere. See: Malcolm H. Oettinger, "Another Three Cheers!" *Picture Play*, December 1930, 34.
[34] Gehring, 79.
[35] Swindell, 103.
[36] Roger Bryant, *William Powell: The Life and Films* (Jefferson: McFarland & Co., Inc., 2006), 65.
[37] Charles Francisco, *Gentleman: The William Powell Story* (London: St. Martin's Press, 1985), 8.

conservative man's man [who] is one of the best-dressed men in the motion picture colony."[38] His friendship with Colman and Barthelmess—who were together known as "Hollywood's Three Musketeers"—was covered in fan magazines and gossip columns, and the trio were regularly featured in stories detailing their extravagant vacations and nightlife at some of Hollywood's most popular clubs.[39]

To quote a *Screenland* article, Lombard and Powell's relationship developed "hastily" from co-stars to a real-life couple.[40] Compared to the coverage of Lombard's later well publicized three-year courtship with her second husband, Clark Gable, fan magazines discourse took the position that Hollywood was shocked by her and Powell's unlikely romance. In spite of Powell's bachelor image—and perhaps as a way for Hollywood to affirm their investment in monogamous marital ideology—he went on record stating that "I want to marry ... I believe that love is the only thing in the world worth having."[41] Lombard, it seemed, was not so sure; just three months prior to their marriage, she allegedly stated that she did not want to marry Powell.[42] After a whirlwind courtship they were married on June 6, 1931 at Lombard's home in Beverly Hills,[43] and went on honeymoon to Hawaii.[44]

Reflecting on Lombard's earlier rejection of marriage, an unnamed *Screenland* columnist hypothesized that she agreed to the marriage, in part, because Powell had become "less selfish ... Bill Powell had forgotten himself. Love had worked its magic."[45] The magazine describes Lombard as "an independent little lady and yet, paradoxically, most dependent" on her mother, from whom she had only ever been apart "no longer than three days."[46] Calling Lombard a "little lady" and the reference to her girlish attachment to her mother was stretching the truth, since she was twenty-two years old and had lived alone for several years. The description magnifies the sixteen year age difference between her and Powell, and sets up the article's strategy of disproving the naysayers in Hollywood who were skeptical of the marriage. It explains how each star "changed" in order to accommodate the other, thus again affirming Hollywood's pro-marriage ideology. By the

---

[38] "William Powell is a Man of Many Vivid Contrasts," *Washington Post*, February 15, 1931, A4. See also: "Inside Facts Concerning a Popular Star," *Washington Post*, June 1, 1930, A4.
[39] James Castonguay, "Myrna Loy and William Powell: The Perfect Screen Couple," in *Glamour in the Golden Age: Movie Stars of the 1930s*, ed. Adrienne McLean (New Brunswick: Rutgers University Press, 2011), 224.
[40] Gary Gray, "The New Mr. and Mrs.," *Screenland*, October 1931, 27.
[41] Bryant, 79.
[42] Ruth Biery, "Why Carole Changed Her Mind," *Screenland*, September 1931, 55.
[43] Gehring, 87.
[44] "Screen News," *Screenland*, December 1931, 128.
[45] Biery, 104.
[46] Ibid.

FIGURE 2.1 *Carole Lombard and William Powell became a real-life couple while making* Man of the World *(Richard Wallace, 1931). The pair were married on June 6, 1931. Although they divorced less than two years later, they remained friends for the rest of Lombard's life.*

columnist's assessment, Lombard matured from a "little lady" to a wife, while Powell gave up his bachelor lifestyle to be a devoted husband and champion of her budding career.[47] Together, Powell and Lombard embodied the fun, chic, and urbane modern Hollywood star couple.

Missing the mark as a Hollywood glamour girl

Once Carole Lombard wed William Powell, there was a noticeable shift in trying to market her star persona in conjunction with his newfound air of sophistication. Just as their individual star personas became linked through matrimony, so too was there a push by Paramount to project a modern urbanity onto their stars' coupledom. There were also ideological and financial incentives to unify Powell and Lombard's star images. In the same way that Lombard's second marriage to Clark Gable "offered a model for childless working couples that combined the 'fun' of their screen roles with

[47] Ibid.

a utilitarian nature," and reflected the "shifting conception of relationships" and marriage during the Depression,[48] Lombard and Powell's marriage signified the lavish and fantastic world of Hollywood stardom.

During Powell's transition from villainous characters to the "Nick Charles" prototype, by early 1932 Lombard had acquired her glamour girl persona. According to Wes Gehring, she was "caught up by the screen's emphasis on high glamour," which reflected the public's "crystallizing agony of the Depression."[49] In 1931 the Hollywood studios began moving away from the shopgirl genre of films made famous by Joan Crawford and Barbara Stanwyck that exploited the economic turmoil caused by the Depression,[50] and began to produce films that satisfied the public's growing demand for glamour, gentility, and elegance.[51] Swindell writes that Paramount had already "successfully marketed Kay Francis in that tradition; and the accent on sophistication was further justified by the exotic appeal of that sensational import Marlene Dietrich ... Carole's new image would be a calculated hybrid of the Dietrich and Francis attributes."[52] Francis brought a mischievous toughness to her worldly heroines, typified in her role as perfume manufacturer Madame Mariette Colet in *Trouble in Paradise* (Ernst Lubitsch, 1932). Meanwhile Dietrich's star persona exuded an unwavering masculine confidence and extreme female sensuality, a combination made more palpable by her German—foreign—origins.

There is a general consensus among Lombard fans and biographers that around the time she acquired her new glamour girl image, Paramount orchestrated a marketing campaign to promote her under the nickname "The Orchid Lady." Silent film buffs might recognize "The Orchid Lady" moniker as having been originally attributed to the silent screen actress, Corinne Griffith. In a June, 1930 article from *Talking Screen,* columnist Dorothy Spensley describes Griffith as the "orchid lady of the screen" and "one of the chief exponents of feminine sex appeal."[53] This particular star persona was based on what the popular press identified as her "patrician beauty ... refinement"[54] and "dainty personality,"[55] showcased in such films as *Mademoiselle Modiste* (Robert Z. Leonard, 1926) and *The Divine Lady*

---

[48] Michael Hammond, "'Good Fellowship': Carole Lombard and Clark Gable," in *First Comes Love: Power Couples, Celebrity Kinship and Cultural Politics*, eds. Shelley Cobb and Neil Ewen (London: Bloomsbury, 2015), 54.
[49] Gehring, 101.
[50] Mary Beth Haralovich, "The Proletarian Woman's Film of the 1930s: Contending with Censorship and Entertainment," *Screen* 31: 2 (Summer 1990), 177.
[51] Gehring, 101.
[52] Swindell, 101.
[53] Dorothy Spensley, "The Orchid Bids Farewell to the Screen," *Talking Screen*, June 1930, 34.
[54] "From Vamp to 'Oomph'," *Photoplay*, August 1939, 32.
[55] "Keeping the Home Fires Burning," *Talking Screen*, June 1930, 68.

(Frank Lloyd, 1929). The original story about Lombard's "Orchid Lady" persona can be traced to Larry Swindell's book, *Screwball,* in which he describes her as an updated version of Griffith's "orchidaceous" image and emphatically claims that she was "going to be 'The Orchid Lady';"[56] his idea has been reproduced in notable recent works such as Robert Matzen's *Fireball,*[57] Kay Young's *Ordinary Pleasures: Couples, Conversation, and Comedy,*[58] Elizabeth Kendall's *The Runaway Bride: Hollywood Romantic Comedy of the 1930s,*[59] as well as on the Lombard fan site *Carole & Co.*[60]

Given the lack of historical evidence, I was skeptical of the veracity of this nickname. In my own research, I came across examples of fan magazine stories and promotional materials that discussed Lombard within the context of Hollywood glamour and high fashion, but none that explicitly describes her as "The Orchid Lady." Eventually, I discovered a two-page spread from a Paramount exhibitors guide accompanying the release of *No More Orchids* (Walter Lang, 1932) that identifies Lombard as a "Lady of the Orchids." It features several hand drawings of Lombard in various glamorous looking outfits, and includes an accompanying blurb describing her as, "One of the most, beautiful, talented, and modish actresses in screendom! More enchanting than ever in this superb drama of a woman who loved to live and lived to love!" This description is the only evidence that I have found that explicitly uses a variation of the "Orchid Lady" nickname to describe Lombard. I would therefore argue that Lombard was never dubbed "The Orchid Lady" in any form of publicly-consumed advertisements or front-facing marketing material, however Paramount did, in fact, use the nickname in their official communication with exhibitors. From the lack of other contemporaneous material supporting Swindell's claim, it appears that this nickname was strictly a marketing gimmick devised by Paramount to be used within the narrow context of advertising *No More Orchids,* and not Lombard's star persona more generally.

In reality, the first step in Paramount's star image rehabilitation was not a new nickname but a change to Lombard's body. This process centered on a well-documented "weight loss" that turned the former "Carole of the Curves" into "svelte Carole Lombard."[61] Just as in the late 1930s, Rita

---

[56] Swindell, 101.

[57] Matzen, 77.

[58] Kay Young, *Ordinary Pleasures: Couples, Conversation, and Comedy* (Columbus: Ohio University Press, 2001), 161.

[59] Elizabeth Kendall, *The Runaway Bride: Hollywood Romantic Comedy of the 1930s* (New York: Cooper Square Press, 1990), 139.

[60] Vincent Paterno, "Going exotic with the orchid lady," *Carole & Co.*, November 15, 2011, accessed March 29, 2017, http://carole-and-co.livejournal.com/741699.html.

[61] "How Sylvia changed 'Carole of the Curves' to Svelte Carole Lombard!" *Photoplay,* April 1933, 51.

Hayworth underwent a public transformation that included "diet and body reshaping through exercise, strengthening and homogenizing her voice with diction and singing lessons," and electrolysis to raise her hairline,[62] Lombard underwent a similar, but less physically invasive transformation. In the April 1933 issue of *Photoplay*, an uncredited columnist profiles how Sylvia, a Hollywood masseuse and "physical culturist," put Lombard on a strict diet and intensive massage regimen to transform her from a "size sixteen to a twelve in four weeks."[63] They also claim Sylvia's intervention determined the fate of Lombard's screen career.[64] Although Lombard was not overweight or even especially plump, the article nonetheless features side by side "before" and "after" shots of the actress meant to validate Sylvia's techniques, and ends with a series of reader letters requesting weight loss tips. Like Hayworth's transformation less than a decade later, Lombard's weight loss also was "accomplished in full view of the public" and "made part of the discourse"[65] surrounding her new glamour girl persona. The article confirms the ordinary/extraordinary paradox that underpins stardom by chronicling the steps Lombard, the former tomboy from Indiana, undertook to become a Hollywood glamour girl.

On a cultural level, Lombard's weight loss speaks to the pressures of physical perfection that contextualized the Hollywood female body in the 1930s. According to Rebecca Arnold, "the slim body that developed in the 1920s and 1930s" was promoted through a larger culture of consumption, made ubiquitous through magazine articles, photographs, and cinematic images.[66] Such an image began in the 1920s through the popularity of flapper fashions, which demanded a "boy-like, flat-chested figure to show off the straight, low-waisted dresses to advantage." It was not uncommon for American women to turn to "starvation diets and vigorous exercise" in an effort to measure up to this new feminine ideal.[67] By the 1930s, cultural ideals of the female body moved toward a more shapely, hourglass figure epitomized by actresses Jean Harlow and Mae West, though there was still an emphasis on a trim physique. In these media outlets, it was always "young, slim"—and, I should add, white—bodies that were on display which, according to Arnold, "reinforced restrictive notions of acceptable

---

[62] Adrienne McLean, *Being Rita Hayworth: Labor, Identity, and Hollywood Stardom* (New Brunswick, NJ: Rutgers University Press, 2005), 33.
[63] "How Sylvia changed 'Carole of the Curves' to Svelte Carole Lombard!," 50.
[64] Ibid.
[65] McLean, 33.
[66] Rebecca Arnold, *The American Look: Fashion, Sportswear, and the Image of Women in the 1930s and 1940s* (New York: I.B. Tauris, 2009), 44.
[67] Sarah Grogan, *Body Image: Understanding Body Dissatisfaction in Men, Women and Children* (New York: Routledge, 2017), 20–21.

body size"⁶⁸ and associated such images with health and vigor. Given the pervasiveness of such images in popular media at the time, it is perhaps no coincidence that the *Photoplay* article about Lombard's physical transformation includeed a self-help and reader question section. Not only did the magazine encourage readers—who were overwhelmingly female—to feel "invested ... in the culture of Hollywood"⁶⁹ and, specifically, Lombard's stardom by showing how she suffered from the same weight issues as the average American woman, but it also offered a solution to the—presumed—dissatisfaction they had with their own bodies. Glossing over the untenable financial costs and time commitments of Lombard's weight loss regimen, the article encouraged readers to embark on their own physical transformations, and by doing so, perpetuates the negative cultural correlation between a healthy female body and the Hollywood star figure. Meanwhile, through the self-help and reader participation angle it encouraged readers to feel "invested ... in the culture of Hollywood"⁷⁰ and, specifically, Lombard's stardom.

To publicize Lombard's new "svelte" body and to get audiences invested in her new persona, Paramount assigned her to a string of films that showcased glamour including *No More Orchids*,⁷¹ *The Eagle and the Hawk* (Stuart Walker, 1933), *Brief Moment*, *White Woman*, *Bolero*, and *Lady By Choice* (David Burton, 1934). However, unlike Francis or Dietrich, her star persona was not yet entirely identifiable. She looked glamorous and wore the season's latest fashions, but the image was not yet sufficiently anchored in film parts and media discourse, so it appeared insubstantial. Moreover, Lombard was not given enough acting opportunities to demonstrate that she could be more than just a pretty face. While several of these titles did well at the box office and proved that Lombard had the potential to be a bankable star, in virtually all the aforementioned films her role is primarily decorative. Her brief performance in *The Eagle and the Hawk* as an unnamed woman on a park bench is indicative of this trend.⁷² Lombard plays the ambiguous "Beautiful Lady," a sign of just how unimportant her acting skill is to her

---

⁶⁸Rebecca Arnold, *Fashion, Desire and Anxiety: Image and Morality in the 20th Century* (New Brunswick, NJ: Rutgers University Press, 2001), 63.

⁶⁹ Marsha Orgeron, "'You Are Invited to Participate': Interactive Fandom in the Age of the Movie Magazine," *Journal of Film and Video* Vol. 61, No. 3 (Fall 2009):16.

⁷⁰Marsha Orgeron, "'You Are Invited to Participate': Interactive Fandom in the Age of the Movie Magazine," *Journal of Film and Video* Vol. 61, No. 3 (Fall 2009):16.

⁷¹ This film title may also be part of the source of misinformation about Lombard as the "Orchid Lady." Its working title was "Orchids and Onions," but was allegedly changed to *No More Orchids* in post-production after Lombard allegedly complained to Columbia Studios head, Harry Cohn, "I'm ready for some other angle. No more orchids for me." See: Ralph Wilk, "A Little from Lots," *The Film Daily*, August 13, 1934, 8.

⁷² Given the year this film was made, she plays a curiously small role in only one scene and has almost no dialog.

performance. In her major scene, Lombard's character walks through Central Park with First World War flier Jerry (Fredric March), her body draped in a long silk coat with an oversized white fur collar. The pair sit on a park bench and her character says almost nothing as Jerry recounts his frustration with war. The dim moonlight illuminates the fur trim of her coat, which shrouds her face in a fluffy white halo. Lombard is framed almost entirely from the neck up, and at one point the film cuts to a jarring extreme close-up of her face. She says and does virtually nothing, only staring off camera at March while looking the part of the "Beautiful Lady." If Lombard's glamour girl persona was to be a "calculated hybrid" of Francis and Dietrich, her limited performance in *The Eagle and the Hawk* would suggest that Paramount fell short in developing it beyond the superficial.

Lombard's new persona came at a definite cost, as it prioritized her beauty and glamour over her acting. Swindell's assessment that "she was a clotheshorse in all of her 1931 pictures following *It Pays to Advertise*"[73]

FIGURE 2.2 *Carole Lombard is pictured alongside Fredric March in* The Eagle and the Hawk *(Stuart Walker and Mitchell Leisen, 1933). Her character's name, The Beautiful Lady, signifies the extent to which Lombard's star persona in the early 1930s centered around glamour.*

---

[73] Swindell, 113.

accurately sums up the disconnect between her image and her untapped acting skills. With the exception of *Lady by Choice* and *Brief Moment* that offer some glimmers into her acting potential, Lombard's performances in these titles confirm how heavily Paramount was initially invested in Lombard as an image of a glamorous star. Stephen Gundle notes that the Hollywood studios looked for raw beauty when cultivating new talent, but that "personality had to shine through on screen. Stars have to have a magnetism and a talent for holding attention."[74] Lombard did indeed have a physical magnetism that derived from her youth, her toned figure, and her familiar blonde hair and blue-eyed, fair complexion. In her Sennett films she was known for her athletic beauty and physical vigor, but her new persona carried an aura of delicate, sensual beauty. Lombard may have looked the part of a young Hollywood movie star but there was a shallowness to her glamorous studio image that made her seem cold and distant. This new image was based on surface beauty and elegance, and her film parts gave little indication of the vibrant personality that had been evident in some of her earlier films.

In promotional photos of the period, Lombard often wore clothes and ornate jewelry that highlighted her status as a Hollywood fashion icon and the extravagance that her profession signified. Throughout the early 1930s, Paramount marketed Lombard as a fashion conscious star. She was often featured in full-length fan magazine portraits showcasing the season's latest fashions, and in articles where she would offer beauty and fashion tips. This also illustrates how Hollywood cinema created mass desire for glamour. Gundle writes that the industry "created a unique blend of the aristocratic, fashionable, sexual, theatrical, and consumerist appeals that had emerged and uneasily coalesced in Europe and America. This blend ... exercised an unprecedented influence over global aspirations, desires and lifestyles."[75] Stars like Lombard "turned glamour into a corporate product," and fashion became integral to the way they personified "Hollywood fantasy."[76] A fan magazine article about Hollywood's emergence as a fashion hub entitled "Hollywood snubs Paris" heralds Lombard for her "great natural chic." Columnist William P. Gaines portrays Lombard as being intuitively fashionable, writing "She wears clothes beautifully; can put them on and forget about them."[77] In this description, Lombard becomes the clothes she wears as if they were a second layer of skin.

Fan magazines capitalized on Lombard's glamorous persona by bestowing upon her an instinctual fashion sense. In a 1931 article from *Screenland* released around the time of her marriage to Powell, columnist

---

[74] Stephen Gundle, *Glamour: A History* (Oxford: Oxford University Press, 2008), 179.
[75] Gundle, 175.
[76] Ibid, 178.
[77] William P. Gaines, "Hollywood Snubs Paris," *Photoplay*, April 1934, 79.

Betty Boone opens her article with the line "She looks New Yorkish,"⁷⁸ connecting Lombard's name to what was then—and still is—considered the hub of American fashion. In his essay on Hollywood and the fashion industry, Charles Eckert writes that in 1930 industrialist Bernard Waldman established the Modern Merchandising Bureau (MMB) in New York City as a "fashion middle-man" for the film studios, overseeing the industrial production of cheaper alternatives to Hollywood fashions for mass consumption.⁷⁹ New York quickly became the epicenter for American fashion and merchandising, and a place that manufactured commodities that gave fans tangible connections to their favorite stars. As a reflection of the synthesis between high fashion and industry, the MMB transformed the elite Hollywood fashions worn by the privileged few into cheaper versions that the masses could afford.

Lombard was not remotely connected to New York City, and the description erroneously displaces her real-life history as an Indiana-born California girl with a false image of modern urban stylishness. Boone asks if clothes should be considered a female hobby: "Carole is scornful. 'Clothes a hobby?' she echoes incredulously. 'Clothes should be a business, a very serious business to every woman, whether she likes it or not.'"⁸⁰ Whether this is an actual quote from Lombard or not is unclear, however such a statement is used in the article as a confirmation of her meticulous grasp of fashion. Lombard allegedly promotes the idea that fashion is a direct reflection of one's womanhood, arguing that clothes should be an essential part of "every" woman's life. The article reinforces the film industry's deep associative bonds between femininity and fashion, in which stars became "mannequin[s'] modeling clothes, furs hats and accessories that they would wear in upcoming films."⁸¹ Star publicity photos and advertisements became constructed images of desire and fantasy for the millions of fans who looked to their favorite stars for the latest trends. The article signals Lombard's status as a Hollywood style icon, and the ideas of commerce and industry upon which her glamorous star persona was indirectly built.

In spite of the mountain of publicity material concerning Lombard's so-called intuitive glamour, there is evidence that her studio-engineered persona was falling flat. Around the time of Lombard's divorce from Powell on August 16, 1933,⁸² there was a noticeable shift in fan magazine discourse toward Lombard's off-screen reputation as Hollywood's number-one "party

---

⁷⁸ "What About Carole Lombard?", 83.
⁷⁹ Charles Eckert, "The Carole Lombard in Macy's Window," in *Movies and Mass Culture*, ed. John Belton (London: The Altlone Press, 1999), 103.
⁸⁰ "What About Carole Lombard?", 111.
⁸¹ Eckert, 104.
⁸² Swindell, 127.

girl."[83] Robert Matzen writes that even though Lombard was still playing a glamour girl in her films, by 1934 she "had entered her party phase,"[84] during which time she became infamous for hosting elaborately themed parties such as her "Venice Beach Pier Party"[85] or her "Hospital Party." While Lombard's glamour girl persona connoted grace and refinement, overwhelmingly fans came to associate her image with the quirky and "eccentric private person they read about in their favorite magazines."[86] In a *Photoplay* article entitled "How Carole Lombard Plans A Party," she was described as having the ability to design "parties based on an idea, usually an absurd idea at that, and carry them to a sublime finish."[87] Readers of such articles would have also been familiar with candid photos of Lombard at Hollywood nightclubs like Ciro's, the Mocambo, Café Trocadero, and the Cocoanut Grove. She was frequently featured in fan magazine articles that profiled her rumored romantic liaisons with George Raft and screenwriter Robert Riskin, as well as her boyfriend, crooner Russ Columbo. Lombard's "glamour girl" and "party girl" personae may, at first glance, seemed incompatible. However, upon further consideration I argue that the two sides worked symbiotically. Given the close relationship between the Hollywood studios and the fan magazines, articles about Lombard's vibrant and unbuttoned "party girl" reputation would not have been permissible without studio consent. Therefore, although they did not obviously "fit" in with Lombard's glamour girl image, I argue that they had a definite purpose.

In what appears to be an orchestrated effort to salvage her "glamour girl" image, fan magazines quickly began to take note of the missing piece in Lombard's on-screen persona. In an article from a 1932 issue of *Photoplay* entitled "30 Girls in a Race for Stardom," "columnist" Cal York[88] writes:

> It is strange about Carole Lombard. She's the Constance Bennett screen type in appearance and ability, and yet–here's a little secret–exhibitors, who are the boys who buy pictures for the theaters, are not wasting any

---

[83] Despite what the "party girl" label implies, it is not a reference to any salacious behavior but simply Lombard's reputation for throwing elaborately themed parties. See: Robert Matzen, "Party Girl," *Thoughts about life in general and old Hollywood in particular,* date unknown, http://robertmatzen.com/tag/carole-lombard-party-house/.

[84] Matzen, 17.

[85] Ted Smits, "Hollywood Stars Drop Dignity to Romp at Amusement Resort; Carole Lombard Sets Hot Pace," *St. Petersburg Evening Independent*, June 17, 1935, 8.

[86] Gehring, 124.

[87] Lang Hunt, 95.

[88] According to Anthony Slide, there was no such person at *Photoplay* named Cal York. "Cal" was short for California and "York" for New York, which Slide explains is "indicative of the two editorial offices providing the column's stories." See: Slide, 8.

time crying for Lombard pictures–yet. Somehow she hasn't piqued the public curiosity to date ... Carole has the same potentialities [as Bennett], but she's not front page copy ... glamour is largely dependent upon a fantastic background which Carole hasn't acquired–yet![89]

The repetition of the word "yet" suggests that *Photoplay*, the exhibitors, and even the public were still waiting to be impressed by Lombard. The article draws comparisons to Constance Bennett who, along with Miriam Hopkins and Bette Davis, were actresses that were often linked to Lombard because of their similar platinum blonde hair and pale complexions. Her resemblance to other Hollywood starlets was so striking that in 1930 Herbert Cruikshank of *Motion Picture* magazine called her the "three-in-one girl," writing "Imagine Constance Bennett with Jeanne Eagels's voice and you have Carol Lombard."[90] On the first comparison, Cruikshank has a point: both Bennett and Lombard had well-defined square jawlines, big, expressive eyes, and chin-length, bleach-blonde hair. However, in my opinion, Lombard's voice is quite unlike Eagels's. Ignoring her put-on posh English accent,[91] Eagels's voice is far more punchy than Lombard's, who generally spoke in a less enunciative and softer tone. Nevertheless, Cruikshank's overall argument that Lombard's star persona was largely indistinguishable from her peers is valid. To be a top star Lombard had to carve out a niche of her own, but at Paramount she "was the only studio girl who was a leading lady without her own stardom."[92] She had garnered a degree of recognizability and much potential, but had not yet distinguished herself from the swath of other actresses in either appearance or skill set.

In light of the lukewarm critical reception of Lombard's glamour girl persona, one could argue that the coexistent stories about her "party girl" antics were planted to provide depth to Lombard's stardom and distance her from stories about her divorce from Powell and his refined, man-of-the-world persona. In some of her films, Lombard may have appeared cold and remote, but stories and photos documenting her whirlwind social life reminded readers that she was, in fact, young, energetic, and someone with whom audiences could easily relate. By 1933 Lombard was a newly single 25-year-old star, and there was a relative "compatibility" between the "textual and extra-textual image as promulgated in popular discourse."[93]

---

[89] Cal York, "30 Girls in a Race for Stardom," *Photoplay*, April 1932, 75.
[90] Herbert Cruikshank, "Three-In-One Girl," *Motion Picture*, November 1930, 74.
[91] Eagels was born and raised in Kansas City, Missouri.
[92] Swindell, 115.
[93] Adrienne McLean, "The Cinderella Princess and the Instrument of Evil: Surveying the Limits of Female Transgression in Two Postwar Hollywood Scandals," *Cinema Journal* Vol. 34, No. 3 (Spring 1995): 36.

The new Carole Lombard personified the youthful gaiety and exotic elegance of 1930s Hollywood, all of which made her a more dynamic and accessible film star in a way that her "glamour girl" persona alone could not.

Conclusion

It is difficult to pinpoint the exact end date of Lombard's glamour girl period because she was still being promoted through that angle even after *Twentieth Century* was released in 1934. Paramount eventually gave up their efforts by 1936 once it became clear that Lombard's screwball comedies were commercially viable, a decision largely fueled by the release of three extremely successful films *Love Before Breakfast* (Walter Lang, 1936), *The Princess Comes Across* (William K. Howard, 1936), and *My Man Godfrey*. She also began her widely publicized relationship with Clark Gable in 1936, and there was therefore an ideological imperative to shift her persona away from its associations with Powell to Gable's no-nonsense masculinity because it symbolized the unity of their new star coupledom. The relative ease with which Paramount altered their publicity tactic demonstrates just how artificial the glamour girl persona was to begin with.

In an effort to uphold a legitimate star-character screwball symbiosis, fan magazine stories from the late 1930s profiled how Lombard supposedly resented the derogatory clotheshorse label.[94] In a 1937 interview with Ben Maddox from *Photoplay*, Lombard allegedly explained "Personally I resent being tagged a 'glamour girl.' It's such an absurd, extravagant label. It implies so much that I'm not." Later, Maddox quotes Lombard as saying, "When I want to do something I don't pause to contemplate whether I'm exquisitely gowned. I want to live, not pose! My ambition is to be an excellent actress … I don't believe in being lavish that way."[95] Maddox describes Lombard as possessing an "irresistible quality" of honesty that "begins at home. She isn't hypocritical in her opinions; but more important, she isn't fooled by herself."[96] His description and the quotes attributed to Lombard encapsulate the one of the reasons for the greater success and appeal of Lombard's screwball persona. Maddox's story makes her relatable in a way that her glamour girl persona could never be by ostensibly uncovering the personality behind the star image, citing her humility and honesty as cornerstones of her unpretentious disposition. By contrast,

---

[94] Emily Carman, *Independent Stardom: Freelance Women in the Hollywood Studio System* (Austin: University of Texas Press, 2016), 27. See also: Morgan, 132.
[95] Ben Maddox, "The Real Down-Low on Lombard," *Photoplay*, January 1937, 16.
[96] Ibid.

Lombard's glamour girl persona was far too esoteric for mass audiences; it made Lombard relevant primarily as an image, but it was not an indicator of her talent or star potential. However little Lombard's glamour girl reputation did to advance her career, it did confirm Paramount's interest in her as a star. In less than a decade, Lombard went from bit player to picture personality to female lead, and was making considerable headway in her uphill climb to Hollywood stardom. Although she had not yet achieved the level of success, and financial and career security of her screwball years, this period proved to be a time of immense growth and adjustment for her career and star persona.

3

The queen of screwball comedy

As the reigning "Queen of Screwball Comedy" during the 1930s, it is surprising that Carole Lombard does not have a more prominent presence in film and comedy scholarship. What has often been described as her vitality and energy[1] is no more apparent than in her screwball performances; the synthesis of star and character is so closely knit that she was said to have personified the screwball genre.[2] From Stanley Cavell's seminal *Pursuits of Happiness* (1981) onwards, Lombard has a smaller than expected presence in the academic corpus, typically overlooked in favor of other popular screwball stars like Katharine Hepburn and Irene Dunne. There are exceptions to this systemic neglect including Wes Gehring's extensive comparison of screwball and rom-com,[3] James Harvey's chapter about Lombard in *Romantic Comedy in Hollywood: From Lubitsch to Sturges* (1998) and Tamar Jeffers McDonald's analysis of *My Man Godfrey* in *Romantic Comedy: Boy Meets Girl Meets Genre* (2007). It is not my desire to discredit the existing body of screwball scholarship nor do I wish to diminish the work of other screwball actors. However, the limited attention to Lombard's performances from the screwball canon leaves a gap in the comprehensive understanding of one of the genre's key players. This situation points to the need to reevaluate the canon, a task that requires us to take a second look at films, actors, and their performances. Given Lombard's immense success in the genre during the late 1930s, as well as the strength of her posthumous reputation as a screwball comedian, she is perhaps the most obvious figure to start such a reevaluation. Therefore, an analysis of Lombard's screwball films will hopefully initiate further

---

[1] For example, see: Glady Hall, "Lombard – As She Sees Herself," *Photoplay*, November 1938, 34; Katharine Hartley, "What's Become of the Good Scout?" *Modern Screen*, August 1938, 26.
[2] Noel F. Busch, "A Loud Cheer for the Screwball Girl," *Life*, October 1938, 48.
[3] See Wes D. Gehring, *Romantic vs. Screwball Comedy: Charting the Difference* (Maryland: Scarecrow Press, Inc., 2002), 29–96.

inquiries into the state of the present canon and, more broadly, new ways of thinking about female performance in comedy.

In contemporary popular and academic discourses, Carole Lombard is best remembered as a screwball star. Existent biographical accounts uniformly reference the daffy screwball heroine, or "madcap Carole,"[4] drawing parallels between star and film personae. For instance, in conjunction with the New York City Film Forum's 2008 retrospective honoring Lombard's centennial, the *New York Times* published an article outlining her lasting appeal as a screwball comedian, in which columnist Terrence Rafferty reflects, "Carole Lombard, blond, beautiful and fearless, was the pre-eminent screwball of her mad, desperate time." He concludes by saying that Lombard's specialty was to "make people laugh," and that she will always be remembered as Hollywood's greatest screwball star.[5] Articles such as this recycle the rhetoric that contextualized Lombard's star persona in the late 1930s, particularly her innate proficiency in film comedy and the incongruity between her conventionally beautiful physical appearance and her on-screen "madcap" antics. While enjoyable on a cursory level, they provide only superficial readings of her films and star persona, and ultimately fail to define what made her comic style so noteworthy.

Some of this posthumous reflection may also have to do with the fact that Lombard is closely connected to the origins of the screwball comedy genre. The word "screwball" was first used in sports journalism as early as the 1880s to describe baseball star Mickey Welch's pitches.[6] The first known example of "screwball" appearing in a cinematic context is in a 1936 *Variety* review about Lombard's performance in *My Man Godfrey*: "Miss Lombard played screwball dames before, but none so screwy as this one."[7] Kathrina Glitre reminds us that "it is initially the central characters who are labeled as 'screwballs,' not the films."[8] Given its cinematographic etymology, it is understandable that the link between Lombard and screwball comedy is so tightly intertwined; Lombard's dizzying performance style can claim to be one of the main originators of cinematic screwiness. However, a quick glance through her filmography reveals that she made more non-screwball films than screwball comedies, and arguably only made screwball comedies between 1934 and 1938, with *Mr. and Mrs. Smith* (Alfred Hitchcock) and

---

[4]Frederick W. Ott, *The Films of Carole Lombard* (New York: Citadel Press, 1972), 19.
[5]Terrence Rafferty, "Forever Screwball, Forever Fearless," *New York Times*, November 20, 2008, 18.
[6]Rob Neyer, "The Screwball: Fading Away," in *The Neyer/James Guide to Pitchers: An Historical Compendium of Pitching, Pitchers, and Pitches*, eds. Rob Neyer and Bill James (New York: Simon & Schuster, Inc., 2004), 52.
[7]"My Man Godfrey," 16.
[8]Kathrina Glitre, *Hollywood Romantic Comedy: States of the Union, 1934–65* (Manchester: Manchester University Press, 2006), 23.

her final, posthumously released black comedy *To Be or Not to Be* (Ernst Lubitsch, 1942) which has some clear screwball undertones. Considering that by 1934 Lombard had been acting in films in Hollywood for over a decade,[9] around five years in screwball is relatively short in comparison to her nearly twenty-one years as an actress. As discussed in the previous chapter, Lombard worked in genres ranging from the Western, melodrama, horror, and slapstick. She made two dance films, *Bolero* (Wesley Ruggles, 1934) and *Rumba* (Marion Gering, 1935), played torch singers and was featured in singing numbers in both *Brief Moment* (David Burton, 1933) and *Swing High, Swing Low* (Mitchell Leisen, 1937), was a prostitute in the pre-Code drama *Virtue* (Edward Buzzell, 1932) and a nurse in *Vigil In The Night* (George Stevens, 1940). The majority of her career was spent outside of screwball comedy, and it would not be an overstatement to say that she transcended genre boundaries. Nevertheless, Lombard's screwball identity was and still is the primary means by which scholars and historians assess her star persona, and perhaps understandably so: the filmic usage of the word "screwball," as we saw, was first attributed to a descriptive evaluation of Lombard's performance, thus her associations with the genre have been widely disseminated in popular media and academic sources for over eighty years.

This chapter contains detailed textual analyses of five of Lombard's screwball comedies and one black comedy: *Twentieth Century* (Howard Hawks, 1934), *Love Before Breakfast* (Walter Lang, 1936), *My Man Godfrey* (Gregory La Cava, 1936), *Nothing Sacred* (William Wellman, 1937), *Mr. and Mrs. Smith* (Alfred Hitchcock, 1941), and *To Be or Not to Be* (Ernst Lubitsch, 1942). In light of the reoccurring observation about Lombard's "blonde and beautiful" physical appearance in relation to her physicality, I make the argument that Lombard's body and voice were central to her screwball persona because they conveyed her characters' emotional and psychological ranges. The Lombard heroine's inexhaustible curiosity, charming optimism and youthful spunk give us the sense that physical comedy is a channel through which she can release her abundant energy.

While this chapter's primary focus is Lombard's screwball performances and accompanying star persona in six specific films, it also expands more broadly into discourses about female comedy and bodily performance. Thus, as previously stated in my introduction, Lombard's stardom is a vessel to explore ideas about gender and comedy, and the inherent tension in being considered a beautiful comedian. I also discuss Lombard's body in terms of how she embodies the demarcation between feminine beauty and rough-and-tumble physicality, as well as address the role of Lombard's beauty in gendered power terms. Lombard's performances opened up a space in

---

[9] Her first film was Alan Dwan's *A Perfect Crime* (1921), but she started working steadily in Hollywood in 1925.

screwball comedy for female physicality, and her screwball films support the idea that a female comedian can be feminine and still be a participant in male-dominated comedy. She challenges the "pretty versus funny" trade-off that has long plagued female comedy,[10] giving credence to the claim that women do not need to sacrifice their appearance to be taken seriously as comedians. Finally, woven through my analyses is a discussion of Lombard's so-called "natural" screwball star persona. With each screwball film Lombard's star persona aligned itself more closely with her on-screen roles, virtually melding two sides into one cohesive figure in such a way that reflected the necessary synchronicity for a marketable star image in classical Hollywood cinema.[11] By the mid 1930s, Lombard embodied screwball in her on- and off-screen personae, and physical comedy was a key component of her screwball image.

A few notes: the films are arranged chronologically to track Lombard's screwball performance style. As indicated in my introduction, the methodological approach of this chapter is based on the fact that there has yet to be a comprehensive scholarly account of Lombard's performances in screwball comedy. It may run the risk of appearing overburdened with textual analyses, but the current absence of scholarly probes into Lombard's performances necessitates exhaustive close readings. I have chosen to omit *Hands Across the Table* (Mitchell Leisen, 1935), *True Confession* (Wesley Ruggles, 1937), *Swing High, Swing Low* (Mitchell Leisen, 1937), and *Fools for Scandal* (Mervyn Le Roy, 1938). This was less a result of personal taste and more about the need to avoid redundancy in my observations, since there are some noticeable similarities between these titles and the ones I have chosen. Instead, I have included *To Be or Not to Be* in this chapter because, although not a screwball comedy per se, its spirit and tone are "screwball-esque," and the ideas around Lombard's body that I discuss in this chapter are also relevant to this film. What follows is an account of Lombard's screwball comedies that will, for the first time, break down the reoccurring features of her performance style.

Screwball comedy

Before we delve into Lombard's screwball comedies, it is helpful to briefly outline the origins and characteristics of the genre. Screwball comedy refers to a body of Hollywood films made between 1934 and

---

[10]Linda Mizejewski, *Pretty/Funny: Women Comedians and Body Politics* (Austin: University of Texas Press, 2014), 5.
[11]Barry King, "Articulating Stardom," in *Star Texts: Image and Performance in Film and Television*, ed. Jeremy Butler (Detroit: Wayne State University Press, 1991), 181.

the mid 1940s.[12] It began as an offshoot of romantic comedy,[13] and was described by film critic Lewis Jacobs as a "revival of comedies of satire and self-ridicule."[14] Although screwball comedies continue to be made to this day, most historians agree that screwball's "classical" period was during the 1930s, when filmmakers used comedy to reflect on the financial, social, and geopolitical unrest of the Great Depression.[15] In the darkest days of the Depression, Hollywood cinema served a social purpose by distracting audiences from the economic reality of their everyday lives. According to Thomas Renzi, the Depression "stifled faith in the American dream" and the belief that anyone could make something of themselves with the right amount of luck, perseverance, and drive.[16] This manifested in such screwball films as *My Man Godfrey* (Gregory La Cava, 1936), *Easy Living* (Mitchell Leisen, 1937), *Topper* (Norman Z. McLeod, 1937), and *Holiday* (George Cukor, 1938) through the ridicule of "the leisure life, often in the 'high-society' style."[17] Wealth and poverty are portrayed in sharp contrast to magnify the economic and class divide of its characters. This is illustrated most effectively in what is arguably Lombard's most famous screwball comedy, *My Man Godfrey*. In the opening scene, dizzy Manhattan socialites Irene (Lombard) and Cornelia Bullock (Gail Patrick) search for items for a scavenger hunt at the city dump, which doubles as a temporary refuge for homeless men. Such juxtapositions offer humorous critiques of upper class frivolity, while acknowledging the urgent sense of despair rooted in contemporaneous American society.

Screwball films combine "high comedy, such as … [the] comedy of manners, with low slapstick comedy."[18] Renzi identifies "daffiness, eccentricity, self-deprecation, satire, and physical and verbal battles between the sexes" as the main elements of the screwball genre.[19] Central to all of these themes is the adversarial yet egalitarian relationship of the male and female characters,

---

[12]The official end date is open to debate, and some scholars consider 1938 as the "end" of the classical screwball period. For example, see: Jane M. Greene, "A Proper Dash of Spice: Screwball Comedy and the Production Code." *Journal of Film and Video* Vol. 63, No. 3 (Fall 2011): 48; Lewis Jacobs, *The Rise of American Film: A Critical History* (New York: Harcourt, 1939), 535–536.
[13]Thomas C. Renzi, *Screwball Comedy and Film Noir: Unexpected Connections* (North Carolina: McFarland & Company, Inc., 2012), 6.
[14]Lewis, 535.
[15]Gehring, 4.
[16]Renzi, 39.
[17]Gehring, 30.
[18]John Belton, *American Cinema/American Culture*, 4th ed. (New York: McGraw-Hill Education, 2012), 180.
[19]Renzi, 6.

which Andrew Sarris argues reflected "male and female polarities."[20] The combative nature of the screwball couple's relationship and the prevalence of slapstick physicality functioned as covert references to sex.[21] Screwball's furtive approach to sex reflected the moral limitations that were imposed upon the Hollywood studios by the Production Code Administration (PCA), a regulatory body that was officially formed on June 13, 1934[22] through the combined efforts of the Motion Picture Producers and Distributors of America (MPPDA) and the Studio Relations Committee (SRC) in order to avoid the implementation of federal censorship laws.[23] Any reference to sex in the Production Code era had to be "incontrovertibly bound to love, and by extension to monogamy and marriage."[24] Physical comedy was therefore used by filmmakers as a replacement for overt sexual expression. Tamar Jeffers McDonald writes "as the filmmakers began to realize the restraints they were working under ... they began to find imaginative ways to exploit them." She goes on to explain that "while, under the Production Code, a comedy could not display an active sexual relationship between an unmarried woman and man, it could hint at the continuation of a sexual relationship between a couple once married, now neatly divorced or separated."[25] To that end, Tina Olsin Lent reminds us that play and childlike antics—two common forms of screwball physicality—"functioned as a substitute for overt sexuality" which helped to show "the prohibitions and restrictions imposed by the Production Code."[26] The Code's ban on explicit references to sex led to indirect modes of representation, so physicality along with verbal humor became virtually one of the few ways producers could convey latent sexual desire.

Along with these external censorship requirements, another reason for screwball's gendered tension is the "heroine's relative independence," which is "countered all too often by punishing, resentful heroes whose punching fists, spanking palms, and generally threatening mouths serve as the forces of masculine reaction."[27] Tina Olsin Lent and Sara Ross both identify links between the 1920s flapper and the 1930s screwball woman. Lent defines the flapper as someone who "challenged earlier codes of feminine behavior" through her consumption of commodities, but as one who "broke with the

---

[20]Andrew Sarris, *You Ain't Heard Nothin' Yet: The American Talking Film, History & Memory, 1927–1949* (New York: Oxford University Press, 1998), 93.
[21]Ibid, 97.
[22]Doherty, 61.
[23]Doherty, 67.
[24]Jane M. Greene, "Manners Before Morals: Sophisticated Comedy and the Production Code, 1930-1934" *Quarterly Review of Film and Video* Vol. 23, No. 3 (2011): 245.
[25]Tamar Jeffers McDonald, *Romantic Comedy: Boy Meets Girl Meets Genre* (New York: Columbia University Press, 2007), 22.
[26]Lent, 328.
[27]Sikov, 28.

feminist ideas of political and economic equality."[28] The flapper's conspicuous consumption established women, for the first time, as active participants in the American economy. But in light of the limited opportunities afforded to women to enter the workforce, most often the flapper remained financially dependent on others—read: men. The flapper's role in the consumer revolution "masked her continued and more profound conformity to the dominant ideology of women's subordination ... and her primary role as wife and mother."[29] Sara Ross argues that the flapper's independence was often used as a source of comedy in silent films such as *The Plastic Age* (Wesley Ruggles, 1925) and *Mantrap* (Victor Fleming, 1926), explaining that "comedies concerning modern girls eased the threat of the representation of them as sexual beings by making light of and/or satirizing their behavior."[30] This suggests a societal uneasiness toward the flapper, as she "pushed the boundaries of acceptability" with her frankness, dress, and overt sexuality since she represented a departure from her conservative and chaste Victorian predecessor.

By contrast to the self-assured screwball woman, the male screwball figure is typically considered both an "anti-hero" and childlike,[31] which is conveyed most frequently in the absentminded professor character trope found in such films as *Bringing Up Baby* (Howard Hawks, 1938), *Ball of Fire* (Howard Hawks, 1941), *The Lady Eve* (Preston Sturges, 1941), and *Monkey Business* (Howard Hawks, 1952). Screwball comedy created a space for actresses like Carole Lombard, Katharine Hepburn, Claudette Colbert, and Jean Arthur to play confident and self-assured heroines, while actors such as Cary Grant, Melvyn Douglas, Henry Fonda, and Gary Cooper frequently took on the roles of the dependent and sometimes aloof males.

Finally, on a formal level, screwball films combined both modern technology of the 1930s and editing and storytelling practices from silent comedy. Ed Sikov explains that the displacement of explicit sexual relations manifests both at the narrative and formal levels, generating a "sense of confusion about romance and human relations usually expressed by verbal and sometimes physical sparring."[32] The aural tempo of screwball films is "fast-paced and contentious," which was made possible by such developments of sound technology as multitrack recording and mixing that were standard Hollywood practices by 1931.[33] By contrast, the dynamic cinematographic and editing techniques often found in screwball films such

---

[28]Ibid, 316–317.
[29]Ibid, 317.
[30]Ibid, 409.
[31]Gehring, 31.
[32]Ed Sikov, *Screwball: Hollywood's Madcap Romantic Comedies* (New York: Crown Publishers, 1989), 19.
[33]Ibid. See also: Tom Brown, *Spectacles in "Classical" Cinema: Musicality and Historicity in the 1930s* (New York: Routledge, 2016), 86.

as cross-cutting, quick cuts, and tracking shots are reminiscent of the silent comedies of the 1910s and 1920s.[34]

Twentieth Century (*Howard Hawks, 1934*)

In 1934 Lombard starred in what has since been deemed one of Hollywood's first screwball comedies, Howard Hawks's *Twentieth Century*. Along with *It Happened One Night* (Frank Capra, 1934), the two films have been widely credited as having jumpstarted the 1930s screwball trend.[35] But in 1934 this new type of comedy, ripe with what one Variety reviewer described as "psychopathic ward tendencies,"[36] was not immediately identified as "screwball." One review described the film as a "smart comedy" with a "breathless pace" that was attributed to screenwriters Ben Hecht and Charles MacArthur and director Howard Hawks.[37] Nowhere in this or other reviews is the word "screwball" used, which indicates that the film was categorized as a screwball comedy only after the genre became popular and its generic characteristics were critically and commercially defined.

The receptions of each comedy could not have been more different; *It Happened One Night* garnered extraordinary box office success after several lackluster weeks, and eventually became the first Columbia production and the first of only three films to win Academy Awards in all of the five major categories.[38] *Twentieth Century*, on the other hand, premiered on May 3, 1934[39]—just months before the PCA came into full effect[40]—and was met with glowing critical reviews but did "dismal" business at the box office.[41] The reason for its poor public reception is not entirely certain, though *Variety* predicted that the film was "probably too smart for general consumption."[42]

---

[34]Sikov, 20. See also: Renzi, 10.
[35]Wes D. Gehring, *Romantic vs. Screwball Comedy: Charting the Difference* (Lanham: Scarecrow Press, 2002), 11.
[36]"My Man Godfrey," *Variety*, Wednesday, September 23, 1936, 16.
[37]"20th Century," *Variety*, Tuesday, May 8, 1934, 14.
[38]Joseph McBride, *Hawks on Hawks* (Lexington: The University Press of Kentucky, 2013), 324. The other two films are *One Flew Over the Cuckoo's Nest* (Miloš Forman, 1975) and *The Silence of the Lambs* (Jonathan Demme, 1991).
[39]Mordaunt Hall, "John Barrymore in '20th Century'; Actor Revels in Role of Egomaniac Producer – 'Double Door' – The Murderer and the Governor – A Molnar Novel," *The New York Times*, May 13, 1934, X3.
[40]Thomas Doherty, *Hollywood's Censor: Joseph I. Breen and the Production Code Administration* (New York: Columbia University Press, 2007), 97.
[41]Douglas Churchill, "The Year in Hollywood; 1934 May Be Remembered as the Beginning of the Sweetness-and-Light Era," *The New York Times*, December 30, 1934, X5.
[42]"Film Reviews – 20th Century," *Variety*, May 8, 1934, 14.

The film performed "under initial hopes" in a mid level city like Baltimore, making a mere $15,000 during its first week in theaters,[43] while in New York it played for only one week before closing at Radio City Music Hall.[44]

Based on the Ben Hecht-Charles MacArthur Broadway play of the same title and directed by Howard Hawks, *Twentieth Century* stars Lombard as Lily Garland, a lingerie model turned theater ingenue. After being discovered by Broadway producer, Oscar Jaffe (John Barrymore), Lily, and Oscar quickly become New York's most famous theater couple. Lily discovers that she cannot handle Oscar's temperamental personality, so when she is offered a contract with a major Hollywood studio, she heads west. Oscar's career plummets after Lily's departure, and after a failed preview show in Chicago, he and his cast skip town. On the 20th Century Limited train back to New York he unexpectedly bumps into Lily, and opportunity strikes. In an attempt to bolster his dying career and to gain funding for his upcoming production of *The Passion Play*, Oscar devises a plan for Lily to sign another contract with him.

Both *It Happened One Night* and *Twentieth Century* upset conservative gender dynamics by presenting strong-willed heroines that, to varying degrees, challenge the agency of their heroes. Screwball narratives are often predicated on the adversarial relationship of the male and female protagonist.[45] Screwball women are unapologetically confident, and their films give them both a voice and the physical means to establish equal footing with their male counterparts.[46] These generic characterizations are relevant when we consider the development of screwball. Romantic comedy historian Jane M. Greene divides screwball comedy into two chronological phases: the insane and sophisticated cycle. The former lasted from 1934 to 1938, and is marked by "far fetched lunatic behavior" reminiscent of silent slapstick comedies. The insane cycle films offer "perfunctory lessons" about morality that are "thinly plotted excuses for eccentric antics."[47] *Twentieth Century* fits Greene's "insane cycle" description: its characters are exaggerated figures that seem too grand and over-the-top to exist anywhere other than the cinema, and they make no effort to abide by any conscious moral code. Screwball comedies like *Twentieth Century* are carnivalesque worlds bursting at the seams where social order often gets disrupted—at

---

[43]'Villa' Balto's Big One at $19,500; '20th' 15G, Mild," *Variety*, May 8, 1934, 9.

[44]Todd McCarthy, *Howard Hawks: The Grey Fox of Hollywood* (New York: Grove Press, 1997), 204.

[45]Thomas C. Renzi, *Screwball Comedy and Film Noir: Unexpected Connections* (North Carolina: McFarland & Company, Inc., 2012), 6.

[46]Ed Sikov, *Screwball: Hollywood's Madcap Romantic Comedies* (New York: Crown Publishers, 1989), 19.

[47]Jane M. Greene, "A Proper Dash of Spice: Screwball Comedy and the Production Code," *Journal of Film and Video* Vol. 63, No. 3 (Fall 2011): 47.

least temporarily—gender dynamics are reversed, and stability is thrown out in favor of unrestrained lunacy.[48] Its theatrical setting is also no coincidence, as the theater celebrates excess and grandeur.

By early 1934, Carole Lombard was gaining ground as one of Hollywood's most promising starlets, but given her relatively minor star status and Barrymore's experience and theatrical lineage, the decision to cast her was unexpected. For all her public and critical acclaim, she was still not considered a "great" film actress.[49] Screenwriter Ben Hecht explained that the key to casting the right actress to play Lily was to find someone who could hold their own with Barrymore, and that Columbia's primary consideration in accepting Paramount's loan-out of Lombard "was not ability, but personality."[50] In light of the weakness of Lombard's "official" glamorous studio persona and the growing coverage Lombard's "party girl" reputation was receiving in the popular press, Columbia hoped that Lombard's vibrant off-screen personality would shine through on screen.[51] Many stories have circulated regarding Lombard's inexperience compared to Barrymore's, including a famous pep talk with Hawks where he asked her how she would respond if a man talked to her the way Oscar does to Lily. Lombard reportedly answered, "I'd kick him in the balls."[52] Lombard added to this mythologizing, later reflecting that while making *Twentieth Century* she learned to "loosen something inside of me that's been tied up all my life, and to release an entirely new source of energy."[53] Whether true or the work of a savvy studio publicist, these types of press stories have a legitimate function because they demonstrate that Lombard could hold her own with veteran actors like Barrymore, and that her off-screen persona was well suited for the film's madcap rhythm.

Screwball characters have been described as "childlike" people unable to fully integrate into their social environments.[54] Oscar is a megalomaniac living in his fantasy world, and he grooms Lily from meek Mildred Plotka into a female version of himself. Both are stunted by their egos, but while Oscar is unequivocally blinded by his greatness, Lily remains conscious of both of their shallow personalities, telling Oscar on the train that "We're

---

[48]For more on the carnivalesque see: Mikhail Bakhtin, *Rabelais and his World*, first Midland books edition, trans. Helene Iswolsky (Bloomington, IN: Indiana University Press, 1984).
[49]Dorothy Manners, "She Won't Put On An Act!", *Modern Screen*, October 1934, 43.
[50]Larry Swindell, *Screwball: The Life of Carole Lombard* (New York: William Morrow & Company, Inc., 1975), 141.
[51]Ibid.
[52]Wes D. Gehring, *Carole Lombard: The Hoosier Tornado* (Indianapolis: Indiana Historical Society Press, 2003), 120.
[53]Robert Matzen, *Fireball: Carole Lombard and the Mystery of Flight 3* (Pittsburgh: GoodKnight Books, 2014), 52.
[54]Gehring, 180–181.

not people, we're lithographs ... We're only real in between curtains." These types of statements are evocative because they suggest that while Lily is just as self-absorbed as Oscar—declaring at one point to her boyfriend, George, "I'm too big to be respected!"—unlike Oscar she is, at times, conscious of her narcissism. We are constantly reminded of Lily's background and rise to stardom, whether it be repeated references to her real name, or Oscar's derogatory remarks about her working-class roots. Lily's assessment of herself reveals how she "plays the part" of Lily Garland, acting out her own identity as a means of conforming to Oscar's vision of what she should be. This is where her physical comedy and voice come in: Lombard astutely exaggerates her body movements and vocal delivery to show how Lily tries to fit into Oscar's world. Larry Swindell suggests that the narrative is predicated upon "seduction," with "Jaffe playing on Lily's ego" to win her back into his confidence.[55] Lily transforms from a neophyte into a conceited egomaniac much like her mentor and as her confidence builds, so do her theatrics. By *Twentieth Century*'s conclusion, she and Oscar become virtually indistinguishable. For the first time since her Sennett days, Lombard used physical comedy to convey her character's emotional fragility. An analysis of Lily's bodily movements and changes to her vocal tone in two scenes will reveal the importance of Lombard's body and voice as the primary means of conveying Lily and Oscar's psychological likeness. Additionally, these scenes demonstrate how Lily's body functions as the lynchpin that motivates the struggle for autonomy between herself and Oscar.

Consider the contrast between the film's opening scene and Oscar and Lily's final showdown. In both scenes, Lily's body and voice are critical to the power struggle between herself and Oscar. In the opening sequence Lily is still identified as Mildred Plotka, the lingerie model "from the sticks" trying to get her big break on Broadway. Lombard plays the scene with a self-conscious timidity that reflects Lily's inexperience. Her movements are subtle and she stays in the background of most of the shots, revealing that Lily wants to draw as little attention to herself as possible. Lily speaks to Oscar in a quiet whimper, an almost apologetic tone. Her voice trembles in intimidation, as if she is about to burst into tears. She wears a modest black dress with simple white detailing, while her light blonde hair remains untouched and hangs just above her shoulders. She looks like meek Mildred Plotka; she has not yet transformed into Lily Garland.

Oscar presides over rehearsals and immediately takes notice of her ungraceful acting. Lily nervously steps into her role as Mary Jo Calhoun, a Southern Belle in Jaffe's latest melodrama, and her character's first act is to walk through the front door of her plantation house. Lily pushes open the imaginary door and bounds to the front of the stage toward the camera

---

[55]Swindell, 142.

where her face is framed in close-up. She walks quickly with a wide stance, swinging her arms front and back at her sides to match the rhythm of her stride. Her eyes dart around the stage anxiously and she smiles timidly, her inexperience wears on her face like a nervous mask. Just as she opens her mouth Oscar interrupts and says, "Just a moment, my dear. That's the way an ice man would enter the house." He instructs her to try the entrance again. The film cuts back to a medium shot of Lily, her eyes cast downward to the floor to convey her embarrassment. In her second attempt she succumbs to Oscar's authorial control of her body by modifying her performance. Lily wrings her wrists nervously—a reoccurring action Lombard does in her films to occupy her hands—and walks toward the camera. She lifts her arms outwards and hollers "Daddy!" in a screechy Southern twang. We cut to a reaction shot of Oscar wincing at her unladylike bellow; he points out that "the Old South does not yodel" and instructs her to try again.

As their rehearsal continues, Oscar modifies her performance until it perfectly suits his vision. He even goes so far as to draw "tracks" on the stage floor to ensure Lily hits every mark and instructs her to restart the scene over and over until she hits each one perfectly. In a long shot that

FIGURE 3.1 *In* Twentieth Century *(Howard Hawks, 1934), Oscar Jaffe (John Barrymore, pictured top left) draws chalk lines for ingenue Lily Garland (Lombard, pictured bottom right) during a play rehearsal. This film is considered one of the first screwball comedies.*

frames her entire body, Lily apologetically begins again, bursting through the imaginary door with a renewed sense of confidence in her performance. Oscar stops her by saying she is "off the track," and she freezes in place. Lily looks down at the line and without any instruction turns around and walks back to her starting position. The scene dissolves into an overhead shot of the stage; it is covered with dozens of chalk lines. The actors are slumped lifelessly in chairs across the stage to indicate that the rehearsal has been going on for hours. Lily is lying across several chairs near the bottom of the frame as fellow cast member, Anita (Billie Seward), wafts smelling salts under her nose. The maze of chalk lines reveals the extent to which Oscar guides Lily through the scene, controlling her physical and vocal performance until they are to his standard.

This opening sequence confirms the initial power dynamics of their relationship. Lily is his creation and Oscar is her self-professed Svengali; he molds her into what he wants, even giving her a new name that sounds more theatrical. Her body and voice are the main sites in the transfer of control, as he teaches her the "proper" way to act and how to behave like a star. In this opening scene we get the sense that Lily is slowly losing control of herself to Oscar. Even when Oscar's tactics prove too much for her to handle and she pleads that she "can't stand it any longer," he still retains his hold over her, demanding that she continue the rehearsal; despite her protestations and exhaustion, Lily obeys. After their play opens and the pair are in Lily's dressing room, she asks him in a meek, almost tear-filled voice "Was I alright? Was I what you wanted?" which indicates that at that point in the film, she is desperate for his approval.

As Lily's confidence grows, she begins to push back against Oscar's unchallenged control and eventually walks out on his production. The pair meet on the Twentieth Century cross-country train, where Oscar decides to woo Lily back into a new contract so that he can obtain funding for his latest production, *The Passion Play*. After a brief absence from the narrative action, we rejoin Lily in her compartment where she is traveling with her boyfriend, George (Ralph Forbes). They get in a heated argument after Lily confesses that she never loved George, and that Oscar was the only man in her life. George tells her that they are through and storms out. In a medium shot, Lily begins to whimper loudly and sits down on the bench. Lombard sticks her bottom lip out and scrunches up her eyes to convey Lily's feigned frustration. In a quivering voice, she shouts "Why do they keep hammering at me? Hammering, hammering!" Lombard bounces her legs up and down, bringing her knees in toward her chest. She holds up her balled fists beside her head, and pounds them at her temples in rhythm with her legs. Her exaggerated movements convey Lily's newly acquired hammy temperament. Lombard raises the level of her voice to a high, squeaky pitch and projects loudly to indicate that Lily is acting like a spoiled brat to gain attention. In the midst of Lily's outburst her maid, Sadie, walks in from the adjoining

FIGURE 3.2 *Lily's feigned outburst reveals her emotional and behavioral similarities with mentor, Oscar.*

compartment. Sadie takes no notice and attempts to corral Lily into the other compartment. Lily suddenly stops her cries. Without missing a beat, she turns her head toward Sadie and in a loud, slightly deeper pitch she yells, "Stop pushing me!" before angrily stalking toward the compartment door.

In this scene, Lombard performs a comically excessive version of what James Naremore calls the breakdown of "expressive coherence." He describes this performance trait as taking root in "the presentation of self in society ... that assures others of our sincerity"[56] in social situations. Naremore's theory draws from the work of sociologist Erving Goffman, who writes that "while in the presence of others, the individual typically infuses his activity with signs which dramatically highlight and portray confirmatory facts that might otherwise remain unapparent or obscure."[57] Goffman explains that in all social interactions, we put on a "front" for our audience in order to fit into society or achieve our goals. He describes this as a form of "impression management," where an individual "presents

---

[56] James Naremore, *Acting in the Cinema* (Berkeley and Los Angeles: University of California Press, 1988), 70.
[57] Erving Goffman, *The Presentation of Self in Everyday Life* (Edinburgh: University of Edinburgh, 1956), 19.

himself and his activity to others ... in which he guides and controls the impression they form of him."[58] Naremore argues that films and the theater operate within different parameters compared to social interactions, and typically actors "dramatize situations in which the expressive coherence of a character either breaks down or is revealed as merely an 'act.'"[59]

When George is present Lily pretends to be overly dramatic, erratic, and emotionally sensitive, but in private, her demeanor is relatively calm and collected. It is therefore important that Lily abruptly stops her hysterical outburst only when George leaves her compartment, because it reveals that she consciously acts the part of a mercurial film star. The layers of Lombard's performance show us that Lily's erratic temper is a performative tactic that she has acquired from Oscar who, earlier in the film, threw a similar tantrum when he learned of her contract with a Hollywood studio. Lily's behavior in this scene is part of her movie star masquerade; a mood she can snap out of at a moment's notice for other people's benefit and to get her own way.

Oscar and Lily's final confrontation contrasts with the earlier dressing room scene. Lily is much more hostile and unwilling to entertain Oscar's ideas. Lombard's voice drips with venom as Lily acknowledges Oscar, asking "What do you want, scorpion?" The slight low angle of the shot accentuates their similar statures and we notice that they are practically the same height. It is a minor visual cue that reinforces their likeness, and reveals that she has finally mustered enough courage to stick up for herself. Lily confronts him about making her use chalk to show her how to move, and the embarrassment she felt when he had to teach her how to "talk like a parrot." Oscar confesses that he is planning a production of *The Passion Play* and suggests that Lily play the part of Mary Magdalene. They are framed in a medium shot, inches away from one another, their noses practically touching. Lombard maintains a calm but firm voice as Lily tells Oscar to get out of her compartment. Oscar jumps in place and the whole set shakes, the vibrating camera confirms the intense rage Barrymore imbues in his performance. Lily swings her arm behind her ready to hit him, and screams at the top of her lungs, "Get out of here you fake, you swindler!" She hits him, but Oscar grabs her by the forearms to calm her down. Lombard demonstrates Lily's resistance by writhing from side to side trying to loosen Oscar's grip. Lily pushes herself away from him and as his hold loosens she falls backward. The film cuts to a medium shot of Lily on the compartment bench with Oscar towering above her. She draws her knees into her chest, and swings her feet in and out in a boxing motion to hit him on the chest. Oscar points at her and yells, "I taught you everything you know. Even your

---

[58] Ibid, preface.
[59] Naremore, 70.

name: Lily Garland, I gave you that!" To indicate the extent of Lily's disgust, Lombard uses the force of her entire body to kick at Barrymore, and lets out a series of violent high-pitched screams that punctuate her character's physical attack. Oscar may have taught her how to act like an actress, but in doing so he has unknowingly given her the confidence she once lacked to stand up to him. She uses her body and voice to distance herself and to remind him that while he may have helped to "create her," he no longer controls her.

Despite Lily's protestations, Oscar tricks her into signing another contract and the film's final scene is almost a duplicate of the opener. Back in the same theater, Lily begins rehearsal for Oscar's latest play, but he continues to instruct her on how to act. The film comes full circle and we realize that Lily had only momentarily escaped Oscar's influence, and is now back under his thumb. The roundness of the narrative speaks to the carnivalesque qualities of the gender roles that screwball comedies like *Twentieth Century* put forth. In his study of the Middle Age carnival, philosopher Mikhail Bakhtin defines the medieval carnival as a "second world and second life outside of officialdom, a world in which all people participate more or less" as equals.[60] According to Kathleen Rowe, comedy challenges patriarchy by putting "men and women on an equal footing," and the couple "must be well matched, at least temporarily." However, she concedes that like the end of the medieval carnival, which signals the return to hierarchical social relations, by the conclusion of most screwball comedies the male character's "social and sexual power [is] restored." The screwball heroines find themselves once again subordinate to the male protagonist in an effort to recoup the narrative's conservative social order.[61]

The ephemerality of the screwball couple's equality is evident in the fluctuating dynamics of Lily and Oscar's relationship. Lily's self-confidence momentarily disrupts the balance of power between the two protagonists. Their relationship follows an arc built upon a struggle for control: at the outset, Lily submits body and mind to Oscar, and he builds her into a perfect replica of himself, a mini Oscar. Gaining access to her body is integral to their pairing as it implies a sexual conquest—she admits to George that Oscar is the only man she has "been" with—as well as agency over her movements, her gestures, her voice, and her acting. All of Oscar's efforts are not without consequence: the climax of their struggle for power finds Lily trying to regain her identity back from him; her kicking and screaming are learned mannerisms in line with the theatrical behavior he has taught her. But the film's conclusion and Lily's eventual contract signing restores the

---

[60]Mikhail Bakhtin, *Rabelais and his World*, first Midland books edition, trans. Helene Iswolsky (Bloomington, IN: Indiana University Press, 1984), 6.

[61]Kathleen Rowe, *The Unruly Woman: Gender and the Genres of Laughter* (Austin: University of Texas Press, 1995), 118.

FIGURES 3.3 & 3.4 *Lily confronts Oscar over his controlling behavior. These film stills capture how Lombard uses physicality to represent Lily's frustration.*

balance of power. *Twentieth Century*'s circular narrative recoups whatever agency it temporarily affords Lily over her own body. Just as the medieval carnival ends with a restoration of social order and rank, *Twentieth Century* reconfigures Oscar and Lily's relationship back to its initial starting point, and uses her body and voice to negotiate her new identity.

As Lily Garland, Carole Lombard proved that she could hold her own against a well-established star like Barrymore, and she aptly maneuvered between verbal and physical humor to add depth to her performance. A *New York Daily News* review quoted in a full-page *Variety* advertisement proclaims that Lombard "gives the best performance she has ever given."[62] *Variety* journalist Cecilia Ager writes "Carole Lombard in '20th Century' doesn't even look like Carole Lombard,"[63] an observation that verifies how atypical a role Lily Garland was for Lombard at this stage of her career. Ager goes on to praise the actress's visceral performance and how it mirrors her energetic off-screen persona, writing "Miss Lombard has found strength and vitality and good health again … She's exchanged her makeup mask for a human being's face."[64] Reflecting on her experience in *Twentieth Century*, Lombard was said to have told *Photoplay* that the "simple truth about acting" was to be able to "dig down deep into your understanding of the human being you were attempting to create, and living and thinking and being that character every moment the camera was turning."[65] The same article explains that while working for Sennett, Lombard learned how to handle her body and such techniques like where to place her hands while they were inactive,[66] all of which allowed her to hone her comic performance style and to give her characters depth and dimension. Such articles were meant to add credibility to Lombard's comic performance by showing that she approached her work as a serious craft. *Twentieth Century* is just the first in a long line of physical comedy based screwball performances, and as Lombard's career progressed, it increasingly became a fundamental component to her screwball persona.

Love Before Breakfast (*Walter Lang, 1936*)

In *Love Before Breakfast,* one of Lombard's many loan-outs—this time to Universal—Lombard plays Kay Colby, a socialite trying to resist the advances of a high-powered oil executive named Scott Miller (Preston Foster). After

---

[62]"N'York Critics Echo Fan Mag Raves!," *Variety*, May 8, 1934, 26.
[63]Cecilia Ager, "Going Places," *Variety*, May 8, 1934, 57.
[64]Ibid.
[65]George Madden, "The Evolution of a WOW!" *Movie Mirror*, December 1936, 100.
[66]Ibid, 49.

Scott sends Kay's boyfriend, Bill Wadsworth (Cesar Romero), to work in Japan he makes an earnest play for her affection. Despite Kay's extensive resistance throughout most of the film, the pair eventually marry when she realizes that she can no longer hide her feelings for Scott. This is the first film since *Twentieth Century* that permitted Lombard to incorporate physicality into her comic performance; her character gets punched, bruised, and battered all the while maintaining her unwavering sense of confidence. An analysis of Lombard's appearance in two scenes and the film's promotional campaign will demonstrate the interplay of physicality and beauty at the core of her star image, and the techniques used to create textual and extra-textual connections between star and character.

The first scene to deploy Lombard's physical comedy results in her character getting punched in a bar brawl. After seeing Bill off on his voyage, Kay and Scott head to a bar for some drinks. They get into an argument and Kay furiously stalks off to the other side of the room. She gets harassed by a group of fraternity boys, and when Scott tries to intervene a fight breaks out—but since the lights in the bar get turned off, we do not see any fighting. The police arrive and haul all of the patrons away in a police van. In the van, Kay and Scott are framed in close-up; the camera only reveals the left sides of their faces. Kay stares straight ahead motionless, barely opening her mouth to speak. Lombard's voice is deeper than usual and she speaks quickly, both reoccurring techniques she uses to convey her character's anger. Kay sarcastically compliments Scott on his dirty fighting tactics and quips, "I must give you credit for your good left hook." The film cuts in closer, and Kay turns her head to reveal that her right eye is swollen and covered by a big bruise. The camera pulls back to show Scott who begins to laugh uncontrollably, while an infuriated Kay glares at him.

The balance between Lombard's physicality and her remarkable physical beauty are at play in this scene, and bring forward her performance history with physical comedy. Barry King explains the difference between a star's and an actor's performances, with the former described as "personification" and the latter "impersonation." Impersonation refers to an acting style where "the 'real' personality of the actor should disappear into the part ..."[67] Conversely, personification is an intertextual process where "the actor as a private individual is already constituted as a sign within the host culture, insofar as his or her behavioral and physical attributes have been read and will be read as cues to their personality."[68] Personification tethers a star's performance to their already established public persona,[69] but as Karen Hollinger argues, the demarcation between the two sides are not as clear

---

[67]King, "Articulating Stardom," 130.
[68]Ibid, 131.
[69]Ibid, 141.

cut as King's definition would suggest.[70] She cites James Naremore, whose analysis of Cary Grant provides an "example of the acting effectiveness of personification."[71] Writing about Grant's self-reflexive performance in the train scene from *North by Northwest* (Alfred Hitchcock, 1959), Naremore observes "'Cary Grant' is displayed not simply as a famous personality who is performing a role but as the very essence of stardom—that is, as a remote, glamorous object who emits a glorious light simply by being 'himself.'"[72] The natural quality of Grant's performance masks his immense skills as an actor, which Naremore claims is evidence that "a vivid star personality is itself a theatrical construction."[73]

For a 1930s audience likely familiar with Lombard's star image, her well-known slapstick history would have provided a context for her bruised face and physical performance. In the same way that Grant's gesture with his sunglasses references his star "aura" and "overwhelms the fictional circumstances" of *North by Northwest*,[74] the black eye extends beyond the film's narrative to the boisterous, roughhousing comedy of Lombard's early career. It also reinforces the unique relationship between Lombard's physical comedy and her femininity. Brett Mills argues that female physical comedy upsets gender politics because it "refuses to conform to the convention of the female body as needing to take up as little space as possible, and only to be looked at for male sexual pleasure."[75] Kay's presence in the fight complicates the physical comedy gender divide. By participating in the scuffle, Kay firmly rejects the notion that she needed Scott's defense against the aggressive collegiate boys, and demonstrates that she possesses the physical stamina and athletic ability to partake in this form of male oriented comedy.

Lombard's growing presence in screwball comedy adds further layers to Kay's involvement in the bar brawl. Henry Jenkins argues that a star's overall image contextualizes their individual film roles, explaining, "the polysemic and fully articulated star image often overpowers the character played in any given film … Classical cinema minimizes the gap between star image and character, typically by casting stars into roles closely corresponding to their preexisting image."[76] A star's image precedes the roles they play, and in many cases, impacts on how their performances are interpreted by

---

[70]Karen Hollinger, *The Actress: Hollywood Acting and the Female Star* (New York: Routledge, 2006), 47–50.
[71]Ibid.
[72]Naremore, 221.
[73]Ibid, 234.
[74]Ibid, 221.
[75]Brett Mills, *Television Sitcom* (London: British Film Institute, 2006), 117.
[76]Henry Jenkins, "'A High-Class Job of Carpentry': Towards a Typography of Early Sound Comedy," in *Movie Acting, the Film Reader*, ed. Pamela Robertson Wojcik (London: Routledge, 2004): 112.

audiences and critics. The star–character symbiosis that was beginning to take shape in *Twentieth Century* is also evident in *Love Before Breakfast*. Just as Lombard's studio was separating her star persona from her glamour girl image, this film was exploiting the public's familiarity with Lombard's new independent and tough image. It is interesting to note that Kay is the only woman in the police van, a detail that suggests we should consider her as being on par—physically, at least—with the men; she must suffer the same consequences regardless of her gender. The fact that she is the only one to bear physical traces of the fight complicates this nominal equality—a point I will return to later. Given the context of Lombard's stardom, it is understandable that Scott is unfazed by the black eye. We can accept his laughter because of Lombard's strong image, and the qualities of her stardom that Kay Colby was built upon.

Kay's face bears the effects of her involvement in the bar brawl, but also signifies the duality of Carole Lombard's star persona. The left side emphasizes Lombard's natural beauty, while the right side reflects the physical aspect of her comic performance. The lighting makes the automobile scar on her left cheek visible and like Kay's roughhousing, connects Lombard's on- and off-screen personae. Typically airbrushed out of Lombard's promotional photos but referenced in virtually all of the biographical material about her, the scar's prominence in this and other Lombard films points to the accident that threatened her life and career, as discussed in the previous chapter. As a signifier of Lombard's accident, it adds a weariness to her face. When Kay turns to reveal her black eye, we are reminded that, despite Lombard's extraordinary beauty, she uses her body as part of her comic performance. When she turns her head her scar becomes more noticeable due to the lighting, and in combination with the black eye heightens the impression of physical violence. Like the slapstick comedy in her Sennett films or the kicking and screaming in *Twentieth Century*, the dual imperfections symbolize the malleability of her body and the significance of physicality to her star persona.

Another example of the juxtaposition between Lombard's physicality and beauty is the penultimate boat scene. At this point in the narrative, Kay has reunited with Bill and has ignored her feelings for Scott. When Scott invites her to a party on his boat, she stubbornly decides instead to go sailing with Bill. Both parties are on their respective boats when a terrific storm hits. Kay and Bill's small craft is no match for the storm, and the two get tossed about below deck. Lombard repeatedly gets knocked around, and is relentlessly pounded by waves of incoming water that drench her entire body. The heavy surges of water pummeling the boat throw Kay off balance, adding to the sense of panic that radiates from Lombard's already frantic movements. Typical of Lombard's performances, she also expresses Kay's fear and desperation through her wavering, low-toned voice that makes it seem like she is on the verge of tears.

Kay quickly recognizes the danger of their situation and pleads with Bill to leave, but he is too inebriated. Scott sends over a rescue team but Kay adamantly refuses their help; she screams at the top of her lungs and stomps her feet like a bratty child for them to leave. Kay's stubbornness is not a result of some sadistic pleasure for danger, but rather because she wants to leave the boat on her own terms. Accepting help from Scott would be a defeat of her fierce independence and an admission that she needs his protection. Eventually, she is physically restrained by the rescue party and dragged off her boat to safety, but not before she carries Bill to the top deck of the boat. It is interesting that Kay is the one who drags Bill out of danger; both the water and the weight of Bill's body put considerable demands on Lombard's athletic-but-slim frame. Kay gets drenched from head to toe, soaking her loose hair, sporty sailing outfit, and tennis shoes. In this scene, Bill is the passive figure—too drunk to think or move coherently—while Kay remains active and tries to take control of their situation. The clear gender reversal and the combination of these physical pressures confirm the malleability of Lombard's body and Kay's independent femininity.

Feminist film scholars have noted the transgressive potentials available to comediennes. Theorist Nancy Walker explains that "For a woman to adopt this role means that they must break out of the passive, subordinate position mandated for them by centuries of patriarchal tradition ... To be a woman and a humorist is to confront and to subvert the very power that keeps women powerless ...."[77] One can sense the influence of Bakhtin's theory in Walker's idea as she acknowledges the disruptive potentials in female comedy performances. Comedy offers women a platform to address their social circumstances or a particular societal malaise. A female comedian's body is central to their star persona, and they are often assessed by their appearance. Films that highlight the female body afford scholars the opportunity to engage with issues like gender, sexuality, race, and age.[78] Focusing on Lombard's body opens up a space to unpack the politics of the female body in classical Hollywood comedy. As mentioned in this chapter's introduction, Lombard's physical appearance primarily rested on the balance between her conventional beauty and her athleticism; she could be photographed convincingly in either a sexy bathing suit or in sports attire, and neither image destabilized her clearly coded all-American white femininity.

Both the "all-Americanness" and "whiteness" modifiers of femininity are important not only to Lombard's gender, but also to the sense of power implicit in our readings of her performance and star persona. According to

---

[77]Nancy Walker quoted in Susan Horowitz, *Queens of Comedy: Lucille Ball, Phyllis Diller, Carol Burnett, Joan Rivers and the New Generation of Funny Women* (Amsterdam: OPA, 1997), 5.
[78]Mizejewski, 10.

FIGURES 3.5 & 3.6 *In* Love Before Breakfast *(Walter Lang, 1936) Kay Colby (Lombard) gets a black eye after being punched in a police wagon. Lombard's performance in this film represents the balance between physicality and physical beauty underpinning her star image.*

Frances B. Cogan, the concept of the ideal American girl was popularized in the mid nineteenth century as a moral and physical standard of "real womanhood."[79] Such women "required not only a physically fit body, a healthy outlook on life, and a well-balanced mind but the correct education to use each to its best advantage."[80] This definition privileges youth—"a physically fit body" implies strength and vigor—moral conservatism—"a healthy outlook on life" suggests an acceptance of established social and cultural values—and wealth and privilege—"correct education" means gentility and manners, which were expected from girls and women of an upper class background. It also noticeably ignores the underlying racial bias: ideal American womanhood could only be bestowed upon white American women.

Richard Dyer argues that "the equation of being white with being human secures a position of power."[81] Although there are what Dyer calls "variations of power amongst white people" that are related to class, gender, and other social differences, "white power none the less reproduces itself regardless of intention, power differences and goodwill, and overwhelmingly because it is not seen as whiteness, but as normal."[82] The types of power Dyer writes about can be political and economic, but also social, relating to the opportunities and prejudices one faces as a result of their racial identity. Roles such as Kay Colby did not exist for nonwhite actors in the 1930s.[83] Nor could a nonwhite woman in a 1930s Hollywood comedy act as stubborn, self-assured, and romantically capricious as Kay because of the institutional, social, and cultural limitations governing nonwhite bodies. "All-American" is a racially charged term that is synonymous with whiteness, and this ties back to our understanding of Lombard's performance and her ability to be comically transgressive without undermining her femininity. Kay can enter into combative situations with Scott and Bill and still be a likable character precisely because Lombard looked and—for the most part—acted in accordance with the white American female ideal. Kay's feisty, independent nature, and antagonistic relationship with the film's male protagonists may have been seen as progressive, but they were also non-threatening because of Lombard's racially and socially privileged femininity.

Nevertheless, there are limits to Lombard's comic transgressions. The assault on Kay's body in both scenes alludes to the "independent female" quality of Lombard's image and highlights the boundaries of her physicality

---

[79]Frances B. Cogan, *All-American Girl: The Ideal of Real Womanhood in Mid-Nineteenth Century America* (Athens: The University of Georgia Press, 1989), 61.
[80]Ibid.
[81]Richard Dyer, *White: Essays on Race and Culture* (New York: Routledge, 1997), 9.
[82]Ibid, 9–10.
[83]Thomas Cripps, *Slow Fade to Black: The Negro in American Film, 1900–1942* (New York: Oxford University Press, 1993), 112.

in relation to her beauty. Kay's black eye, in comparison to Scott's unscathed face, shows the disparity of their relative physical strengths. Similarly, the rescue team he sends to save her and his subsequent paternal scolding imbues her with a childish obstinacy; she would not have gotten soaking wet had she not refused to leave the boat. All of this is not to deny Kay's transgressive intentions, but in each scene the film unfavorably compares her defiled face and body with Scott's—slightly more—powerful brawn and brain. Although Lombard's physicality affords her the chance to partake in a form of male oriented comedy, in this context, it is also used to signal her weakness. The film achieves this by eroticizing her black eye, and falsely equating her physical beauty with passivity.

The film's publicity campaign confirms my argument, and addresses the wider ideological tension between violent physical comedy and beauty. The promotional posters feature a drawing of Lombard sporting Kay's black eye. This same image was used to advertise the film in both domestic and foreign markets, and has since circulated on film memorabilia like buttons, mugs, and clothing. The image works off shock value and foregrounds the juxtaposition of her uncharacteristically male physicality and her glamorous femininity. Lombard's blonde hair frames her face in a yellow–orange hue that creates an angelic halo around her head. She smiles and is wearing bright red lipstick, and her other eye is made up with heavy dark lashes and eye shadow roughly the same color as the bruise. Lombard looks unfazed by the bruise, wearing it as if it were part of her makeup.[84] Her head rests gently on her left shoulder and her gaze is cast off into the distance as if to imply a flirtatious timidity.

The posters speak to Lombard's performance history, but they also reference a glamour not quite in tandem with the violence that the black eye connotes. Stephen Gundle defines glamour as an outgrowth of "the dreams of commercial society,"[85] describing it as an "enticing and seductive vision … whose purpose it is to dazzle and seduce whoever gazes on it."[86] The posters aestheticize domestic violence and present a complacent image of female abuse. They exude a mix of coquetry and the aftereffects of violence;

---

[84] A similar casual attitude to female abuse can be seen in *The Golden Arrow* (Alfred E. Green, 1936), a Bette Davis film that was released nearly three months after *Love Before Breakfast*. Toward the end of the film, Daisy (Davis) gets hit in the eye with a tennis ball and develops a black eye. To denounce rumors about her marriage and social position, and to win back her estranged husband Johnny's (George Brent) affections, she explains to her social circle that the black eye was the result of a physical fight. Unlike Lombard's film, however, Daisy does not ever participate in any sort of on-screen altercation, and the black eye was not used in any marketing campaign. Nevertheless, since *The Golden Arrow* wrapped production in early March—and retakes, including this scene, were filmed several weeks later—one could argue that *Love Before Breakfast* may have inspired Davis's black eye gag.

[85] Stephen Gundle, *Glamour: A History* (Oxford: Oxford University Press, 2008), 7.

[86] Ibid, 5.

brutality and beauty are quite literally fused together. There is a troublesome indifference in Lombard's expression, as she appears complicit in promoting this sexualized vision of female abuse. The image evokes a passivity toward physical aggression, an aestheticization of male assaults toward women. I would argue that both the film and the posters downplay this issue, but unlike the posters, the film contextualizes the bruise through the dynamics of Scott and Kay's relationship, and gives Kay an opportunity to respond to his violent outburst. *Love Before Breakfast*'s posters undermine whatever empowered intent the film affords Lombard and ultimately recoup her physical comedy into a sexually charged and seductive yet uncomfortable image.

Love Before Breakfast falls short of capturing the electric rhythm and congenial spirit of the Lombard–Barrymore pairing in *Twentieth Century*, and Lombard's chemistry with Preston Foster and Cesar Romero is one-dimensional. Neither Bill nor Scott are very likable characters and frankly, it is hard to believe Kay would waste so much energy on either of them. Critical reviews were mixed, with one rather harsh *New York Times* reviewer describing it as "a story thin to the point of emaciation" based upon "meagre materials."[87] *Variety* called the film "the old plot malarkey wrapped up in fancy trimmings," but projected that it would be a high grosser at the box office because of its "fairly good entertainment" value.[88] *Love Before Breakfast* was considered a major picture for Universal and, as predicted, did fair business, proving that Carole Lombard's star status was growing. The film opened nationwide on March 9, 1936 and grossed $18,000 in its first week in a mid level city like Cleveland, but failed to edge MGM's *Wife vs. Secretary* (Clarence Brown, 1936) from the top spot.[89] Meanwhile, it grossed $40,000 in its first week at The Roxy in New York.[90] *Hands Across the Table* and *Love Before Breakfast* were the first fully-fledged "Carole Lombard pictures," both of which she carried as the top-billed star. Lombard was also able to bring her own technical crew from Paramount to Universal, including her longtime cinematographer, Ted Tetzlaff.[91] Unlike *Twentieth Century* where she played second lead to John Barrymore, these films marked a surge in Lombard's career where she began to receive full star treatment and billing. This trend would increase exponentially throughout the rest of the 1930s, with 1936 being a turning point for Carole Lombard's screwball career.

---

[87]"Movie Reviews," *Love Before Breakfast*, March 14, 1935, K18.
[88]"Film Reviews," *Variety*, March 18, 1936, 17.
[89]"'Wife' 25G, Quins $20,000, Give Lent Trimmin' in Cleve.," *Variety*, March 11, 1936, 11.
[90]"Strike Over, Weather Better, B'way OK; Dionnes Nice $85,000 1st Week, 'Klondike Annie' 50G, 'Breakfast' 40G," *Variety*, March 18, 1936, 9.
[91]He worked with Lombard on ten films. See: Frederick W. Ott, *The Films of Carole Lombard* (New York: Citadel Press, 1972), 26.

My Man Godfrey (*Gregory La Cava, 1936*)

Carole Lombard is arguably best remembered for her Oscar nominated performance as Irene in Universal Studio's *My Man Godfrey*. It contains such generic tropes as fast-talking dialog, madcap antics, and a "female-dominated courtship"[92] that have since come to define screwball comedy. The film was released on September 6, 1936 and was met with instant box-office success and positive critical reviews. Lombard was widely praised for giving "one of the most deft and devastating comedy performances,"[93] and the film received six Academy Award nominations including one for Best Actress.[94] Set in New York in the midst of the Depression, it tells the story of its eponymous character, Godfrey "Smith" Parke (William Powell), and heiress Irene Bullock. Godfrey, the son of an established American family, is masquerading as a "forgotten man," a destitute war veteran, living in a New York City dump. Irene and her sister Cornelia (Gail Patrick) meet him while playing a scavenger hunt, and Irene offers him a job as the family's butler. She falls madly in love with Godfrey, and despite his willful resistance to her advances, by the end of the film she cajoles him into marriage.

Irene has been described as "the most exhilaratingly anarchic child–woman" in screwball.[95] The reference to her childlike demeanor may imply that Irene is lacking depth, but Lombard brings an endearing quality to her performance that prevents Irene from becoming one-dimensional. Irene is arguably one of the most complex figures in the film because she reveals glimmers of her humility, and her relationship with Godfrey is the catalyst for the film to engage with contemporary issues like unemployment and poverty. That being said, Irene never loses her impish naïveté, and her social conscience remains secondary to her immaturity and love for Godfrey. Lombard was cast at the request of William Powell, who believed that her screwball talents would be well suited for daffy-yet-lovable Irene.[96] His hunch proved correct, and Lombard plays Irene with a high-strung spirit and passion, traits that were also identifiable in her star persona. Much like her previous screwball films, Lombard primarily relies on her body and voice to convey Irene's emotional state of mind. An analysis of Lombard's bodily movements and vocal delivery in two scenes will illustrate the incongruity between Irene's underdeveloped intellect and physical maturity. Furthermore, I will explore contemporary publicity to show

---

[92]Gehring, 178.
[93]Madden, 49.
[94]Ibid, 94.
[95]Elizabeth Kendall, *The Runaway Bride: Hollywood Romantic Comedy of the 1930s* (New York: Cooper Square Press, 2002), 153.
[96]Gehring, 132.

how these inconsistencies in Irene's character mirror the beautiful/physical juxtaposition that underpinned Lombard's screwball persona.

We are first introduced to Irene as she bounds out of a taxi at the city dump, breathless and full of vitality. The streetlight overhead catches the sparkles on her silver dress and casts an effervescent shimmer across her face that matches her bubbly personality. She and Cornelia are on the hunt for a "forgotten man" for their scavenger hunt, the reason for their visit to the dump. After they spot Godfrey, Irene yells to Cornelia, "You're not gonna get away from me, I saw him first!" Lombard runs toward the camera and giving us a glimpse into Irene's restless spirit, while the line itself indicates her character's competitive relationship with Cornelia and her childlike disposition. Godfrey bristles at their intrusion and knocks Cornelia into a pile of ashes, then proceeds to interrogate Irene. The pair are framed facing each other in a close-up and in a breathy, soft voice and talking exceedingly fast, Irene confesses that she has always wanted to push Cornelia into a pile of ashes. Suddenly, she cups her right hand over her mouth and lets out a very hearty, high-pitched chuckle. Lombard also uses her body to indicate Irene's amusement, throwing her head and upper body back and forth in rhythm with her laughter.

FIGURE 3.7 *In* My Man Godfrey *(Gregory La Cava, 1936) Lombard plays opposite her ex-husband, William Powell. He agreed to play the title role only if Lombard was cast as the scatterbrained heiress, Irene Bullock.*

Growing impatient, Godfrey asks her if she is capable of following an intelligent conversation and inquires about the scavenger hunt. Irene explains that a scavenger hunt is about finding objects that nobody wants, at which point Godfrey interjects, "Like a forgotten man." Struck by the recklessness of her game, Irene's smile disappears and she replies softly, "I don't want to play games with human beings as objects, it's kinda sordid when you think of it, I mean when you think it over." As she says the line, Lombard slows down her delivery and speaks with a quiet intensity, and looks directly at Powell to indicate Irene's sincerity. Without missing a beat Irene smiles and looks around at her surroundings. With an upbeat lilt in her voice she asks, "Can I ask why you live in a place like this when there are so many other nice places?" Bemused, Godfrey tells her that his doctor said it was good for his asthma. Staring into Godfrey's eyes, Irene says matter-of-factly "Oh, my uncle has asthma." The tone in her voice carries a hint of innocence and solemnity, revealing that Irene fails to understand Godfrey's sarcasm. She beams because she and Godfrey are engaging in what she considers to be an intelligent conversation, while Godfrey looks bemused by her naïveté. It is important that Irene misunderstands Godfrey's answer because it shows how unaware she is of his hardships, and the economic turmoil outside of her upper class bubble. Irene's infantilization is comically excessive, and she consistently vacillates from blissful ignorance to critical self-consciousness throughout the film. The overall shift in Irene's conversation and tone is initially disconcerting, but is itself part of *My Man Godfrey*'s comic mechanism. Irene's exaggerated lack of awareness is a form of social criticism, employed for comic purposes to expose the disconnection between the film's upper and lower class characters.

Irene suffers from an overwhelming lack of discipline and self-control. She engages with contemporary social issues only on a personal level through Godfrey, and the film frames her slight social conscience as a by-product of her obsession with him. The extent of Irene's immaturity becomes clear in the tantrum scene, which begins when her father, Alexander, calls the family together in their living room to discuss their dwindling fortunes. Irene saunters into the room wearing elaborate gold lamé lounging pajamas and a matching black and gold embroidered long jacket paired with black heels. Her blonde hair frames her face, and her face is covered with minimal makeup to complement her casual-yet-sophisticated outfit. Her "lounging pajamas" are exceptionally glamorous for a casual evening at home, and Lombard—then aged twenty-eight—looks too mature and sophisticated for a girl that is meant to be eighteen or nineteen.

Itching to provoke Irene, Cornelia suggests that they fire Godfrey. As the family sounds their agreement, the film cuts to a close-up of Irene on the verge of tears. Lombard's bottom lip trembles as she stares down to the ground to show that Irene is holding back her tears. Irene sniffs and her whimpering grows louder. She walks toward Alexander and leans her head on his shoulder much in the same way a young child would with their parent. Irene then lies down on the sofa facing her family, giving them a clear view of her feigned suffering. Lombard exaggerates her groans by making them excessively loud and drawn out, and Angelica pats Irene's head while repeating "There, there," and "Now, now, darling" the same way a mother would to their crying baby. Irene's ostensibly juvenile flailing and the juxtaposition between her physical maturity and immature antics call attention to the fact that her family—primarily Angelica—indulges her bad behavior. Angelica suggests they call a doctor, but Irene yells "I don't want a doctor, I don't want an ice pack, I want to die!" Lombard draws out her delivery of the word "die" and flails her arms out over the edges of the sofa, both performance techniques designed to reinforce Irene's disingenuous suffering.

Angelica instructs her "protégé" Carlo (Mischa Auer) to amuse Irene. He musses his hair, jumps on the couch on all fours to mimic a monkey. As he does this, the film cuts to a close-up of Irene's face. Her whimpers subside and Lombard opens her mouth in a dumbfounded grimace to show that, for a minute, Irene realizes Carlo is acting just as nutty as she is. Irene's crying subsides as soon as she is reassured Godfrey is in the room. Basking in the success of her charade, she smiles at Godfrey, who is watching the family in silent disbelief. Holding her hand over his and staring up at him with a smug smile across her face, Irene whispers in a way a child does when they have a secret, "I'm not really having a spell." Godfrey leans down to hear her, and as he does film cuts to a close-up of their heads. Irene reaches up to grab his face and kisses him.

Lombard uses her body and voice to push Irene's adolescent behavior to its limit. She extends Irene's theatrics beyond the verbal and into the realm of the physical, her flailing body working in tandem with her over-the-top cries. Irene throws tantrums to get her own way, a technique far too childish for a woman of her age. Part of *My Man Godfrey*'s marketing campaign was predicated on Irene's comic immaturity: in conjunction with the film's release, Universal Studios released a promotional booklet entitled *Diary of a Debutante*. The twelve-page pink booklet is a "reproduction" of Irene's diary filled with entries meant to be in her handwriting. It was conceived as a publicity gimmick by Joe Weil, head of Universal's publicity department, to introduce readers to Irene before the film, so that they would be in "the right frame of mind to pick up the picture."[97] The diary contains her musings about Godfrey such as, "he came over and patted my hand. M-mm what a thrill!" Through the juxtaposition of the written text and the accompanying images, the diary exposes the disparity between Irene's mature sexuality and childish behavior. In doing so, it also reveals how the film uses Irene's naïveté to engage with sexual innuendo.

---

[97] "Astor Influence," *Variety*, September 9, 1936, 25.

THE QUEEN OF SCREWBALL COMEDY 101

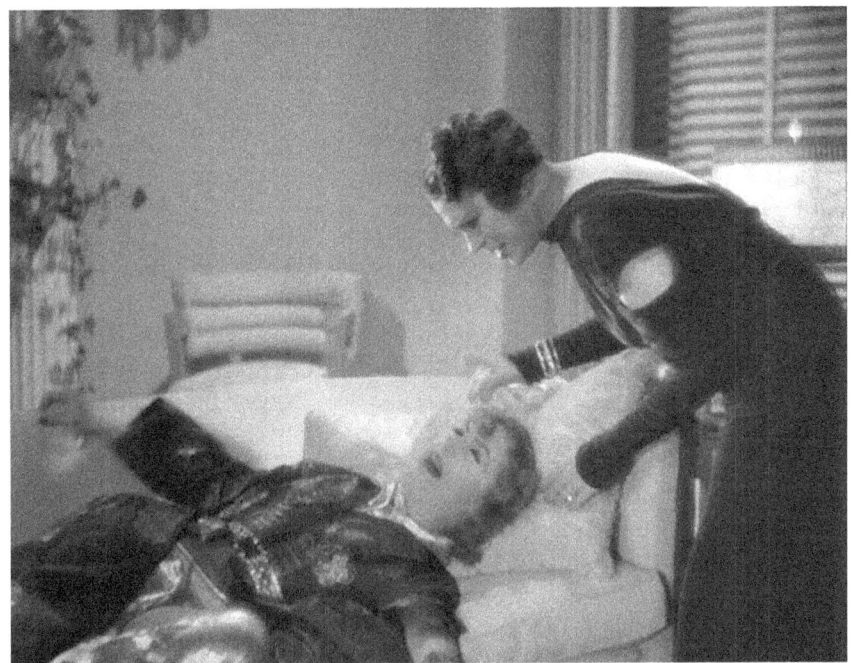

FIGURES 3.8 & 3.9 *Lombard uses her body and voice to convey Irene's feigned hysterics.*

One such example of innuendo is when Irene and her maid, Molly, are discussing Godfrey in the Bullock's kitchen. Molly is seated at the kitchen table sewing buttons on Godfrey's suit jacket. Irene asks "It's his, isn't it? Do you always sew his buttons on?" to which Molly replies, "Sometimes." Irene gently strokes the sleeve with her hand and admits, "Oh, I'd like to sew his buttons on sometime when they come off. I wouldn't mind at all." Her tone is serious enough to convey Irene's innocence, but Lombard says the line with subtle emphasis on the words "come off" that we know she is talking about something other than buttons. Looking Irene in the eye, Molly answers, "He doesn't lose very many." Irene answers, "He's very tidy" to which Molly echoes, "Yes, he's very tidy." Taken at face value, the exchange is innocent, yet the women's sideways glances and tongue-in-cheek deliveries create a space for the phrase "sew his buttons" to be interpreted as a euphemism for Irene's lust. This reading is plausible, in part, because of the comic duality in Irene's character, but also because of Molly's role as the Bullock's servant and the close—sometimes sexual—relationship that exists between domestic servants.[98]

The photos included in Irene's "Diary" confirm the incongruity in Irene's character. In one, Lombard looks at the camera with her head slightly tilted upwards and heavy, sultry eyelids. The light shining from above casts a shadow on her face that accentuates her high cheekbones. She wears a white blouse with a deep V-neck clearly unsuitable for a teenage debutante. As already mentioned, Lombard was twenty-eight when she made *My Man Godfrey*—a full ten years older than Irene in Eric Hatch's novel. Like the tantrum scene, the diary exposes the inherent conflict that lies in between Irene's character and the reality of Lombard's persona; the two sides do not produce a cohesive figure.

The discrepancy between Irene's physical and mental age is also a variation of the inconsistency at the core of Lombard's screwball persona. After recognizing that Lombard's glamorous studio image was not resonating with audiences, Paramount quickly shifted their focus on to her vivacious and earthy personality to create a symbiotic connection between her star image and her film roles. By 1936, publicity stories and images frequently appeared in fan magazines that validated her new on-screen persona. During this time, Lombard was described as "a raucous, rowdy girl, who even in dungarees looks lovely enough to eat with a spoon ..."[99]

---

[98]The implication being that Molly has a sexual history with Godfrey, and can therefore speak with a degree of authority about his habits. In the screwball genre, the romantic entanglements of hired help is addressed most notably in *If You Could Only Cook* (William A. Seiter, 1935). Released less than nine months before *My Man Godfrey,* the film stars Herbert Marshall as an automobile executive and Jean Arthur as an unemployed woman who pose as a married couple so that they can secure jobs as a butler and cook.

[99]Elizabeth Wilson, "It Looked Good for a Laugh at the Time," *Silver Screen*, January 1941, page unknown.

Her penchant for practical jokes and wacky, elaborately themed parties was legendary, including the previously mentioned "Venice Beach pier party" and her "Hospital party" where guests were forced to exchange their dinner clothes for hospital gowns and were served their food in bedpans.[100]

Around the time *My Man Godfrey* was released Lombard's "party girl" reputation was at its peak. Fan magazines offered readers insight into Lombard's entertaining savvy, including tips on how to throw the best possible party.[101] Later, Lombard supposedly claimed that her party girl reputation was "entirely misjudged,"[102] but Robert Matzen explains that it was a "means to an end to position [her] as the type of personality just right for screwball."[103] In her discussion of typecasting, Pamela Robertson Wojcik writes that in each film "the Hollywood star creates a role homologous with themselves." Through the sum total of a star's film performances and the publicity discourse about their off-screen persona, the Hollywood studios and their respective publicity departments are able to establish an identifiable and definable star "type."[104] The press stories and photographs published in the mid 1930s added verisimilitude to Lombard's screwball performances by strengthening the close parallels between her star persona and her characters, like Irene. Her false tantrum therefore makes sense, since her outrageous behavior had some grounding in Lombard's already established "authentic" screwy persona. Although Irene's personality has a literary precedent, given the dark undertones of Eric Hatch's novel, one could argue that the cinematic version of Irene is arguably more closely aligned with Lombard's off-screen persona as a "party girl." Director Henry Jaglom once described Lombard as a "road-company Garbo,"[105] an image that simultaneously evokes an ethereal physical beauty and an earthy sensibility. She was far more attractive than the "girl next door," but her quirky personality kept her relatable for the average film spectator, a combination that speaks to the ordinary–extraordinary paradox that star studies scholars have identified at the heart of public perceptions of stardom.[106]

Over the course of a few years Lombard became the antithesis of her glamour girl persona. Along with the burgeoning focus on her no-nonsense

---

[100]Ibid.
[101]Julie Lang Hunt, "How Carole Lombard plans a party," *Photoplay*. February 1935, 67.
[102]Edith Dietz, "She Scoffs at the Terrors of Filmland," *Screen & Radio Weekly* (December 1934), 5.
[103]Robert Matzen, "Party Girl." *Thoughts about life in general and old Hollywood in particular*, date unknown, http://robertmatzen.com/tag/carole-lombard-party-house/.
[104]Pamela Robertson Wojcik, "Typecasting," *Criticism* Vol. 45, No. 2 (Spring 2003), 231.
[105]Henry Jaglom *My Lunches with Orson: Conversations between Henry Jaglom and Orson Welles*, ed. Peter Biskind (New York: Metropolitan Books, 2013), 62.
[106]John Ellis, "Stars as Cinematic Phenomenon," in *Star Texts: Image and Performance in Film and Television*, ed. Jeremy Butler (Detroit: Wayne State University Press, 1991), 303. See also: Edgar Morin, *The Stars* (London: Evergreen Profile Books, 1960), 51; Richard Dyer, *Stars*, new edition (London: Palgrave MacMillan, 1998), 47.

nature, there was a newfound simplicity to Lombard's clothing and private hobbies like fishing and skeet shooting that was a stark contrast from the fast-paced nightclub life of her earlier days. Irene's tantrum foregrounds Lombard's malleable screwball body at a time when it was becoming the focal point of her star persona for different reasons. In early 1936 Lombard had begun dating Clark Gable, who was an avid outdoorsman, hunter, and fisherman. In order to demonstrate Gable and Lombard's compatibility, fan magazines widely publicized the fact that Lombard took up his hobbies with great gusto; by 1938, she was described by *Life* as "the best woman skeet shot in Hollywood."[107] Once news of their relationship broke in the popular press, she was often featured in "candid" publicity shots wearing simple clothes like plaid lounging pajamas, cowboy boots, or jeans, all items that Lombard the glamour girl would never wear. She was also photographed doing sporty activities like shooting or fishing. In late 1938, she attracted a great deal of publicity after she bought a ranch in the San Fernando Valley, and in an interview with host Cecil B. DeMille on the *Lux Radio Theater* adaptation of *My Man Godfrey*, she explained how she was spending her free time studying farming in a college level correspondence course.[108] Despite having an official residence in Bel Air, Lombard spent the following months renovating the ranch in anticipation of moving in with Gable once they were married—a plan that was contingent on his divorce proceedings with his estranged wife, Rhea. Lombard's unexpected interest in ranch life was, in part, motivated by the relationship with Gable. But it also served to authenticate her screwball persona: it created a bridge between star and character, and conversely, her work in screwball comedy established a new set of parameters to contextualize her stardom.

The shift in Carole Lombard's post 1936 stardom underscores the fusion of star and character, and cemented Lombard's feisty heroines as a quintessential screwball "type." Lombard's on-screen personality brought to life the frenetic eccentricity that could not be captured in print, and as John Ellis suggests, "film performance will present the completeness of the star, the real mystery at which [auxiliary publicity materials] only hint."[109] Ellis points to film as being the missing piece of the puzzle that is the star image. Richard Dyer, on the other hand, argues that every medium carries their own information that contributes to a star's image. He writes, "star images are always extensive, multimedial, intertextual" but that "not all these manifestations are necessarily equal."[110] He notes the intertextuality of a star's image, but unlike Ellis does not see film as being the necessarily dominant medium in building a star's meaning. This is crucial to unpacking

---

[107] Busch, 50.
[108] "My Man Godfrey," *Lux Radio Theater*, May 9, 1938.
[109] Ellis, 305.
[110] Dyer, *Stars*, 3.

Lombard's screwball persona, as so much of her on-screen persona is tethered to her physical, tactile engagement with her co-stars and spaces. Lombard's spunky off-screen personality cannot quite be captured in textual accounts, and characters like Irene add visual rhythm, movement, and animation to otherwise static publicity accounts of her screwball traits. Likewise, publicity stories add a deeper layer of "truth" to her on-screen screwball personality, confirming that Lombard's diegetic eccentricities have roots in her "real life." Put together, the publicity images and press stories worked with Lombard's film roles to create a compact symbiotic exchange between her star image and her screwball heroines.

Released on September 6, 1936, *My Man Godfrey* was a massive hit at the box office. It was recorded as having the biggest opening day in eighteen months in St. Louis, and grossed $18,000 in its first week.[111] Meanwhile, in Detroit it made an impressive $30,000 in its first week,[112] and set records for opening weekend sales in Pittsburgh, making $10,000 and prompting several theaters to add additional show times each day.[113] *New York Times* arts columnist Douglas W. Churchill argued that *My Man Godfrey* marked the birth of a cycle of zany comedies, writing that the film "convinced [Hollywood] of the value of a deliberately disordered mind."[114] His comment was likely a reference to Irene's eccentric antics, but Irene is "zany" without being a parody. Lombard does not let Irene become superficially screwy. She injects a warmth into her performance that makes Irene likable in spite of her maddening immaturity. Irene's tantrum speaks to the growing force physical comedy was playing in Lombard's screwball persona. This would only increase exponentially in the coming years, with *Nothing Sacred* marking the apex of physicality in Lombard's comic performances.

Nothing Sacred (*William Wellman, 1937*)

By early 1937 Lombard was at the end of her Paramount contract, and quietly began intense negotiations with her agent, Myron Selznick, for a contract with his brother, the independent producer David O. Selznick. With a string of established screwball hits and an Oscar nomination to her name, Lombard was at that point one of Hollywood's biggest stars.

---

[111]"'Zieggy' $23,000, 'Swing Time' $17,500, 'Godfrey' $18,000, St. Louis' Big Week," *Variety*, September 9, 1936, 8.
[112]"'Asking' With Spitalny Gals $26,000, Mich.," *Variety*, September 16, 1936, 9.
[113]"'Adverse' $22,000, 'Hussy' $20,000, Both Terrif on Raised Pittsburgh Sales," *Variety*, September 9, 1936, 10.
[114]Douglas W. Churchhill, "Lunacy Hath Charms at the box office," *New York Times*, July 11, 1937, L10.

She was also in the advantageous position to demand a more lucrative contract. The trio settled on a three-picture deal at $175,000 per film,[115] and a freelance contract that also granted Lombard final approval on her future projects. Shortly after signing, Lombard began working on Selznick's Technicolor screwball comedy, *Nothing Sacred*. Written by screenwriter Ben Hecht and directed by William Wellman, the film stars Lombard as Hazel Flagg, a small-town girl who is misdiagnosed with deadly radium poisoning. When slick city reporter Wallace Cook (Fredric March) hears about Hazel's illness, he invites her to live out her last days in New York in order to get a story for his newspaper. Hazel is eager to escape her town, so she accepts Wally's offer although she knows by then she is not ill. Hazel quickly discovers that the well-meaning New Yorkers are disingenuous, their false sympathy exposes the phoniness of the big city.[116] Wally finds out the truth about his city but also about Hazel's illness, so in order to prevent public outrage and keep his job, the pair must find a way to keep her hoax a secret.

Nothing Sacred is undeniably one of Lombard's most energetic screwball comedies and it gives her several opportunities to show off her skills at physical comedy. The film harkens back to the rough-and-tumble comedy of Lombard's Sennett days, and builds upon her already established athletic screwball persona. Lombard gets tossed around, falls, and throws punches but unlike *Love Before Breakfast* where the actual blow was off screen, she receives an on-screen punch in the face and throws one in return. In many ways, *Nothing Sacred* could be considered as a "next step" film from *Love Before Breakfast* in Lombard's physical comedy oeuvre. Similar issues regarding the interplay between her beautiful appearance and earthy physicality that are at play in *Love Before Breakfast* are also present in *Nothing Sacred*. Lombard's physical beauty still remains at the core of her comedy, but Hazel is altogether less demure and more unapologetically aggressive than Kay Colby. During the film's climax in which Hazel boxes with Wally, she is stripped of any hint of glamour or sex appeal. She is wearing a full-length robe and scarf that cover her entire body, and this costuming detail draws our focus to her physical performance. With each confrontation Hazel proves that she can hold her own with Wally, which more broadly reflects the progressive potentials for female physical comedy. I will analyze Hazel's appearance and physical interactions with Wally in the boxing scene and the film's publicity campaign to demonstrate how the juxtaposition of beauty and physicality was more relevant to the marketing of *Nothing Sacred* than to the narrative itself. In addition, I will argue for *Nothing Sacred*'s cultural significance as part of a trend of mid 1930s

---

[115]Swindell, 219.
[116]Harvey, 204.

Hollywood comedies that moved toward a more egalitarian representation of gender roles through physically active female performances.

The fight scene takes place in Hazel's hotel room where she has been holed up in bed feigning her illness. As Wally enters the room the camera pans to Hazel, who is wrapped under the covers, wearing a robe and a hot water bottle tied around her head. Lombard's eyes are closed and she mumbles softly to give Hazel's performance its intended effect. Wally has just learned that his editor, Oliver Stone (Walter Connolly), has invited the renowned Viennese doctor, Emil Eggelhoffer (Sig Ruman), to examine Hazel and fears that her lie will be exposed and that they will be made laughing stocks of the city. Hazel is unaware of Dr. Eggelhoffer's impending visit, so she continues her charade by pretending that she has not heard Wally's plea for help.

Wally explains that the best way to make Hazel appear like she is dying is to get her "gasping, panting and covered in a cold sweat inside of five minutes"; unlike the subtle sexual innuendo in *My Man Godfrey,* in this scene the sexual subtext is made all too clear by the dialog and the physical sparring, which is indicative of the "erotic tension" between the sexes that characterized 1930s screwball comedies.[117] Wally suggests that they play fight and slaps her bum to get her out of bed. To indicate Hazel's disregard for Wally's plan, Lombard falls backward dramatically on the bed and flings the covers over her head. As Christina Lane astutely observes, Lombard's heroines' "high theatrics and vulnerable excess often slide into self-conscious role playing."[118] Hazel's over-indulgent reaction is indicative of the layers of performance at play in this scene, and Lombard allows us to see Hazel's "tiny flicker" of wavering belief in her own performance.[119] Wally grabs and drags Hazel to the edge of the bed by her legs, and punches her hot water bottle off of her head before lifting her to her feet. He shakes her violently while shouting, "Because I love you, because I'm going to marry you and I don't want to spend my honeymoon at Sing-Sing blowing kisses to you in the exercise yard!" The film cuts to a reaction shot of Hazel, who appears astonished by his brazen outburst. Lombard conveys Hazel's rage by yelling and swinging her fists energetically at March's face. Wally kicks Hazel's bum and she falls face first onto the bed. Lombard uses the bedsprings to gain momentum and prove Hazel's physical resilience: she bounces back up without much effort and continues to box her fists at March. The film cuts to a shot of Lombard's face over March's shoulder, and her expression further conveys Hazel's determination: she scrunches up her mouth, squints her eyes and punches him in the stomach.

---

[117]Tamar Jeffers McDonald, *Romantic Comedy: Boy Meets Girl Meets Genre* (New York: Columbia University Press, 2007), 97.
[118]Christina Lane, "A Modern Marriage for the Masses: Carole Lombard, Clark Gable, and the Cultural Front," *Quarterly Review of Film and Video* Vol. 33, No. 5 (January 2016), 414.
[119]Terrence Rafferty, "Forever Screwball, Forever Fearless," *New York Times*, November 20, 1938, 18.

However, given the underlying sexual innuendo of the scene one could also interpret her expression as a visceral acknowledgment of sexual pleasure. Wally puts both hands around Hazel's waist and throws her back on the bed; she jumps up and slowly walks toward him throwing her balled-up fists toward his abdomen. She screams, "I hate you, I hate you, I just hate you," and swings her arms at his body in rhythm to her shouts.

The film cuts to a long shot that shows Wally grabbing Hazel's body in a bear hug. Lombard continues to use the weight of her entire body to throw punches, but slows down her movement to show that Hazel is getting worn out by the prolonged physical exertion. She screams in a raspy voice, "Let go of me, let go of me!" and as Wally eases his grip, Hazel falls backward into a large bouquet of flowers that occupies the room's fireplace. The film cuts to a medium shot of Hazel sitting amongst the flowers, looking worn out but determined not to let Wally get the best of her. One cannot ignore the obvious sexual connotation of such a shot, particularly given the symbolic association between flowers and female genitalia. Hazel has reached her near climax, and Lombard conveys this by snarling "I just hate you!"

FIGURE 3.10 *In what is arguably Lombard's most physically demanding role, Hazel Flagg is punched and kicked by her love interest, Wallace Cook, in* Nothing Sacred *(William Wellman, 1937). This action was deemed inappropriate by the Production Code Administration's head, Joseph Breen, but he ultimately agreed to leave it in the film because it would "cause great difficulty to delete it."*

Lombard then sticks her tongue out, a teasing, childish reaction to show that Hazel is not giving up her fight. Hazel stands, lifts her fists into a boxing position and begs, "Let me hit you just once!" This is the—sexual—climax of their physical encounter, and Lombard conveys this in her performance by speeding up her arm movement. With each punch, Hazel's accuracy weakens and her movements slacken. Lombard uses the entire length of her arm rather than just her fists, and begins to punch the air around March's body to show that Hazel is rapidly losing energy.

Hazel slinks onto the floor as Wally gives her instructions for when she regains consciousness. With her eyes closed, she mumbles "What do you mean when you come to?" Lombard slurs her words together to indicate Hazel's disorientation. He grabs Hazel again by the collar and pulls her to her feet. Overwhelmed by the physical fervor, she murmurs, "Yeah, yeah, let me sock you just once, just once on the jaw and I don't care what happens!" Her body is as limp as a rag doll and she is unable to stand on her own. Wally pulls her to her feet and says, "Say goodnight to Papa." Framed in close-up, Lombard's mouth gapes open to indicate Hazel's delirium and confusion. Hazel replies, "Well what are you going to do?" The film cuts to a long shot of Wally, who takes a step back and punches her chin. The film cuts back to the close-up of Hazel's face. Lombard's eyes are closed and her lips mouth something inaudible. The film cuts again to the same long shot, and Lombard stands motionless to show that Hazel is in shock and is disoriented from the barrage of physical attacks. Wally delicately pokes Hazel's chest with his finger, and Hazel drops backward onto the bed, knocked out cold.

Hazel's physical assault is emblematic of what Henry Jenkins calls "the narrative consequences" of impersonation within the screwball diegesis.[120] Feigning her illness and conspiring with Wally to keep their secret from his newspaper "contributes to the plot development"[121] by creating an environment where their antagonistic relationship could blossom into love; it also prefigures their final escape and union at the end of the film. Due to the extensive physical interaction between Lombard and March, the film's sexual undertones are more obvious than in *Love Before Breakfast* and *My Man Godfrey*. However, this scene is jarring, primarily because of the degree of equal physical contact between Wally and Hazel. Until this point *Love Before Breakfast* and, to a lesser extent, *Twentieth Century*, were two of Lombard's most physically demanding sound comedies, with her character Kay receiving a black eye in the former film. Unlike *Love Before Breakfast*, where viewers do not actually see any violence take place nor is Lombard's character given a chance to fight back, here it is explicit.

---

[120] Henry Jenkins, "'A High-Class Job of Carpentry': Towards a Typography of Early Sound Comedy," in *Movie Acting, the Film Reader*, ed. Pamela Robertson Wojcik (London: Routledge, 2004), 120.
[121] Ibid.

FIGURES 3.11 & 3.12 *Hazel's feisty personality is on display in these stills from* Nothing Sacred. *This film and, in particular, Lombard's performance, led to a trend in the late 1930s of films that featured female physicality.*

In the next scene, Hazel gives him a swollen jaw to match her own, their dual facial deformations signal their equal physical skill and reflects what Jenkins describes as the "stylistic consistency between the film's performers" that is typical of the screwball genre.[122] Hazel's retaliation is a step closer toward an egalitarian mode of physical comedy that was not afforded to heroines like Kay Colby or Lily Garland. Earlier I cited Alex Clayton's comments regarding the historical absence of women performing physical comedy, a situation which he claims is caused by widespread societal misconception regarding the delicacy of female bodies. This scene refutes Clayton's contention that screwball women were relegated to "comic props"[123] and supports the historical frameworks put forth by historians such as Kay Young and Susan A. Glenn, both of whom insist that physical comedy has long been an integral part of female comic spectacle. According to Jenkins, screwball comedy "owes relatively little to the vaudeville aesthetic,"[124] but Young argues that female physical comedy in romantic comedies is, in fact, a "legacy of 'live' vaudeville."[125] Similarly, Glenn describes the prevalence of female physicality in theater and film as a reflection of the rising popularity of "New Humor," a "visceral, fast-paced, physically demonstrative, and sometimes violent style of comedy."[126] There is also evidence to suggest that female physical comedy was a growing trend in late 1930s Hollywood cinema.

By 1937, there had been a rise in the number of female actresses such as Lombard, Katharine Hepburn, Barbara Stanwyck, and Jean Arthur that performed forms of roughhousing physical comedy, so much so that scenes like the one from *Nothing Sacred* became a point of contention among critics and censors alike. In a memo to David O. Selznick, PCA chief, Joseph Breen, voiced his objections with Wally kicking Hazel's bum during the fight scene. He wrote that he would permit the shot because it "would cause great difficulty to delete it" and that he was "reluctantly approving the film."[127] Breen's sentiment becomes clearer if one interprets the scene as sexual innuendo; Wally's kick is linked to a part of the female body that is closely related to sexuality. Breen's apprehension points to how much of *Nothing Sacred*'s humor is based on the physical tension between sexes, and he might have also feared that the kick appeared misogynistic. By including

---

[122]Jenkins, 120.

[123]Clayton, 154.

[124]Jenkins, 120.

[125]Kay Young, *Ordinary Pleasures: Couples, Conversation, and Comedy* (Columbus: The Ohio State University Press, 2001), 101.

[126]Susan A. Glenn, *Female Spectacle: The Theatrical Roots of Modern Feminism* (Cambridge: Harvard University Press, 2000), 41.

[127]Joseph Breen to David O. Selznick, October 21, 1937, History of Cinema: Hollywood and the Production Code, Reel 13, Motion Picture Association of America: Production Code Administration Records, 1927–1967. Margaret Herrick Library Special Collection, Los Angeles.

it, the PCA could be accused of condoning female abuse and, given the hotel room setting, validating perverse sexual pleasure. But aside from the sexual innuendo, the scene makes almost no overt reference to Hazel's gender. Her costume and aggressive mannerisms desexualize her body to such an extent that we are almost meant to set aside their gender difference, in spite of the obvious sexual undertones of their physical altercation. Her body becomes "instrumentalized ... a prop or tool to induce laughter,"[128] the means to bring about a narrative resolution. The word "instrumentalized" runs the risk of implying female objectification and sadistic sexual contact. But since Hazel is already desexualized from the outset, and because Lombard frequently uses her body in her comedy, I would argue that it can also be an unexpectedly empowering term. We cannot ignore the fact that Hazel is given the chance to punch Wally back, her punch being the final outburst of physical assault. Lombard uses her body to engage in a typically "male" form of comedy, and Hazel's scrappiness assures us that she is his relative physical equal. Her body is an instrument because it receives and dishes out physical violence, with her final punch functioning as a negation of the bodily and sexual objectification Wally's kick initially evokes.

Physical confrontations like the one in *Nothing Sacred* were becoming increasingly common in Hollywood productions by the mid 1930s, and they were not limited to screwball comedy. A few months after *Nothing Sacred*'s release, *New York Times* film critic Bosley Crowther penned a sarcastic article hailing the demise of "fragile femininity" in contemporaneous cinema. He writes:

> The very thought of a gentlewoman being struck by a gentleman was beyond comprehension of the most unregenerate script writers— or purposes of the picture, that is. And the contrary notion of a lady throwing anything more damaging than butternuts and epigrams was even more horrifying ... One after another pictures have come along in which some of the most feminine of screen ladies have been compelled not only to submit to terrific kickings-about—usually at the hands, or feet, of the heroes—but also to respond with their share of right and left hooks to the jaw.[129]

Crowther identifies Lombard's performance in *Nothing Sacred*, as well as Myrna Loy in *Double Wedding* (Richard Thorpe), Barbara Stanwyck in *Breakfast for Two* (Alfred Santell) and Miriam Hopkins in *Wise Girl* (Leigh Jason), as examples of actresses who used physical comedy in films from

---

[128]Muriel Andrin, "Back to the Slap: Slapstick's Hyperbolic Gesture and the Rhetoric of Violence," in *Slapstick Comedy*, eds. Tom Paulus and Rob King (New York: Routledge, 2010), 230.
[129]Bosley Crowther, "Females of the Species," *New York Times*, January 16, 1938, X5.

1937. He predicted that in the coming years more actresses would begin to use physical comedy more frequently, and cites "the most carefully restrained damsel," Jeanette MacDonald, and her role in *The Girl of the Golden West* (Robert Z. Leonard, 1938) to show how pervasive the trend was in Hollywood in 1937.[130] The article suggests that by the mid 1930s actresses had more opportunities to exercise their physical prowess, and the range of examples in Crowther's article as well as the national press attention female physicality was attracting contradicts the claim that Hollywood actresses were discouraged from using physical comedy techniques.

Henry Jenkins writes that throughout the late nineteenth and early twentieth centuries, film critics took a skeptical position toward female comedy, which he surmises was "probably tied to the dominant comic tradition's function as a release of male anxieties and fears."[131] During this period, comedy was overwhelmingly performed by male comics whose jokes were oriented toward predominately male audiences; women were left out of the comic sphere. The rise in the mid 1920s of female comedians such as Marie Dressler, Polly Moran, and the comedy duo Anita Garvin and Marian Byron disrupted the male-dominated industry because they "posed a potential new threat to male authority and masculine dignity, intensifying the tensions that masculine-centered comedy sought to resolve."[132] Jenkins extends his argument to the cultural reluctance toward female physical comedy in the early sound period, arguing that actresses who performed physical comedy routinely used their bodies as a "grotesque parody of traditional femininity, as an unfit object for male desire."[133] He uses the example of actress Winnie Lightner, who would often be framed from unflattering low angles and in extreme close-ups to exaggerate the mass of her body. Lightner would also "thrust her face and hands into the camera, often staring unflinchingly into the lens" to excessively represent her "assertive and domineering" persona.[134] Her engagement with the camera demonstrates her self-awareness of her image as an "unruly" woman and her deliberate disruption of gender identity. In addition to her unconventional performance style, Lightner was frequently "surrounded by highly effeminate or physically inadequate men" like Frank Fay in *Show of Shows* (John G. Adolfi, 1929) or Charles Butterworth in such films as *Side Show* (Roy Del Ruth, 1931) and *Manhattan Parade* (Lloyd Bacon, 1931), who acted as foils to her overbearing and "mannish" comic persona.[135]

---

[130]Ibid.
[131]Henry Jenkins, *What Made Pistachio Nuts?: Early Sound Comedy and the Vaudeville Aesthetic* (New York: Columbia University Press, 1992), 256.
[132]Ibid.
[133]Ibid, 260.
[134]Ibid.
[135]Ibid, 262.

Although the tone and vocabulary of Crowther's article points to the unresolved cultural debate about the nature of female humor and female oriented comedy, by the mid 1930s there seemed to be a reluctant acceptance that women could be considered legitimate performers in screen comedy, a fact that was due, in large part, to women's "increased presence in public life."[136] Kristine Brunovska Karnick notes that between 1926 and 1936, there was a surge in female comedy teams, female comics and actresses in Hollywood, and the breadth of images of strong, assertive women in comedy "opened up a space for transgression" by "exposing the mask of femininity."[137] Despite his opinion that "a gentlewoman being struck by a gentleman is beyond comprehension," Crowther's article is indicative of the change in public and critical perceptions about female comedy, because he acknowledges that actresses like Lombard could perform roughhouse physical comedy without relying on (self) deprecating humor that pokes fun at their failure to conform to traditional conceptions of feminine appearance and behavior.

Significantly, the heroines in Crowther's examples all target their physical outbursts toward the opposite sex. In *Double Wedding*, Myrna Loy hits William Powell over the head with a painting; in *Breakfast for Two*, Barbara Stanwyck roughhouses with Herbert Marshall; and in *Wise Girl* Miriam Hopkins throws punches. With the exception of Lombard they perform these physical routines while dressed impeccably, their hair coiffed and makeup not a bit out of place. Collectively their actions suggest that physical comedy need not be a threat to one's femininity; it adds depth to their characterization and shows that they can stand up to the men without having to sacrifice physical or emotional qualities that have been culturally coded as "feminine." Physical comedy requires a negotiation, not a negation of their characters' femininity. Hazel is a perfect example of this, as she vacillates quite effortlessly between rough-and-tumble comedy and delicate femininity in both the film and its marketing campaign. In the scene I described above, Wally makes no concessions for his actions, nor does it inhibit him from hitting her because she is a woman. By contrast to the camera angles frequently used in Lightner's films that showcase the comic spectacle of her "unruly" persona, Hazel's fight sequence is composed almost entirely of over-the-shoulder and long shots. Unlike Lightner, Lombard does not break the fourth wall, and Hazel's transgressive behavior is instead framed to refute the notion of the supposed fragility of the female body. Hazel wears a "gender neutral" outfit consisting of a full-length robe and scarf; by not sexualizing her body through costume or framing we are forced to evaluate their physicality based primarily on their agility as boxers, not

---

[136]Kristine Brunovska Karnick, "Community of Unruly Women: Female Comedy Teams in the Early Sound Era," *Continuum: Journal of Media & Cultural Studies* Vol. 13, No. 1 (1999): 77.
[137]Ibid, 79.

their gender difference. Lombard's energetic performance demonstrates that Hazel can withstand Wally's punch because her skill makes her a worthy match for him.

In contrast to the film scene, the marketing campaign for *Nothing Sacred* overtly references the duality of Lombard's star persona. The advertisements for several foreign markets feature caricatures of the two leads with Hazel throwing a punch at Wally while in seductive outfits. For example in the Latin American lobby cards, Hazel's robe does not resemble the one she wears in the film; its low-cut neckline exposes her cleavage, and its open lower half reveals her legs which are bent cartoonishly at the knees. Hazel's figure is also contorted at an impossible angle, with her head facing toward the left and the rest of her body facing the right. These lobby cards goes to great lengths to make Lombard look more alluring than she does in the film. By contrast, in the film scene Lombard is wearing minimal makeup and her hair gets mussed as she is put through Wally's physical barrage.

Hazel's costume and mannerisms embody the contradiction at the heart of Lombard's star persona. On the one hand, she has high levels of energy and is spirited, on the other she has enormous sex appeal. Whereas the *Love Before Breakfast* posters alluded to this tension but ultimately reaffirmed the limits of Lombard's physicality, here it works in tandem with her femininity to create an equally evocative image. As I have argued earlier, the masculine and feminine sides of Hazel's character take their roots in Carole Lombard's off-screen persona. Around the time *Nothing Sacred* was released, Lombard became increasingly outspoken about the newfound expectations for modern women, and was a proponent for women entering the workplace. In a June 1937 *Photoplay* article entitled "How I Live By A Man's Code," Lombard shares how she maintains her femininity as a "modern career girl." Rejecting the idea of a male-dominated society, she explains, "I don't believe it's a man's world. A woman has just as much right in this world as a man and can get along in it just as well if she puts her mind to it."[138] Lombard pushes for an egalitarian existence between men and women, but concludes that to thrive in the business world it is essential that women "be feminine"—I will return to a fuller discussion of this article in chapter 5.

Nothing Sacred speaks to the negotiated femininity that Lombard cultivates in the *Photoplay* article. Hazel embodies Lombard's push for female autonomy, and her retaliation against Wally's abuse with her own punch at his jaw is her way of establishing her own ground. The punch back is the physical comedy equivalent of the gender dynamics Lombard speaks about in the *Photoplay* article, as it sets the precedent for the way we are to understand her character. Hazel can roughhouse with Wally and get a punch or two in return; her identity in that scene is not solely predicated

---

[138]Hart Seymore, "Carole Lombard tells: 'How I Live By A Man's Code,'" *Photoplay*, June 1937, 13.

on her gender. Yet at the same time, the film makes repeated references to Hazel's gender and femininity, such as when she is honored at the "Heroines of History" ball—advertised on the nightclub marquee as a celebration of "Tootsies of All Nations"—or in the glamorous portrait of her on the cover of *The Morning Star*. These moments are antithetical to the version of tough femininity presented in the fight scene, for in both examples Hazel appears uncharacteristically passive, poised, and restrained. However inconsistent these moments are to the film's depiction of Hazel, it is plausible that she can be both excessively combative and charmingly genteel because of the duality of Lombard's own star persona.

Nothing Sacred was released in time for the 1937 Thanksgiving holiday weekend, and opened to positive reviews. Marian Squire of *Variety* described it as a "novelty in the color picture line, being among the few to concentrate on the picture and take the color in its stride."[139] She also acknowledges the beautiful/comic paradox in Lombard's persona, writing that despite her "sartorially glamorous" appearance in several key scenes, Lombard also "gets kicked and bopped on the jaw, but is dunked in the river by Mr. March."[140] Selznick International's head publicist, Russell Birdwell, came up with several publicity stunts to promote the film including making Lombard "Mayor for a Day" in Culver City, and designating the film's opening day in her hometown of Fort Wayne as "Carole Lombard Day."[141] The latter event included a ceremony at Lombard's childhood home that dedicated it as a historical building.[142] Despite all of Birdwell's publicity tactics, although *Nothing Sacred* did well during its opening week at the box office, it performed below the numbers predicted by the critics. It made $19,000 in its first eight days in Cincinnati[143] and $17,000 in Philadelphia.[144] Meanwhile, according to a full-spread advertisement in *Variety* taken out by United Artists, *Nothing Sacred* made $115,000 during its first week run at Radio City Musical Hall,[145] but just $77,000 the following week due, in part, to "all-day rain and cold" wintry conditions.[146] Despite big gains in its first weeks, United Artists recorded a total loss of $400,000.[147]

---

[139]Marian Squire, "The Girls' Eye View," *Variety*, December 1, 1937, 6.
[140]Ibid.
[141]Swindell, 232.
[142]Ibid.
[143]"'Sacred' $19,000, 'Damsel' 12G, Cincy," *Variety*, December 9, 1937, 9.
[144]"Philly Grid Mobs No Pix Help; 'Fathers,' Flesh 21G, 'Sacred' 17G," *Variety*, December 1, 1937, 10.
[145]"United Artists advertisement," *Variety*, December 1, 1937, 32–33.
[146]"Pre-X-Mas Drops B'way H.O. Pix Sharply; 'Sacred' $77,000 2nd Wk., 'Zola' 2nd $30,000, 'Damsel' $16,000," *Variety*, December 8, 1937, 7.
[147]David Thomson, *Showman: The Life of David O. Selznick* (London: Abacus, 1993), 262.

FIGURES 3.13 & 3.14 *Although Hazel is tough and combative, she is also conventionally feminine in appearance. Hazel's contradictions speaks to the complexity of Lombard's own star persona.*

Mr. & Mrs. Smith (*Alfred Hitchcock, 1941*)

Carole Lombard's penultimate film and final screwball comedy, *Mr. & Mrs. Smith*, is a departure from the intense physical comedies she made during the 1930s. Directed by Alfred Hitchcock as a "friendly gesture" at Lombard's request[148] and coproduced by Lombard herself,[149] the film tells the story of a wealthy Manhattan couple named Ann (Lombard) and David Smith (Robert Montgomery) who, through a geographical technicality, find out they are not legally married. When Ann turns down David's proposition to remarry, he must find a way to win her back to restore order to their domestic life.

Mr. & Mrs. Smith was released on January 31, 1941 to generally positive reviews. *Variety* described it as a "light and gay marital farce, with accent on the laugh side."[150] The same review praised Lombard's performance for her "zest and enthusiasm, and in the best comedy vein."[151] *Mr. & Mrs. Smith* was Lombard's unofficial "comeback" film after a two year hiatus from comedy,[152] during which she experimented with dramatic films. RKO reported that the film made a profit of $750,000,[153] a sum that confirmed the public's preference for Lombard in a light, comic setting. It also validated Lombard's career shift away from both melodrama and the rough physical screwball comedies of the 1930s. *Mr. & Mrs. Smith* reflects Lombard's contemporaneous off-screen status by grounding Ann's newfound independence through its opposition to married life. In 1941, Lombard was married to Clark Gable and her private contentment arguably became one of the primary factors that framed her post 1939 star persona, as will be explored in the next chapter. Carole Lombard, the once self-governing career woman, was now hinting at the possibility of retiring from the screen to be a stay-at-home mother.[154] Ann speaks to this tension in Lombard's public persona by being trapped between financial and psychological independence and her obligation to and love for David.

Far from whimsical Irene Bullock or feisty and combative Lily Garland and Hazel Flagg, Ann nevertheless embodies their independent spirit and spunk. But she is also cool, mature, and possesses an "indirect" sex appeal,

---

[148]François Truffaut, *Hitchcock*, revised edition (New York: Simon & Schuster, 1985), 139.
[149]Swindell, 278.
[150]"Review: *Mr. & Mrs. Smith*," *Variety*, January 22, 1941, 16.
[151]Ibid.
[152]Gehring, 209.
[153]Richard Jewell, "RKO Film Grosses: 1931–1951," *Historical Journal of Film, Radio and Television* Vol. 14, No. 1 (1994): 56.
[154]Don Worth, "Will Carole Lombard's Marriage End Her Career?" *Motion Picture* July, 1939, 56.

making Lombard a precursor to the famous Hitchcock blonde, a character type that François Truffaut described as "the paradox between inner fire and the cool surface."[155] Ann fulfills what Sabrina Barton calls "the blonde-function," whereby the presence of Hitchcock's female characters enables an exploration of "the structuration of the male subject"[156] and of "male desire."[157] This is achieved through the "comedy of remarriage" plot structure: despite David's initially complacent attitude toward marriage, he realizes that he is far more satisfied with his life with Ann than he initially admits. Furthermore, the Smith's domestic troubles reveal that Ann also enjoys being married. Although Ann goes to great lengths to impress upon David that she is content with being single—first, by getting a job in a department store and then by going on dates with her boss, Mr. Flugle (Francis Compton), and David's law partner, Jeff (Gene Raymond)—in reality, these are all calculated efforts to make David realize how much Ann means to him. Significantly, the film's remarriage narrative arc is as much centered on the Smith's legal and moral reunion as it is an acknowledgment of their sexual chemistry. An analysis of Ann and David's verbal banter, body language and visual and dialog-driven innuendo in two scenes will reveal the extent to which the Smith's sexual compatibility governs their marriage and eventual reconciliation.

Like the other screwball comedies analyzed in this chapter, *Mr. & Mrs. Smith* was produced during a time when Hollywood studios were entrenched in self-censorship, in relation to the PCA that was discussed in the introduction. Regulation occurred at the level of production—such as scripts, blocking, and performance—and post-production—through editing, sound, and scene transitions—and transferred artistic and narrative control away from Hollywood directors, writers, and producers to the industry regulators.[158] The PCA took a morally conservative view on sex and relationships, and championed "the sanctity of the institution of marriage and the home."[159] Several screwball scholars see the remarriage genre as a proclamation of a conservative and monogamous heterosexual hegemony.[160]

---

[155] Truffaut, 224.

[156] Sabrina Barton, "'Crisscross': Paranoia and Projection in *Strangers on a Train*," *Camera Obscura*, Vol. 9, Nos. 1–2 (1991): 76.

[157] Steve Cohan, *Masked Men: Masculinity and the Movies in the Fifties* (Bloomington: Indiana University Press, 1997), 12.

[158] Ibid, 69.

[159] Ibid, 352.

[160] Kathrina Glitre, *Hollywood Romantic Comedy: States of the Union, 1934–65* (Manchester: Manchester University Press, 2006), 17. See also: Thomas Schatz, *Hollywood Genres: Formulas, Filmmaking, and The Studio System* (New York: McGraw-Hill, 1981), 171; Richard Neupert, *The End: Narration and Closure in the Cinema* (Detroit: Wayne State University Press, 1995), 181; Steve Neale and Frank Krutnik, *Popular Film and Television Comedy* (London: Taylor & Francis, 2002), 155–156.

Kristina Brunovska Karnick explains that this occurs at the narrative level by the repetitive "boy and girl separate but fall back in love" story arc, and with each retelling the genre engrains a "set of culturally determined though nevertheless powerful goals and ambitions" promoting heterosexual marriage.[161] Kathrina Glitre argues that within the context of the Production Code's "moral guardianship," it was unviable for Hollywood studios in the 1930s to "explicitly reject marriage as the framework for a heterosexual relationship."[162] Heterosexual monogamy was the only morally "correct" and legal option for couples during this period; alternative lifestyles did not fit the mold and were therefore rejected, hidden, or criminalized.

In light of such a narrow framework, the PCA functioned "to mediate conflict between the industry and various external regulatory agencies ... in doing so, it served the industry's political and economic interests."[163] If the studios pushed the boundaries of "unacceptable" moral behavior too far they would risk government intervention in their productions, potentially resulting in a loss in revenue or financing and less control from the studios over their films.[164] Glitre writes that despite the limited room for maneuver afforded to the studios, they did not always offer positive affirmations of the pro-marriage ideology.[165] The Hollywood studios could sidestep the Code's morality through visual or dialog-driven innuendos, subtlety, and the intonations and gestures of an actor's performance. Thomas Doherty explains that by the mid 1930s, filmmakers and audiences alike became well versed in "the grammar of a unique film language, a sophisticated dialogue built on gentle implication, unspoken meaning, elaborate conceits, and winked signals."[166] Audiences learned to "decipher and decode allusions, nuances and ellipses," and directors "abided by the letter of the law while stretching its spirit."[167] Like other "remarriage" comedies and several of the screwball films discussed in this chapter, *Mr. & Mrs. Smith* follows the Code's rules about sex and marriage, yet it also "stretches its spirit" through extensive and often thinly veiled innuendos concerning the Smiths' sexual relationship. Given the strict conservative family values set up by the Code, the film offers a surprisingly flimsy conclusion to legitimate the Smiths'

---

[161]Kristine Brunovska Karnick and Henry Jenkins, "Comedy and the Social World," in *Classical Hollywood Comedy*, eds. Kristine Brunovska Karnick and Henry Jenkins (New York: Routledge, 1995), 279.
[162]Glitre, 44.
[163]Lea Jacobs, "Industry Self-Regulation and the Problem of Textual Determination," in *Controlling Hollywood: Censorship and Regulation in the Studio Era*, ed. Matthew Bernstein (New Brunswick: Rutgers University Press, 1999), 88.
[164]Ibid, 88.
[165]Glitre, 44.
[166]Doherty, 97.
[167]Ibid.

common-law marriage. It leaves the question of whether or not the Smiths will officially remarry unanswered, and offers instead a portrait of sexual reconciliation. In doing so, the film challenges the PCA's moral stature, and ultimately undercuts the pro-marriage ideology it vaguely enforces.

Sexual innuendo is at the crux of the film's comedy, and colors our understanding of Ann and David's relationship. In the film's opening scenes, we are introduced to the couple in their bedroom, where they have been in hiding amidst a three day argument. Coy references to their sexual chemistry run throughout the scenes, including when Ann insists that all marriage ceremonies should include the provision "You are not allowed to leave the bedroom after a quarrel unless you've made up." They reflect on their latest spat while cuddled in bed, and Ann playfully touches David's nose as he holds her head gently on his chest. Their affectionate body language and the soft, gentle tones of their voices show us that the couple are very much in love but also, more precisely, that their quarrel was resolved sexually. This overt display of affection continues into the breakfast scene, which begins with a shot of Ann playing "footsie" with David under the table. This image is an early sign of Ann's flirtatious and teasing personality—which becomes more apparent as the film progresses—and an example of their mutual sexual attraction.

The shot of Ann and David's feet becomes a revealing visual cue to the changing dynamics of their relationship. In a moment of brutal honesty, David reluctantly admits that he would not get married again if he had a second chance. The film cuts to the same shot under the table, and we see Ann's feet slowly slide down David's shins. The camera then cuts to a reaction shot of Ann's face, and Lombard portrays her character's indignation and hurt pride by staring coldly at David while anxiously wringing her hands. This second reaction shot is superfluous because of how effective the foot shot was at capturing Ann's feelings. It is significant that the initial "reaction" shot after David's admission cuts to their feet and not their faces as one would expect, because it reminds us of the important role physical chemistry plays in the Smiths' relationship.

The concluding scene of *Mr. & Mrs. Smith* also demonstrates how sexual innuendo occurs in the film's dialog, framing, and editing. After spending weeks trying to persuade Ann that he wants to get remarried, David discovers that Ann and Jeff are spending the weekend at a ski chalet in Lake Placid. He follows them up to the resort and pretends to be frostbitten and delirious to regain Ann's sympathy. However, his plan backfires when Ann spies him sitting in bed smoking a cigarette. In their final showdown, David grabs her in a headlock in an effort to make her come to her senses. When Jeff—who is in the adjoining cabin—fails to come to her rescue, Ann realizes that she wants nothing to do with either man. She furiously calls Jeff a "mouse" and a "lump of jelly" for not coming to her defense, and firmly tells David "but I'm not taking you!" Disillusioned by David's pompous attitude and Jeff's meek chivalry, Ann rejects both men by telling them that neither live up to her expectations of what a man should be.

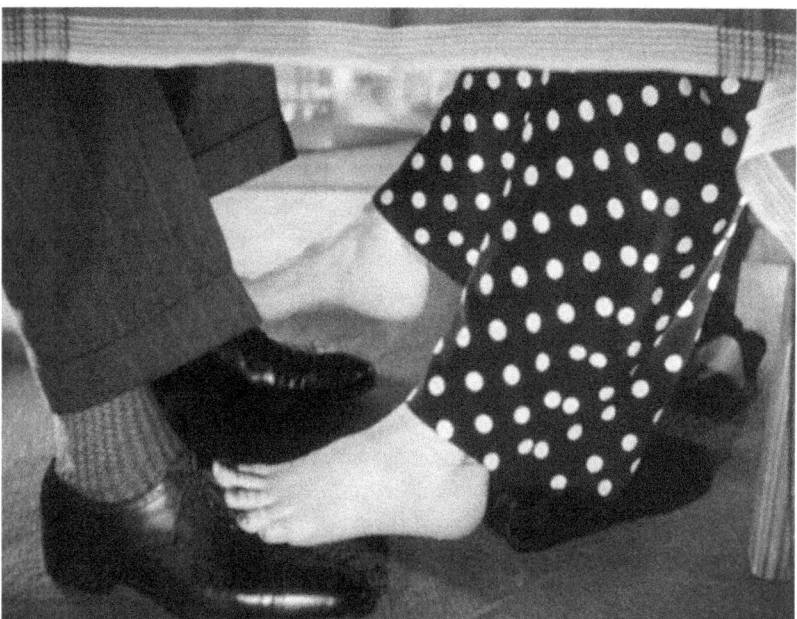

FIGURES 3.15 & 3.16 *Ann (Lombard) and David (Robert Montgomery) Smith play footsie under the breakfast table in* Mr. & Mrs. Smith *(Alfred Hitchcock, 1941). These shots cleverly reveal the couple's mutual sexual attraction and emotional range.*

Back in her own cabin, Ann puts on her skis in order to go back to the main lodge. David follows her into the cabin and suggests that she spend the night with him. The film cuts to a close-up of Ann's face: she looks up at him, she shakes her head and says in a sassy tone "Not on your life." David notices that Ann is having difficulty putting on her skis and offers to help her. In a medium shot, David kneels down and fiddles with her skis as Ann sits helplessly on a chair. Lombard conveys Ann's feigned indifference toward David by defiantly avoiding eye contact. She also shrugs her shoulders in exasperation to show that Ann has no choice but to accept David's help. The film cuts back to a wider shot, and Ann stands up from the chair and begins to wobble around in place, her arms moving about to try to balance her weight. David, who is standing again, playfully pushes her chest with his index finger. Lombard waves her arms in big circular motions to show that Ann is trying to regain balance. Ann falls back down into the chair with her legs flung in the air. As she falls backward, the skis fly above her head and come loose from her boots.

At this point, both the spectator and David become aware of Ann's true feelings toward him; Lombard again performs a breakdown of "expressive coherence." It is clear that Ann's skis are now loose from her boots; if she truly

FIGURE 3.17 *Ann hides her true feelings toward David by pretending to have trouble putting on her skis.*

wanted to get away from him she could have simply put her skis on properly and escape the cabin. Lombard demonstrates Ann's resistance to David's advances through excessively physical—bordering on cartoonish—gestures, which lets us know that Ann is putting on an "act" to get his attention. From the outset, the film makes it clear that Ann is poised and independent: her eagerness to get a job at the department store and her indifference when David threatens to cut off his monetary support give the impression that she is capable of taking care of herself—financially and emotionally—without his help. However in this scene, Lombard's excessive fumbling in the chair and uncoordinated body movements make Ann appear uncharacteristically helpless and vulnerable; her performance is our first indication that Ann's difficulty with her skis is disingenuous.

James Naremore argues that films seldom expose their "techniques of representation," and that the breakdown of expressive coherence happens "only at the level of characterization, where we see persons in the drama trying to conceal or repress their 'sincere' feelings."[168] He uses the example of Barbara Stanwyck's performance in *Stella Dallas* (King Vidor, 1937) to illustrate his theory. In the scene where Stella visits her estranged husband's girlfriend, Helen Morrison, to give up her daughter, Stanwyck conveys Stella's apprehension by twisting a pair of gloves on her lap and fiddling with the arm of the couch.[169] Despite Stella's composed outward demeanor, Stanwyck's performance "shows us how 'true' emotions are expressed," and how a character's mannerisms and voice can reveal the depths of their misrepresented feelings.[170] Similarly in *Mr. & Mrs. Smith*, Lombard indicates Ann's feigned distaste for David by flashing a devious grin in a close-up reaction shot when he offers to help her with her skis. It is significant that her smile is captured in close-up when David is not looking at Ann. Lombard's smile is like a cinematic wink to the audience to let us know of Ann's true intentions, and that despite her character's protestations, "deep down" she is willing to give him a second chance.

Eventually, David catches on to Ann's duplicity. The film cuts to a medium close-up of him smiling smugly as he begins to loosen his tie to show that he is going along with her trickery. We cut back to Ann in a reverse medium close-up, her face framed by her skis that are crossed and just out of focus. Ann quickly realizes that David is not buying her charade, and Lombard conveys her character's frustration by glaring off camera at Montgomery's character with narrow eyes and pursed lips. Ann grits her teeth and mumbles, "I'll kill you in cold blood. Sometime, someday when your back is turned I'll stab you." The film cuts to a reverse shot of David while he continues to undo his tie and collar button. The film cuts back to a wide shot of Ann in

---

[168]Naremore, 71.
[169]Ibid.
[170]Ibid.

the chair, and as David walks behind her out of the frame it tracks in toward her as she continues to pretend to kick her legs loose from the skis. Ann knows David is not falling for her game, but she continues to play along to hold his attention; as in the opening scenes, Ann once again relies on flirtation and teasing to mend her fractured relationship.

The film cuts to a medium shot of David dropping his tie on the bed—another subtle hint to the sexual reconciliation that will follow. The film closes with a wide shot of Ann sitting in the chair and her skis in the air. Lombard repeatedly bangs the skis on the ground and screams "David" in a high-pitched voice to convey Ann's feigned protestation. Ann glances up and sees David standing behind her, and the camera begins to track in to a close-up of David's amused face looking down at her. As it moves in, we hear Lombard softly moan "Oh … oh … David" in a breathy voice that indicates Ann has finally given up her disingenuous resistance and has succumbed to David sexually. Lombard's hands appear from the bottom of the frame and reach up to hug Montgomery's character's neck. David looks from left to right at each hand, smiles, and leans down out of the frame. Ann continues to swoon, "David … oh, David," and as she does, her skis come back into the now empty frame and cross over one another. The final score begins to play and the film slowly fades to black, signaling that sex will occur.

This shot is evocative for its sexual connotations and the absence of any moral or legal resolution for the Smith's marriage. In true Hitchcockian subtlety, the crossed skis allude to the sex that is about to take place, but their sexual reunion is about as far as the film takes their relationship: what happens after? Ann never definitively agrees that she will remarry David, nor does she concede that she needs him in her life in any other way than as her sexual partner. The final scene confirms their physical compatibility but it also offers a vague conclusion to the legitimacy of their union. It is important to consider that both Ann and David are turning to sex, not marriage, to rekindle their romance, but in light of the PCA's strict moral mandate, it is surprising that the film does not make more of a conscious effort to confirm that their relationship will eventually be made legitimate. Throughout the film David makes subtle references to the nonlegal status of their marriage, including when he writes her name as "Mistress Krausheimer"—her maiden name—in his calendar. In spite of Ann's mother's insistence in the restaurant scene that "under no circumstances" should Ann sleep with David while they are not legally married, the film makes no sweeping moral gesture to condemn either spouse for their mutual sexual desires. The ambiguity of their affair and the concluding shot open up a space to acknowledge female sexual desire outside of conservative channels like motherhood and domesticity, and reveals how filmmakers worked within the limits of the Code to engage with themes like sex and love.

Just as Ann Smith is largely defined by her marriage, after her own union to Clark Gable in 1939, Carole Lombard's star persona accrued a

FIGURE 3.18 *The final shot of crossed skis is a subtle yet evocative confirmation of Ann and David's sexual reconciliation. Filmmakers in the classical Hollywood period often had to rely on visual or dialog innuendo to work around the Production Code's strict moral guidelines.*

domestic image. Off the screen, Lombard became "Mrs. Clark Gable," and her marriage began to define her stardom much in the same way as Ann's. Through unforeseen circumstances, Ann is presented with the chance to redefine herself outside of her marriage, and in the process she must decide on her future. Lombard faced a similar decision after 1939: should she continue in the film industry, or retire at the height of her stardom and withdraw into domestic life as the wife of Hollywood's top male star? In the years immediately following her marriage, Lombard took a break from comedy and ventured into domestic melodramas. She also slowed down her work schedule, even taking a yearlong hiatus in order to concentrate on starting a family.[171] In this context, *Mr. & Mrs. Smith* is a comic outlier in the post marriage phase in Lombard's filmography; through title and narrative, it subtly reinforces Lombard's own marital status while acknowledging the difficult decisions she was facing about the next phase of her career.

---

[171] Ruth Waterbury, "Our Home, Our Work – and Children," *Movie Mirror.* November 1939, 45.

The absence of extended physical comedy sequences indicates a change in Lombard's screwball personality that was in keeping with her maturing star persona.

To Be or Not to Be (*Ernst Lubitsch, 1942*)

With the rest of the world having been at war for nearly two years, by 1941 the United States had remained absent from the front lines. Despite the federal government's funding of Allied war materials and "Lend Lease" aid sent to Britain, China and the Soviet Union,[172] the U.S.'s isolationist stance remained strong. Ignoring some isolationist supporters who claimed that by injecting propagandistic messages into films Hollywood was "dragging America into war," the studios could not ignore the scale and magnitude of the global conflict.[173] Prior to the United States's official declaration of war on Germany and Japan after the attack on Pearl Harbor on December 7, 1941 the Hollywood studios began producing big budget war films that were meant to inform and motivate the American public into action and support for their country such as *Confessions of a Nazi Spy* (Anatole Litvak, 1939), *The Mortal Storm* (Frank Borzage, 1940), *Escape* (Mervyn LeRoy, 1940) and *Foreign Correspondent* (Alfred Hitchcock, 1940). The question "Will this picture help win the war?"[174] became a practical concern for Hollywood and the federal government's Office of War Information (OWI) at a time when the medium's propagandistic potentials were being exploited to uphold public morale.

In the months prior to the attack on Pearl Harbor, Lombard completed what was to be her last feature film, *To Be or Not to Be*. Her role was initially offered to Miriam Hopkins, but after some disagreements with director Ernst Lubitsch, it was offered to Lombard.[175] It tells the story of a Polish acting troupe headed by Josef Tura (Jack Benny) and his wife, Maria (Lombard), who devise a plan to outsmart the Nazis. After their theater is shut down by the Gestapo due to censorship violations, the actors devise a plan to impersonate members of the Nazi party in order to save their profession and their country. As the only woman in the troupe, Maria relies on a combination of her actorly skill and performative femininity to infiltrate

---

[172]Robert Dallek, *Franklin D. Roosevelt and American Foreign Policy: 1932–1945* (New York: Oxford University Press, 1979), 259.
[173]Clayton R. Koppes and Gregory D. Black, *Hollywood Goes To War: Patriotism, Movies and the Second World War from Ninotchka to Mrs. Miniver* (Berkeley: University of California Press, 1990), 18.
[174]Ibid, 66.
[175]Scott Eyman, *Ernst Lubitsch: Laughter in Paradise* (Baltimore: Johns Hopkins University Press, 2000), 293.

the Nazi party and win the affections of Professor Alexander Siletsky (Stanley Ridges), a Nazi spy masquerading as a Polish resistance fighter. Like Lombard's screwball comedies, her performance in this film is centered on her status as a beautiful comedienne. There is a symbiosis between Lombard's and Maria's appearance: Maria is extremely aware of her beauty, and Lombard uses that character trait to convey Maria's self-absorbed hammy instincts. Maria's costume is an entry point in understanding the role Lombard's own stardom and appearance play in her performance. Maria wears a light colored silk dress in the film's opening sequence, and later in the film during her rendezvous with Siletsky. In both scenes the dress marks the intersection of star and character, signifying Maria's over-the-top theatricality and Lombard's own comic-yet-glamorous sex appeal.

When we are first introduced to Maria, the actors are in the midst of rehearsing their play about Hitler. The director, Dobosh (Charles Halton), and some of the actors are quarreling about a line when Maria enters from a doorway at the back of the stage. She is carrying the fur-trimmed train of her form-fitting white silk dress, which hugs Lombard's body and accentuates her curvy, feminine physique. It is a simple dress with little adornment, except for a cluster of jewels that sit at the gathered folds of the waistline. Her hair is swept into a sleek bun, and she wears jeweled earrings and

FIGURE 3.19 *Carole Lombard radiates an "effulgent dazzle" in her first appearance in* To Be or Not to Be *(Ernst Lubitsch, 1942).*

bracelets. The creamy, silk material accentuates the whiteness of Lombard's skin and pale yellow color of her hair. Lombard radiates an ethereal glow that is characteristic of what Richard Dyer calls an "effulgent dazzle," the effect created when lighting blonde hair in film.[176] Her walk is framed in a long shot in order to document her entire body. She saunters slowly toward the group almost as if she is gliding across the floor, and she swings her hips slightly from side to side in such a way that calls attention to her femininity.

Maria greets Dobosh with a smooth "Good morning," and asks "How do you like my dress?" Dobosh does a double take, and asks if she intends on wearing the dress in the concentration camp scene. She shrugs her shoulders and says, "Why not?" The film cuts to a medium shot of the two as Maria continues enthusiastically, "I think it's a tremendous contrast. Think of me being flogged in the darkness. I scream, suddenly the lights go on and the audience discovers me in this gorgeous dress!" Lombard's delivery confirms Maria's devotion to her craft and public image, and her indifference to the grim foreshadowing of their production. An actor named Greenberg (Felix Bressart) walks up to the pair and says matter-of-factly, "It'll get a terrific laugh." Exasperated, Dobosh turns to Greenberg and replies, "But I don't want a laugh." Looking back at Maria, he protests "That an artist could be so inartistic. You must be out of your mind!" Josef enters the frame and reprimands Dobosh for chastising his wife. He turns to her and says, "Sweetheart, the dress stinks." Maria lowers her voice and says sternly, "You're only afraid I'm running away with the scene."

In this scene Lombard personifies the beautiful comic; she demonstrates Maria's conspicuous glamour, and uses it to convey her self-conscious hammy theatricality. Though Maria is of a genre unlike screwball comedy, she evokes the spirit of the 1930s blonde bombshells—including Lombard in many of her screwball performances—in the way that she owns her physical appearance. Ellen Tremper writes "The platinum or less extreme blonde who took charge of her physical appearance was asserting that attractiveness was hers to define ... [it] was body language for 'Look at me! Enjoy my audacity, and love me for it!'"[177] Lombard gives her audience permission to laugh at Maria, her stardom, and her exaggerated ego, which also speaks to the superficial conditions of Hollywood stardom and glamour more generally. In stark contrast to the drab stage decorations and the Nazi uniforms worn by the other actors, Maria's costume verges on the ridiculous. But the dress is also an important narrative tool used to signify her sexuality—the soft fabric and tight fitting are particularly revealing of her breasts, especially as she appears to wear no bra—a point highlighted by Lombard's own sex appeal. The focus on Maria's appearance foreshadows the eventual influence

---

[176]Richard Dyer, *White: Essays on Race and Culture* (New York: Routledge, 1997), 92.
[177]Ellen Tremper, *I'm No Angel: The Blonde in Fiction and Film* (Charlottesville: University of Virginia Press, 2006), 119.

she has on virtually every man that crosses her path, and the way she uses her sexuality to entice Professor Siletsky and dupe the Nazis.

James Harvey explains that Maria and the other actors suffer from extreme "self-absorption," so much so that sometimes it appears that their behavior is like a "sick joke."[178] The immediacy of war and the spread of fascism in Europe adds an unnerving quality to the film and its characters. Harvey proposes that if the film appears "tasteless," the point is that its tastelessness "finally becomes irresistible."[179] The Nazis and the actors posing as Nazis end up making the same kinds of jokes—for instance, the oft-repeated "So they call me concentration camp Ehrhart?"—and almost every character plays with their identity. The result is a condition where it becomes difficult to distinguish between sides, and where it is virtually impossible to anticipate any character's actions.[180] Maria and her dress play important parts in this so-called "tasteless irresistibility." She feigns ignorance about her outfit's poor taste because her main concern is adding a layer of dramatic "contrast" to her performance in order to uphold her glamorous star image.

In the second scene in which Maria's dress plays an important role, there are two simultaneous layers of performance at play: Lombard performing as Maria, and Maria performing a feminine seduction. Gestapo censorship prevents the actors from performing the play, but Maria finally gets her chance to wear her glamorous dress. Only this time it is not in the Polski theater, but instead while helping her fellow actors infiltrate the Nazi party. Before she leaves Siletsky's room after their initial visit, she tells him she must go home and change into "a more suitable dress." Upon her return, she enters wearing her hair coiffed in the same bun and a fur coat that hangs just below the knee. The pair are framed in a medium shot, and as Maria smiles she says "I'm sorry I took longer than usual. I hope the effect is worth it." Lombard slowly lifts the coat off of her shoulders to reveal the silk dress. Standing just inches away from Maria, Siletsky gazes into her eyes and replies in a low murmur, "I'm willing to die for our Führer at any moment [*pause*] except for the next few hours." Siletsky's lust for Maria is dependent upon the combination of her theatricality and Lombard's attractiveness. The basis of the seduction is Lombard's appearance in the dress, and the believability of her conquest is, at least in part, due to her own star beauty.

Maria also teases Siletsky much as she does Lieutenant Sobinski (Robert Stack) in her dressing room earlier in the film, and it is primarily through Maria's flirtatious personality that the film engages with sexual innuendo.

---

[178] James Harvey, *Romantic Comedy in Hollywood: From Lubitsch to Sturges* (New York: Da Capo Press, 1998), 483.
[179] Ibid, 486.
[180] Ibid.

FIGURE 3.20 *Maria Tura (Lombard) uses her feminine charm and physical beauty to seduce Nazi Alexander Siletsky (Stanley Ridges).*

At one point Maria asks Siletsky to write his name on a sheet of paper—which she later uses to forge his fake suicide note. Upon seeing his signature, she exclaims "My, I hope you live up to that '*y*,' Professor!" Exchanges like this reveal the extent to which Maria uses her sex appeal to disarm Siletsky. Lombard's excessively flirtatious delivery contains what Alex Clayton describes as a "comic twinkle," a conscious performative gesture to make viewers aware that Maria is being entirely disingenuous. Clayton explains that the comic twinkle is an "oblique bodily disclosure of comic intent—call it irony, cheekiness or a certain sense of 'I-know-you-know-I-know'—which *appeals* to our sense of humor" (italics original).[181] Lombard's exaggerated display of coquetry is a form of comedic address, reminding viewers that Maria's attraction to Siletsky is merely a performance. At one point during their exchange, Siletsky kisses Maria. In an over-the-shoulder reaction shot, she raises her hand and murmurs "Heil Hitler" in a mock sensual voice while she gazes off camera with a glazed stare. Maria's ridiculous reaction to the kiss is Lombard's "comic twinkle" moment that literally

---

[181] Alex Clayton, "Play-Acting: A Theory of Comedic Performance," in *Theorizing Film Acting*, ed. Aaron Taylor (New York: Routledge, 2012), 51.

happens behind Siletsky's back and only for the audience's benefit. Maria's behavior prompts Siletsky to let his guard down long enough to be taken to a false Gestapo headquarters—actually the Polski theater—and interviewed by Josef—posing as Colonel Ehrhart—resulting in a frantic chase and his eventual suicide. In his analysis of the dressing room scene with Lieutenant Sobinski, Clayton argues that Sobinski and Maria's rapport "hinges on the precariousness of role-playing." Lombard's performance adeptly "flits between personae, between the shy sparkle of the girl who played Kiki and the sudden solemnity of the woman who played Lady Macbeth."[182] Similarly, in the scene with Siletsky, Lombard "performs" Maria's seductive femininity by showing how she falsely gives in to Siletsky's advances long enough that he momentarily loses sight of his alliances.

From the outset, *To Be or Not to Be* was plagued by controversy. Prior to its release, United Artists executives felt that the title was "too highbrow for the box office" and suggested instead "The Censor Forbids." The new title drew heated criticism from Benny and Lombard, the latter of whom wrote an impassioned telegram to U. A. president, Grad Sears, that read, "In the interest of a picture in which I am an investor as well as a participant ... I consider the title "The Censor Forbids" suggestive and in poor taste."[183] She had reason to be concerned for the film's financial success: her contract stated she would receive $75,000 upfront plus five percent of the profits from domestic and international distribution—a sum that Gable eventually received through her estate.[184] She went on to explain that had the film been proposed to her under the new title, she "definitely would not have accepted ... under any circumstances."[185] The original title remained, and shooting proceeded without incident. The film was initially booked for a February 19, 1942 release; when news of Lombard's death broke, out of respect United Artists decided to push back the opening to March 6.[186] Lombard and Benny received positive critical review, with a *Motion Picture Daily* critic writing that both stars "give smartly turned performances."[187] Lombard's in particular was praised for being the high point of her career, with one *Screenland* reviewer writing that she "exits laughing as she would have wished for ... her best role, her best mood and manner."[188] But perhaps because of its dark humor, the film generated heated condemnation from

---

[182]Ibid, 57.
[183]Eyman, 297.
[184]"Korda not in on 'To Be'," *Variety*, Wednesday, February 11, 1942, 4.
[185]Eyman, 297.
[186]"UA Delays Release of Lombard Picture," *Motion Picture Daily*, Tuesday, January 27, 1942, 4.
[187]"Reviews – *To Be or Not to Be*," *Motion Picture Daily*, Thursday, February 5, 1942, 5.
[188]Delight Evans, "Your Guide at a Glance to the Best Current Pictures," *Screenland*, May 1942, 52.

critics. *New York Times* film critic Bosley Crowther wrote that to call the film "callous and macabre is understating the case,"[189] and points to one particularly cringeworthy exchange between Josef Tura and Colonel Ehrhart. In disguise as Professor Siletsky, Tura asks Ehrhart if he has heard of the "great Polish actor Josef Tura," to which Ehrhart replies that he remembers seeing him once in Warsaw. He adds, "What he did to Shakespeare we are doing now to Poland."

In response to his critics, Lubitsch penned a rebuttal in the *New York Times*. He writes, "Fortunately, I am not the only one accused of [lack of taste]. My co-defendant is the American motion-picture audience."[190] He justifies his film's comic tone by arguing that contrary to critical opinion, the American film audience's "instinct and intuition always guide them in the right direction when it comes to good taste."[191] *To Be or Not to Be* merely uses comedy to show how "this new order and its ideology being are ridiculed," and how the Nazis have become so anesthetized to violence and torture that they talk about their brutality "with the same ease as a salesman referring to the sale of a handbag."[192] Lubitsch was appealing to the American public's collective ego; if the film's comedy was inappropriate, those who laughed at its jokes were equally as guilty.

Contrary to the myth that *To Be or Not to Be* was a major box office failure,[193] the film did fairly good business nationally. Based on advanced booking sales, United Artists predicted it would gross an impressive $1,750,000 in the domestic market.[194] Despite a slow opening weekend caused by an air raid black out, the film made $33,700 during its premiere in three theaters in Los Angeles in late February.[195] When the film opened nationwide in March, it grossed $37,000 during its opening weekend at the Rivoli in New York City,[196] and did steady business in smaller midwestern markets like Kansas City, where it made $14,000 in the first week.[197] In the week following the film's nationwide release, United Artists took advantage of the film's existent success by publishing an ad in *Variety* boasting that it was "being held over" in cities across the country.[198] In spite of the

---

[189] Bosley Crowther, "The Screen – *To Be or Not to Be*," *New York Times*, March 7, 1942, L13.
[190] Ernst Lubitsch, "Mr. Lubitsch Takes the Floor for Rebuttal," *New York Times*, Sunday, March 29, 1942, 3.
[191] Ibid.
[192] Ibid.
[193] Gehring, 223. See also: Harvey, 489.
[194] "Korda not in on 'To Be,'" 4.
[195] "National Box Office Survey," *Variety*, Wednesday, February 25, 1942, 11.
[196] "Spring Temp. Cuts Down N.Y. B.O.: 'To Be' Strong $37 000, 'Invaders,' 40G, Fine, A.&C. Ride for $24 000," *Variety*, Wednesday, March 11, 1942, 9.
[197] "Lombard-Benny Fine $14 000 in Kansas C.," *Variety*, Wednesday March 11, 1942, 10.
[198] "To Be or Not to Be advertisement," *Variety*, Wednesday, March 11, 1942, 26.

widespread critical panning, the national interest in *To Be or Not to Be* vindicated Lubitsch and proved that Americans could find humor in the darkness of war.

Through these textual analyses, I have demonstrated the significance of physical comedy to Lombard's screwball performances. Unlike her screwball contemporaries, physical comedy was a consistent trait in Lombard's screwball comedies, and it came to be a signifier of her dual masculine and feminine sensibilities: her so-called natural athleticism and her conventional physical beauty. In the chapter that follows, I will build upon my discussion of Lombard's screwball persona and how it was reshaped by her romance with Clark Gable, particularly in relation to the domestic image of Lombard that was cultivated post 1939. I will use Lombard's relationship and eventual marriage to Gable as a case study to interrogate the economic and ideological strategies that undergird Hollywood star couples. The Lombard–Gable "golden couple" narrative put forth by Hollywood had very real consequences for the remainder of Lombard's career and her posthumous legacy as a screwball comedian.

4

"Goodbye Carole 'screwball' Lombard; Hello Mrs. 'Ma' Gable": gender, identity, and the classical Hollywood star couple

The tagline for the 1976 biopic, *Gable and Lombard*, states "They don't love like that anymore." Released thirty-four years after Carole Lombard's death and sixteen after her second husband, Clark Gable's, it offers a nostalgic interpretation of one of classical Hollywood's most famous couples. Based on Warren G. Harris's 1974 eponymous biography, *Gable and Lombard* preserves the "golden couple" love story that is found in both contemporary and current press stories about the stars. Obscuring factual accuracy and chronology for the sake of drama, *Gable and Lombard* builds upon existent historical discourses to rejuvenate the myth that the couple were soul mates destined for love. In doing so, it joined the consortium of journalistic and print media outlets that have collectively tied the cultural currency of both stars' personae to their marriage. This state of affairs has resulted in limited analytical understanding about their individual star images and film performances. When Lombard married Gable in March 1939 their personae became woven together in perpetuity; today, it is rare to come across a fan community or scholarly discussion of either star without some mention of the other.

The chapter title comes from a July 1939 *Motion Picture* article entitled "Will Carole Lombard's Marriage End Her Career?"[1] in

---

[1] Don Worth, "Will Carole Lombard's Marriage End Her Career?" *Motion Picture*, July 1939, 22–23.

which the columnist, Don Worth, considers whether Lombard could successfully balance her domestic responsibilities and her career. I have chosen it as the title because it encapsulates the chapter's focus, namely, the trajectory of Lombard's post 1939 star persona, and the ways in which Gable and Lombard's star coupledom impacted Lombard's independent star persona. Such a study makes inroads into the emerging work on star/celebrity couples, particularly how star couples of the classical Hollywood period "had the power to shape hegemonic western notions of romance and intimacy"[2] and gender politics. Worth's article asks the clichéd question of whether a woman can "have it all," and he predicts that Lombard would be eager to give up her professional aspirations because her "pet dream" was to be "a wife and mother – full time."[3] Once Gable and Lombard wed there seemed to be a tension between Lombard's single independent identity and her newfound status as a happily domesticated wife; she suddenly became someone unlike the familiar Carole Lombard star image that had been constructed and reaffirmed in film and popular media. For instance, the same article surmises that when the couple got married it meant "goodbye Carole "Screwball" Lombard; Hello Mrs. "Ma" Gable."[4] This statement is indicative of the change in tone regarding Lombard's public persona, and it and others like it carry troubling gendered implications that suggest a married woman's duty is first and foremost her husband's contentment, even if that means sacrificing her own identity and sense of individual purpose.[5] For a star whose persona was built upon a strong sense of individuality, self-sufficiency, and gender equality, the idea that Lombard suddenly became a shrinking violet is almost impossible to accept. The reality is that by 1939 Carole Lombard's star persona was in a state of flux, caught between her screwball and marital identities. While these sides do not necessarily have to be at odds, in Lombard's case portraying her as a wife and aspiring mother confirmed Hollywood's investment in conservative marital ideology. It seemed inconceivable that Lombard could remain both the daffy "Queen of Screwball Comedy" and "Mrs. Clark Gable" because her screwball personality appeared too wild and untamed for matrimony, and it challenged the prevailing conception of how an American wife in the 1930s was meant to behave.[6]

---

[2]Shelley Cobb and Neil Ewen, "Golden Couples," in *First Comes Love: Power Couples, Celebrity Kinship and Cultural Politics*, eds. Shelley Cobb and Neil Ewen (New York: Bloomsbury, 2015), 9.
[3]Ibid.
[4]Ibid.
[5]Caroline S. Hoyt, "Can the Gable–Lombard Romance Last?" *Modern Screen*, May 1939, 24.
[6]Glenna Matthews, *"Just A Housewife:" The Rise and Fall of Domesticity in America* (New York: Oxford University Press, 1987), 199.

Carole Lombard and Clark Gable: Classical Hollywood's golden couple

Few star couples from the classical Hollywood period come close to matching the immense appeal and unprecedented fascination that Carole Lombard and Clark Gable elicited. What began as a casual reacquaintance at the annual Mayfair Ball on January 25, 1936[7] snowballed into a monumental publicity story filled with mythologized tales of patience, a love triangle, heartache, and tragedy. During the late 1930s and early 1940s, their love affair became a fixture in fan magazines, gossip columns, and newspapers, as the public eagerly consumed details of their long-winded romance and ostensibly idyllic married life. Perhaps more than anything else, the Gable–Lombard romance was the defining factor in both stars' public personae. Beginning in the mid 1930s when the Gable–Lombard affair was becoming a more frequent story in the press, Lombard's persona underwent a significant change. Her reputation as a screwball comedian seemed to contradict traditional conceptions of how a wife was supposed to behave; it was unfathomable that the zany "Queen of Screwball" and "Hollywood's Number One Party Girl"[8] could also be a convincing wife—at least publicly. Using the breadth of publicity material about the Gable–Lombard romance, I will analyze the popular discourse surrounding Lombard's pre and post marital star persona and the underlying tension these sources produced between her screwball identity and her role as a wife. As the Gable–Lombard romance narrative became more pervasive in publicity outlets Carole Lombard's once ubiquitous screwball persona was destabilized, resulting in a projection of the rugged qualities associated with Gable onto her star persona,[9] and a negotiation of the qualities associated with her public and private images.

Gable and Lombard's first star pairing was in Paramount's romantic drama *No Man of Her Own* (Wesley Ruggles, 1932) where, upon completion and in keeping with her reputation as a gag master, Lombard presented Gable with a ham affixed with his portrait. There have been theories put forth

---

[7]Robert Matzen, *Fireball: Carole Lombard and the Mystery of Flight 3* (Pittsburgh: GoodKnight Books, 2014), 79.
[8]"Cal York Announcing," *Photoplay*, March 1933, 48.
[9]Although by 1938 Carole Lombard was the highest paid star in Hollywood, Gable was arguably the bigger star. In addition to being crowned the "King of Hollywood" in 1937, from 1932 to 1943, Gable was ranked in the "Top Ten Money Making Stars" polls; Lombard does not appear in any of the yearly rankings. These polls were based on questionnaires sent to exhibitors by the Quigley Publishing Company and measured the "bankability" of Hollywood stars. See: William R. Weaver, "The Money-Making Stars of a Quarter of a Century," *Motion Picture Herald*, September 28, 1940, 123–124.

that the pair may have begun their affair as early as 1932;[10] however, that timeline is unlikely and no evidence has ever materialized to confirm this rumor. Gable and Lombard did not go public with their romance until 1936, and saw little of each other until the night of the Mayfair Ball;[11] Hollywood fan magazines and gossip columns began writing about their affair almost immediately after the party.[12]

In the spring of 1935 Gable separated from his second wife, Rhea, and fled to South America to avoid scandal after learning that his *Call of the Wild* (William Wellman, 1935) co-star, Loretta Young, was pregnant with his daughter, Judy.[13] Shortly after Gable's return to California he began dating Lombard, and speculation soon arose about the viability of their relationship since he was still legally married.[14] Behind the scenes, however, the Gable–Lombard romance was viewed as a publicity and marketing department's dream. In September 1936, a few months after their relationship became public knowledge, Paramount executive, John Hammell, wrote to Joseph Breen asking that the PCA certify *No Man of Her Own* for reissue. Hammell's letter confirms that the motivation for Paramount's request was "the importance of the cast (Gable and Lombard),"[15] which shows that the studio saw a long-term financial incentive to support Lombard's new relationship, despite the immorality of the Gable–Lombard romance.

It was reported that, by January 1939, Rhea had taken up residency in Reno to obtain a divorce.[16] Meanwhile, Lombard and Gable began house hunting and eventually settled on director Raoul Walsh's twenty-acre ranch

---

[10] Lombard and Gable famously gave each other engraved name bracelets. There are some photos of Gable taken prior to 1936—one dated from 1932—that shows him wearing his bracelet. Additionally, there is photographic evidence that Gable and Lombard both attended a party given by Countess di Frasso in 1935, over a year before the Mayfair Ball and Jock Whitney's "High Noon" party. Although they did not arrive at the party together, their presence in photos fueled speculative rumors about their romance.

[11] Wes D. Gehring, *Carole Lombard: The Hoosier Tornado* (Indianapolis: Indiana Historical Society Press, 2003), 101.

[12] Although the Mayfair Ball is commonly considered to be the event where Gable and Lombard began their romance, Vincent Paterno suggests that it may have possibly begun several months earlier at Jock Whitney's "High Noon" party on February 7, 1936. See: Vincent Paterno, "One more party pic," *Carole and Co.*, October 23, 2008, accessed November 14, 2015, http://carole-and-co.livejournal.com/147855.html.

[13] Gable never publicly nor privately acknowledged Judy as his daughter. See: Judy Lewis, *Uncommon Knowledge* (New York: Simon & Schuster, 1994), 384.

[14] Adela Rogers St. Johns, "Pursuit of the Hollywood He-Man," *Photoplay*, June 1936, 75.

[15] Letter from John Hammell to Joseph L. Breen, September 21, 1936, Motion Picture Association of America, Production Code Administration records, Margaret Herrick Library, Academy of Motion Picture Arts and Sciences.

[16] "The Marital Mixup of Carole and Clark," *Modern Screen*, March 1939, 58–59.

FIGURE 4.1 *Although they did not become an off-screen couple until 1936, Carole Lombard and second husband Clark Gable's screen chemistry is evident in* No Man of Her Own *(Wesley Ruggles, 1932)*.

in the San Fernando Valley town of Encino.[17] After they were married, the Gables were often photographed informally at home alongside their pets and menage of farm animals, as well as performing ranch duties like plowing or collecting eggs. The ranch soon became a symbol of the couple's marital contentment and unaffected star personae. And as Christina Lane notes, such press reports conveyed that their star couple represented a "practical, salt-of-the-earth quality and lack of pretense," making them an idealized couple for Depression era readers.[18] The Gables were glamorous but, more importantly, they were also relatable. After lengthy settlement negotiations with Gable's home studio, MGM,[19] Rhea was finally granted her decree on March 8, 1939.[20] In the gossip press, columnists went into overdrive trying

---

[17] Jean Garceau, *Dear Mr. G-*, Boston: Little, Brown and Company, 1961, 9. It should be noted that Lombard alone paid $50,000 for the ranch because Gable's money was tied up in his divorce proceedings. See: Gehring, 186.
[18] Christina Lane, "A Modern Marriage for the Masses: Carole Lombard, Clark Gable, and the Cultural Front," *Quarterly Review of Film and Video* Vol. 33, No. 5 (2016), 401.
[19] Matzen, 120.
[20] Swindell, 248.

to get an exclusive scoop on when and where Gable and Lombard would finally marry.[21] During one of Gable's breaks from filming *Gone with the Wind* (Victor Fleming, 1939), the couple slipped away from Los Angeles and were married on March 29 in Kingman, Arizona.[22] The following morning they returned back to Los Angeles to Bess Peters's house, where MGM had set up a press conference for eager reporters and photographers waiting to get the first glimpse of Hollywood's newest married couple.[23] The couple, who famously called each other "Ma" and "Pa"—nicknames fitting with their down-to-earth personae and pastoral lifestyle—quickly settled into married life.

If we consider the trajectory of the publicity discourse surrounding the Gable–Lombard romance, their relationship seemed to produce a dichotomy between Lombard's on- and off-screen personae. When she began dating Gable in early 1936, she had already gained fame in screwball comedy. As their romance blossomed, it became clear that in many ways Lombard, the wild and sociable screwball star, was enormously different from Gable. His persona was that of a rugged outdoorsman, and it was reported that he disliked the intense notoriety that came with movie stardom, so much so that MGM publicity made Gable out to be "an elusive male Garbo."[24] Consider one fan magazine observation from 1936: "Carole, the socially mad! Clark, the socially rebellious. It didn't seem possible. Now Hollywood is looking forward to the marriage of this strangely assorted pair."[25] That Gable and Lombard were labeled as "strangely assorted" explicitly acknowledges the gulf between their public personas. The bigger issue that this quotation reveals is the morally objectionable circumstances of their affair, which columnist Frederick Lewis rationalizes by hinting at the possibility of an eventual marriage.[26] From such statements, it is clear that although Lombard and Gable had vastly different star personae, a bigger hurdle in the press coverage was how to strategically reconcile the fact that the couple was committing adultery in plain view.

Writing about Gable and Lombard's affair without undermining the Hollywood studios' conservative moral values was undoubtedly a tricky

---

[21]Ford Black, "Will Clark Gable Ever Marry Carole Lombard?" *Motion Picture*, February 1939, 36.

[22]Swindell, 250.

[23]Gehring, 186.

[24]Lyn Tornabene, *Long Live the King: A Biography of Clark Gable* (New York: Pocket Books, 1976), 368.

[25]Frederick Lewis, "Is Carole Lombard in Love at Last?" *Liberty magazine*, November 14, 1936, 46–47.

[26]Rogers St. Johns, "Pursuit of the Hollywood He-Man." See also: May Mann, "A Date with Clark Gable," *Screenland*, May 1937, 24.

balancing act. It seemed that the best way for fan magazines to overcome this dilemma without appearing complicit was to acknowledge the differences between Gable and Lombard while simultaneously magnifying their compatibility. For instance, one *Photoplay* columnist writes:

> They have a lot in common, these two stars. They both enjoy informality. They like to be themselves. They welcome anything simple and natural which will give them fun. They like getting into old clothes and going to some out-of-the-way place. Also they like dressing up now and then and visiting some public pot. You may see them at an amusement park, laughing like a couple of kids at nothing at all, trying to be as inconspicuous as possible. You may run across them eating in some obscure little hole in the wall, enjoying the music of a four-piece Mexican orchestra. You might see them at Carole's home, playing bridge with friends. You might see them at the arena on fight nights, yelling with gusto "Sock him the kish-kish, Albie; he can't take it there!"[27]

This description is particularly evocative for the way it pinpoints their alleged kindred spirits, yet alludes to the distinct qualities that define each star. It acknowledges their "informalities," yet their down-to-earth personalities are linked to very different star images. Lombard's is clearly linked to her screwball comedy roles; her clowning and penchant for practical jokes imbued her star persona with a lack of presence that was atypical for a Hollywood actress. The amusement park comment is a nod to her Venice Beach Pier party and speaks to the public's familiarity with her gaiety. Lombard's name and "party girl" reputation was synonymous with madcap Hollywood fun. Conversely, the reference to an "obscure hole in the wall" signals Gable's well-known propensity for privacy. Gable's "informality" arguably originated from humble background: he was portrayed as a midwestern guy who, due to his childhood in rural Ohio[28] and adolescence spent, in part, working as a tool dresser at an Oklahoma oil rig,[29] was most at home in a pair of jeans and cowboy boots.[30] The activities mentioned in the *Photoplay* quotation were likely to have been formulated by the columnist at the behest of Lombard and Gable's respective studios, all in an effort to authenticate their star images. Stories such as this demonstrate how the studios' publicity departments worked hand in hand with the gossip press to systematically publish news items that

---

[27]Edward Doherty, "Can the Gable–Lombard Love Story Have a Happy Ending?" *Photoplay*, May 1938, 18.
[28]Chrystopher J. Spicer, *Clark Gable: Biography, Filmography, Bibliography* (Jefferson, NC: McFarland & Co., Inc., 2002), 12.
[29]Warren G. Harris, *Clark Gable: A biography* (New York: Three Rivers Press, 2002), 14.
[30]Kathleen Gable, *Clark Gable: A Personal Portrait* (New Jersey: Prentice-Hall, 1961), 116.

would coincide with a star's carefully crafted public persona. In this case, the task was to maintain Lombard and Gable's distinct star identities while simultaneously demonstrating how, in their own ways, they each represent the antithesis of the Hollywood movie star.

In order to validate the couple's similar outlooks, many publicity stories took this approach a step further and emphasized how Lombard was unlike Gable's first two wives. The couple was described as "the same kind of people cut from the same gusty cloth of life" and for the first time, Gable's "life was suddenly revolving around an intensely vivid girl whose vitality and zest for life was as strong as his own."[31] Columnist Frederick Lewis writes "both Josephine Dillon, his first wife, and Rhea Langham, his second, were thoroughly serious women. Both were ten years older than he." Lombard, on the other hand, was "imaginative, modernistic, unconventional, and oh, so young!—[in her] he finds the exact antithesis of the women he had known."[32] These types of observations highlight the specific qualities that reflect their particular personae. Lombard's screwball identity remains secure because her "zest for living" rationalized why the couple was so well suited.

This strategy helped to smooth over the precarious moral ground of their affair. Since Lombard was portrayed as a screwball comedian, her relationship with Gable was made to appear less threatening to conservative moral standards because of the playfulness her persona added to their relationship. A *Photoplay* article once described Gable as "the married man who is not married and the carefree bachelor who is not free!"[33] Accounts of their tryst downplayed the romantic angle and curiously referred to their relationship as a "friendship,"[34] a discursive tactic meant to placate any disapproving fans and to keep both stars in good moral standing. Labeling Gable a "carefree bachelor" in 1937 was inaccurate given that he and Lombard had been dating for over a year, but the observation likely reminded readers of the murky waters Hollywood columnists faced when writing about the Clark–Rhea–Carole triangle.

Ironically, Rhea faced considerable animosity for blocking her husband from marrying Lombard. Brett Abrams writes that despite being adulterers, Gable and Lombard were overwhelmingly "respected, enjoyed, and liked in the movie world" and "received acceptance in the [Hollywood] community

---

[31]Dennison Hastings, "Clark Gable's Romantic Plight." *Photoplay*, September 1937, 77.
[32]Lewis, "Is Carole Lombard in Love at Last?" 46.
[33]Hastings, "Clark Gable's Romantic Plight," 12.
[34]Adele Whiteley Fletcher, "A Heart to Heart Letter to Carole Lombard and Clark Gable," *Screen Guide*, November 1936, 5. See also: "How Will the Gable–Lombard Romance End?" *Hollywood magazine*, June 1937, 32; Eleanor Harris, "She Knew What She Wanted," *Screen Life*, March 1941, 23.

and in the mainstream media."[35] In an August 1938 article in *Picture Play*, columnist Margaret Dixon Mann considers, "How can it end happily when Rhea Gable won't give Clark a divorce?" She cites Rhea's temperamental incompatibility with Gable as the reason for their separation, and argues that she provided him an "unhappy mode of life" that supposedly interfered with his career and "depressed him mentally."[36] Though Lombard was the other woman technically, early on in the Gable–Lombard affair it was Rhea who was portrayed as the scorned de facto wife standing in the way of her estranged husband's happiness. Abrams explains that this publicity tactic could only work if the studios "believed that the image benefitted the stars and the industry and also could not hurt either star's fan base."

Despite the various press accounts that Clark and Rhea had a happy and loving marriage, in reality, their marriage came about in order to preserve Gable's star image. The pair had met in New York in the early 1930s and moved in together while he was working in the theater. Rhea allegedly fell in love with Clark, but he did not consider her as a serious love interest and eventually wanted to end their affair. Rhea was angry that Clark wanted to leave her so she supposedly threatened MGM executives that she would tell the newspapers about their immoral living arrangements. Fearing the situation would result in scandal and unwilling to risk the time and money they invested in Clark, according to Lombard biographer Michelle Morgan, MGM cited a morality clause in his studio contract and insisted that he marry Rhea to save his reputation.[37] MGM may have taken precautionary measures about Gable's relationship with Rhea nearly half a decade earlier, but they took a surprisingly relaxed approach in their publicity coverage regarding his affair with Lombard. The motivation behind their new discursive strategy is clear: when news of Gable's relationship with Rhea reached MGM executives in 1931, he was not yet a star and any sort of scandal could have potentially career-ending consequences. But by 1936, Gable was Hollywood's top male star and MGM's most bankable asset. The studio's willingness to promote the Gable–Lombard affair was a sign of their combined star power and overwhelming public approval. Collectively MGM publicists, the Hollywood fan magazines and newspapers, and those in charge of Lombard's publicity "promoted Gable and Lombard as the perfect star couple."[38] Rhea was simply an unwanted distraction from the carefully orchestrated romantic narrative.

---

[35] Brett L. Abrams, *Hollywood Bohemians: Transgressive Sexuality and the Selling of the Movie Dreamland* (Jefferson: McFarland & Co. Inc., 2008), 74.
[36] Margaret Dixon Mann, "Happiness Ahead for Clark and Carole," *Picture Play*, August 1938, page unknown.
[37] Morgan, 117.
[38] Abrams, 74.

Critical to the public's acceptance and moral justification of the Gable–Lombard affair was Lombard's screwball persona. Her vivacious personality ostensibly filled a void in Gable's life since she was portrayed as the type of woman that both his first wife, Josephine Dillon, and Rhea Langham were not. The same *Photoplay* article explained that Lombard "has always been a little mad" and that she approaches everything in her life from her first marriage to William Powell, her career, and even herself with laughter.[39] Lombard's screwball persona epitomized youthful exuberance. Conversely, Gable's first two wives were not only considerably older,[40] but there was an implication that their advanced ages resulted in an old-fashioned formality that did not fit his lifestyle. Michael Hammond writes, "Lombard offers a modern counterpart, read sexual one, to the potentially emasculating relationship with 'mothering types' that both Dillon and Langham represented."[41] Neither of Gable's ex-wives faced substantial derision from the press for marrying a much younger man, but there was an assumption that Gable went into both marriages to advance his career. In 1955, Josephine Dillon was interviewed by *Confidential* magazine for a bitter exposé entitled, "The Wife Clark Gable Forgot."[42] She identified herself as his "dramatic coach" and confessed that she helped him fix his appearance for film stardom, saying "he is my creation."[43] By contrast, Lombard was only seven years younger and a "more modern sexualized partner than his previous wives."[44] She was perceived as his emotional and physical equal, a compatible woman that would hold Gable's attention. The couple were of the same generation, had sexual chemistry, and had public personas that seemed to be based upon fundamentally similar personality traits, all of which provided grounding upon which the press could rationalize their affair.

Prior to their marriage there was a legitimate ideological purpose in maintaining the fun and "neurotic"[45] screwball side of Lombard's star persona. Once they were married, it became at odds with her status as Gable's wife. One of the most prevalent narratives found in publicity sources from

---

[39]Hastings, "Clark Gable's Romantic Plight," 77.

[40]Despite what the previous article states, they were seventeen and fourteen years older, respectively.

[41]Michael Hammond, "Good Fellowship': Carole Lombard and Clark Gable," in *First Comes Love: Power Couples, Celebrity Kinship and Cultural Politics*, eds. Shelley Cobb and Neil Ewen (London: Bloomsbury, 2015), 58.

[42]Contrary to what the title claims, Gable did not "forget" Dillon. In his will, Gable left his entire estate to his fifth wife, Kathleen. However, he included a provision that stated Josephine Dillon could live in her house—which Gable owned and paid for—rent free for the rest of her life. There were no similar provisions made for any of his other surviving ex-wives.

[43]"The Wife Clark Gable Forgot," *Confidential*, July 1955, page unknown.

[44]Hammond, 68.

[45]Noel F. Busch, "A Loud Cheer for the Screwball Girl," *Life*, October 17, 1938, 48.

this time was that Lombard adapted herself to accommodate her husband's lifestyle. An article in *Modern Screen* explained:

> One secret of Carole's hold on Clark is that she has completely changed her life to make Clark happy. What Clark wants to do she does, whereas Rhea Gable tried to get Clark to do the things that made her happy ... Though she used to be Hollywood's most amusing hostess, Carole rarely gives or goes to parties anymore. She knows Clark doesn't care for them.[46]

This description points to the conflict between Lombard's two identities. As the "Queen of Screwball Comedy," Lombard was praised for her independent mindset, and she had a physical prowess to match her intellect. Her "party girl" reputation authenticated and strengthened the playful quality of her screwball persona, and as *Modern Screen* later observed, "her parties were like her trademark."[47] But to be a satisfactory wife according to 1930s mores, Lombard had to put Gable's needs ahead of her own,[48] which accordingly required a change in the discourse surrounding her off-screen identity. In keeping with the narrative put forth by the Hollywood studios and the popular press, the Gables' private secretary, Jean Garceau, recalled that Lombard believed "Clark comes first" and that "she set about making herself over for him."[49] This included taking up his pet hobbies like fishing, hunting, and camping, all activities that brought the pair closer together. Garceau recalled, "For Clark she was fulfillment, a pal and partner in everything ... Everything centered around Clark, his likes and dislikes."[50] Garceau implicitly argues that when Lombard transformed her lifestyle to accommodate her husband, she also took a step back from her premarital image. Although Lombard's screwball persona did not disappear completely after her marriage, the discourse about her screwball reputation was repurposed to include a more rugged and understated image that matched Gable's star persona.

Stories about the Gables's atypical Hollywood lifestyle appear in virtually every publicity document written after 1939 and collectively signal the change in Lombard's star persona. In a gossip column from the August 1939 issue of *Modern Screen* entitled "Those Outdoor Gables," the author writes "Those cinematown cynics were betting that Carole Lombard would not so much as take a look at a fishing rod or take a shot at a skeet after she

---

[46]Hoyt, "Can the Gable–Lombard Romance Last?" 24.
[47]Hartley, 87.
[48]Kirtley Baskette, "Hollywood's Unmarried Husbands and Wives," *Photoplay*, December 1938, 74.
[49]Garceau, 82.
[50]Ibid.

FIGURE 4.2 *Carole Lombard and Clark Gable's Encino ranch was symbolic of their atypical Hollywood star personas.*

became Mrs. Clark Gable ... Carole has gotten so that she never thinks of a nightclub any more."[51] Similarly, in the October 1939 issue of the same magazine, a blurb accompanying Lombard's photo reads, "True, there were the days when Carole Lombard used to throw a mean party. But Mrs. Gable is a rancher now."[52] Her existent screwball persona and her penchant for physicality likely upheld the verisimilitude of her outdoorsy persona because they reinforced earlier claims of the couple's fundamental similarities. It was believable for Lombard to become a skillful hunter, fisherwoman, and skeet shooter precisely because of the characteristics that were tied to her screwball persona and the physicality her comic performance style entailed. It may appear that Lombard's sudden personality change was solely for the sake of publicity, but home movies and the Gables' private photo albums dating from 1936 to 1942 confirm that she was a frequent companion on her husband's hunting and fishing excursions.

---

[51] "Good News," *Modern Screen*, August 1939, 55.
[52] *Modern Screen*, October 1939, 83.

The shift in discourse toward Lombard's new marital identity effectively toned down the "party girl" side of her star persona. It reflects not only the ephemerality of the fundamental qualities associated with her screwball persona, but also the extent to which Gable's stardom impacted her own. This change exposes a pervasive patriarchal ideology; while references to Lombard's energy and zest for life did not diminish, instead of it deriving from her screwball image it was channeled into an earthy and homespun image that coincided with Gable's rugged masculinity.

Projecting aspects of Gable's star persona onto Lombard's enabled these publicity sources to preserve the qualities that defined his stardom. By the time the couple began dating Gable was already considered Metro-Goldwyn-Mayer's top male star, and he consistently ranked in the top three of Hollywood's biggest box office draws.[53] In 1937, a nationwide poll of twenty million readers of the *Chicago Tribune – New York Daily News* syndicate voted to crown Clark Gable and Myrna Loy as the "King" and "Queen" of Hollywood.[54] This title was officially bestowed upon Gable and Loy by Ed Sullivan on his weekly NBC radio show, and according to Loy, was used in the marketing campaign for their film, *Test Pilot* (Victor Fleming, 1938).[55] While Loy eventually shed her title, the nickname remained tied to Gable's star persona for the rest of his life—despite his alleged resentment in later years.[56]

The lack of aristocracy in the United States creates a space where Hollywood stars are considered akin to American royalty. In that light, we should not overlook the cultural significance of Gable's "King" moniker and its effect on his and Lombard's star couple image. In her work on F. Scott and Zelda Fitzgerald, Sarah Churchwell notes that by the early 1920s there was a "symbiotic relationship between celebrity and American aristocracy," and that as a star couple the Fitzgeralds embodied "the moment of America's transfer of social power from traditional 'high society' to emergent celebrity culture."[57] This created a space for the Fitzgeralds to take hold in the public consciousness, and become embodiments of the American leisure class. The Fitzgeralds were considered the equivalent of American royalty in the 1920s,

---

[53] "These Are Not Poison at the Box Office," *Look*, July 5, 1938, 20–21.
[54] Warren, 185.
[55] James Kotsilibas-Davis and Myrna Loy, *Myrna Loy: Being and Becoming* (New York: Knopf, 1987), 146.
[56] A month before his death, he was quoted as saying: "This 'King' stuff is pure bullshit ... There's no special light that shines inside me that makes me a star. I'm just a lucky slob from Ohio ... " See: Bill Davidson, *The Real and Unreal* (New York: Lacer Books, 1962), 95.
[57] Sarah Churchwell, "'The Most Envied Couple in America in 1921': Making the Social Register in the Scrapbooks of F. Scott and Zelda Fitzgerald," in *First Comes Love: Power Couples, Celebrity Kinship and Cultural Politics*, eds. Shelley Cobb and Neil Ewen (New York: Bloomsbury Publishing Inc., 2015), 33.

and the same was true for Gable and Lombard in the 1930s. Like aristocracy, Gable and Lombard's star couple image was aspirational, and as I have outlined throughout this chapter, their private lives were well documented in fan magazines and extraneous publicity materials. But due to the origins of Gable's "King" title, they more closely represent Robert Van Krieken's description of "democratized aristocracy."[58] Gable's title was chosen by his fans, meaning that his "royal" status was a result of popularity, not heredity. And unlike F. Scott Fitzgerald, Gable was not born into wealth and privilege but, as I mentioned earlier, circumstances not unlike the average American moviegoer—making him and, by extension, Lombard, examples of tangible and accessible stardom.

Gable's immense fame and unprecedented widespread appeal bolstered his and Lombard's collective star coupledom and increased the publicity value and public interest in her own star persona. Martha Nochimson explains that Gable's star persona was built upon a juxtaposition between manipulated stasis and an inner undefinable energy.[59] His energetic aura radiated from his self-confidence, which itself derived from his emotional and physical dominance over his female co-stars. What is more, Gable was appealing to both men and women: men wanted to emulate him, and women would "fall prey to his powerful brand of modern masculinity."[60] He was a ruggedly handsome, irresistible scoundrel. Since Gable had such an unchanging persona and was a lucrative commodity for MGM, one could argue that there would have likely been an economic imperative to keep his stardom intact. However, considering that by 1938 Lombard was officially Hollywood's highest paid star,[61] there would also have been an incentive to maintain some consistency in her screwball persona, especially when she achieved her greatest success in the genre. It seems illogical for Lombard to suddenly become disassociated from screwball comedy because it brought her such momentous fame and financial rewards.

To a certain extent, Lombard's persona shift reflects both the prevailing gender dynamics regarding a woman's identity and marriage, and the hard to define chemistry and ideological force of the Hollywood star couple. Susan Ware explains that during the 1930s, American white women were "strongly encouraged to limit their aspirations to husband, family, and domesticity; work outside the home, especially for married women, was

---

[58]Ibid.
[59]Martha P. Nochimson, *Screen Couple Chemistry: The Power of 2* (Austin: The University of Texas Press, 2002), 14–15.
[60]Christine Becker, "Clark Gable: The King of Hollywood," in *Glamour in a Golden Age: Movie Stars of the 1930s*, ed. Adrienne L. McLean (New Brunswick: Rutgers University Press, 2011), 253.
[61]*Life*, October 17, 1938, 9.

discouraged."⁶² For many, "marriage would be a significant part of the female life cycle."⁶³ Although Lombard never fully retired from the screen, rumors quickly circulated that she was seeking to give up her career in order to devote her time to taking care of Gable and to start a family.⁶⁴ In telling articles such as "Will Carole Lombard's Marriage End Her Career?" and "What's The Matter With Lombard?" fan magazines surmised that she had to make a choice between life paths. In a roundabout way they answer the questions they pose in their titles by concluding that for women, marriage should take precedence over a career. This attitude delineates the absence of any possible alternative to marriage and motherhood, whether they be the readers of the magazines or even those few who were as financially secure and independent as Lombard. They collectively point to the difficulty women living in the 1930s faced in trying to balance a career and married life.

These types of articles tether Lombard to a more "conventional" mode of white womanhood; a role that she never entirely fulfilled. Synthesizing hers and Gable's star personae downplayed the aspects of her screwball persona that were vestiges of her "party girl" lifestyle, and confirmed the prevailing marital ideology of the period. These sources never explicitly suggest that Lombard should abandon her career, as they and Lombard's industry associates had a vested interest in keeping her active as a star. Instead, they are indicative of a negotiation of competing negative forces: on the one hand, the dominant patriarchal ideology that molded the expectations and possibilities for white American women and on the other, the financial and ideological incentives of the film industry. Acting the part of Mrs. Clark Gable necessitated a disavowal of some of her previous identity and an adoption of Gable's hobbies. Becoming more like her husband likely appeased any lingering public anxiety about Lombard's premarital identity and in doing so, these sources could confirm that she could behave like the wife she was expected to be.

To further this notion, after her marriage Lombard was habitually labeled "Mrs. Gable." Although that was indeed her legal moniker, we cannot forget that her existent star persona was cultivated independent of Gable's. For a star whose image was wholly based upon ideas of female independence and self-sufficiency, the name change clashes with her premarital identity. On the surface, "Mrs. Gable" practically effaces her entire pre-1939 career, and obscures the carefully crafted work and monetary expenditures that went into constructing "Carole Lombard." It is more than just a name, it is

---

⁶²Susan Ware, *Holding Their Own: American Women in the 1930s* (Michigan: Twayne Publishers, 1984), 14.
⁶³Susan Ware, *Beyond Suffrage: Women in the New Deal* (Boston: Harvard University Press, 1981), 27.
⁶⁴Worth, "Will Carole Lombard's Marriage End Her Career?", 23.

a brand that connotes a particular set of physical attributes and personality traits that, when combined, creates Carole Lombard the star. But, while the "Mrs. Clark Gable" label seemed to obliterate Lombard's earlier star persona, in fact, it did not quite do so. Despite what her new nickname suggests, Lombard's star persona remained grounded in a rhetoric of equality and independence, but with a slight amendment.

In a *Movie Mirror* article released shortly after her marriage, a quotation attributed to Lombard suggests that a successful marriage should be an equal partnership, but that women were the unsung champions behind their husband's successes. She was purported to have said, "Back of every great man in history you'll find some woman who spurred him on … The only marriages today that last are those where the husband and wife have a community of interest and you can't have anything in common with a man if you're constantly to be taken care of."[65] This statement sounds like a subtle reworking of her previous stance on gender equality, but in keeping with the overall shift in her public persona, it confirms the way features of her screwball persona were recontextualized to fit her new private persona. Jean Garceau claims that not only did Gable change Lombard, but she also changed Gable by supposedly making him more carefree and less prone to worrying—though Garceau does not divulge how Lombard achieved such a feat other than by simply being his wife.[66] She explains that in private, Lombard brought out the best in her husband, supporting him to become a better version of himself. It is important to note that Garceau's book was published less than a year after Gable's death. Her comments perpetuate the myth that Lombard was content to become a doting wife and champion of her husband's career, thus reaffirming the conservative family values that were put forth by the Hollywood studios. Moreover, Garceau solidifies the romantic narrative that has since shrouded Gable and Lombard's posthumous star images, and her close working relationship with both stars has allowed such an image to remain largely critically unchallenged to this day.

In order to uphold the solidity of the Gable union, Lombard's outspoken views about female independence shifted toward the domestic sphere. But the type of emotional support and equality mentioned in the above quotation also exposes the disconnection between Lombard and the majority of married women of the 1930s. Garceau sustains patriarchal ideology by suggesting that a wife's duty should be to her husband. Adopting her husband's pet hobbies and toning down her social habits proved that Lombard was conforming to the expectations of a domestic ideal, and she became a sort of aspirational figure for the white female

---

[65] S.R. Hook, "How To Get Your Own Clark Gable," *Movie Mirror*, June 1939, 36.
[66] Garceau, 110.

demographic. But Lombard was an anomaly among this very group because she had the luxury of remaining not only financially independent from her husband, but was also the higher paid spouse.[67] Thus, while Lombard could play the part of the emotional supporter to Gable, unlike the majority of American women she was not dependent on him for financial assistance.[68] The label "Mrs. Clark Gable" and the accompanying shift in discourse unified Lombard's post 1939 public persona into that of a doting wife, but also masked the very atypical circumstances that enabled her to make these types of statements in the first place.

The idyllic image of "Mrs. Clark Gable" at least partially explains the collective allure of their star coupledom. Nochimson argues that the ideological impact of star couples "establishes in its totality a comprehensive, dimensional portrait of intimacy."[69] In effect, star couples bring to life conceptual and idealized notions of what it means to be in love. Her argument primarily draws upon classical Hollywood screen couples, however, it is applicable to star couples more generally because like their fictional counterparts, off-screen star couples are also heavily mediated images. Gable and Lombard had been an on-screen couple in *No Man of Her Own* and were praised for their natural chemistry, with one *Picture Play* reviewer citing their ability to "match wits and sex-consciousness."[70] The closest the Gables got to a second screen pairing was in 1941 when Lombard read Ring Lardner Jr. and Michael Kanin's screenplay for *Woman of the Year*.[71] It was rumored that she considered it to be the perfect film for her and Gable, and tried to secure the property. Unfortunately, Lombard discovered that the screenplay was written "especially for Katharine Hepburn … and was purchased by MGM at Hepburn's request."[72] In spite of what would have been an obvious marketing dream and a possible recipe for box office success, the couple never made another film together.

Nochimson explains that, aside from the potential financial rewards screen couples brought to the Hollywood studios, they also lay the foundation for "the way we process ideas of eroticism and intimacy" and reflect the elusive concept of "star chemistry."[73] She identifies four types of screen couples: the Functional Couple, the Thematic Couple, the Iconic

---

[67]Ruth Waterbury, "Our Home, Our Work – And Children," *Movie Mirror*, November 1939, 45.
[68]Ware, *Holding Their Own: American Women in the 1930s*, 125.
[69]Nochimson, 6.
[70]"The Screen in Review," *Picture Play*, April 1933, 60.
[71]Swindell, 287.
[72]American Film Institute *Within Our Gates: Ethnicity in American Feature Films, 1911–1960*, ed. Alan Gevinson (Los Angeles: University of California Press, 1997), 1154.
[73]Nochimson, 7.

Couple, and the Synergistic Couple. Each category builds upon the idea of a couple's on-screen chemistry, but for the purposes of my argument, the latter two are most relevant. She writes that the Iconic Couple "gives enchanting bodies and faces to the gender stereotypes,"[74] and that they are ultimately clichéd examples of Old Hollywood figures. She draws from Clark Gable's on-screen pairings and the idea of "Gable Plus One," which she explains as Gable playing the same character in every film: sexually dominant, patriarchal, and macho. Gable's heroes were "perfectly adaptable to a large number of acting partners," the only requirement being that they be "sexually attractive and possess a headstrong femininity" in order to serve as a "foil" for him to display his masculinity and indefinable charm.[75] For example, during the 1930s, Gable was frequently paired with actresses like Joan Crawford, Jean Harlow, and Myrna Loy, all women whose tough but feminine personae could stand up to his on-screen personality.

Unlike the Iconic Couple, the Synergistic Couple's chemistry was unique only to their particular pairing. Nochimson writes that they made "genuine expressions about intimacy" by breaking conventional narrative patterns of storytelling and that they often "disrupted the formulas [of storytelling] in interesting ways so as to create highly distinctive perspectives on the social practices" embedded within film narratives.[76] The Iconic Couple was often the result of a hackneyed narrative, while the Synergistic Couple broke away from conventions and brought to life the special dynamics that were cultivated by a couple's unique relationship. The Gables were not a screen couple during this period, but Nochimson's analysis of Gable's on-screen star pairings and his individual persona proves useful in thinking about their star coupledom. The power and appeal of their dual star power lay precisely in the combination of the Iconic and Synergistic formulations, in which Lombard played an important role.

Conclusion

Gable and Lombard conform to the "Gable Plus One" equation because she was also the foil to articulate his star persona. Her adoption of his habits and outdoorsy lifestyle, plus the shift in publicity discourse away from her premarital image solidified Gable's masculinity and reaffirmed his status as a dominant and patriarchal male hero. Lombard perfectly fits Nochimson's requirements for the "Plus One" heroine, as she was the

---

[74]Ibid, 9.
[75]Ibid, 11.
[76]Ibid, 9.

epitome of headstrong femininity and sexual appeal. It is worthwhile to reiterate the distinction that I made earlier about Lombard's post marital identity being a watered down version of her earlier screwball image. Becoming Mrs. Clark Gable did not mean a complete rejection of the basic characteristics of her screwball personality, but merely that her tireless energy and championing of gender equality that was once identified as a by-product of her screwball persona, was eventually channeled into her appropriation of Gable's star qualities. Lombard allegedly admitted that her worst trait was that she had "too much energy," and explained "I'm immensely interested in and enthusiastic in everything I do, everything. No matter what it is I'm doing, no matter how trivial, it isn't trivial to me. I give it all I got and love it. I love living. I love life."[77] Her star persona embodied an unwavering enthusiasm for life, which was epitomized in the way that she took up Gable's hobbies like skeet shooting, camping and hunting,[78] and also met Gable's private yearning of meeting a woman who "has a grasp of masculine feelings."[79] Her persona carried the weight of her premarital gusto and high-strung energy, but was now focused on Gable's outdoorsy hobbies in such a way that validated his virile masculinity. In the same way her screwball qualities set the stage to justify their "immoral" love affair, there was an ideological purpose for Lombard's star persona to become similar to Gable's—to be his "Plus One"—because it reinstated the basic characteristics of his stardom which, in turn, created a cohesive and stable image of both Clark Gable the star, and "the Gables."

As the star of what was arguably the most high-profile film of the period, it is likely that the media-induced buzz generated by *Gone with the Wind* made Gable the primary driving force of the Gable–Lombard's iconicity. But Lombard also played an important role in the couple's collective status. To imply that Lombard was simply Gable's "Plus One" does not fully account for the hard-to-define electricity that radiated from their pairing. This is where the Synergistic component comes into play: Lombard was more than just a "Plus One" because she ostensibly fit into Gable's lifestyle in a way that no woman had before. Their pairing was synergistic precisely because of the way they appeared to complement each other and through their shared hobbies, mindset, and approaches to life. The quote attributed to Gable about love being the only thing that was holding them together highlights the idealized portrayal of their married life, an aspiration model for the legions of film fans who eagerly consumed countless stories and images of the star couple. As half of Hollywood's golden couple, a great deal of the

---

[77] Gladys Hall, "Lombard – As She Sees Herself," *Motion Picture*, November 1938, 66.
[78] Faith Baldwin, "Do Hollywood Women Spoil Their Men?" *Photoplay*, May 1939, 80.
[79] Hoyt, "Can The Gable–Lombard Romance Last?" 25.

value and relevance of Lombard's post 1939 star persona derived from her role as Mrs. Clark Gable. As I have shown, this had profound effects on the publicity discourse featured in popular media channels. And yet, for as much as Lombard's star persona veered away from screwball comedy, the ideas of fun, equality and passion that had been attributed to her premarital screwball identity remained intact and were key components in maintaining the spectacle of the Gables' fascinating public romance.

5

Lombard gets dramatic: melodrama, domesticity, and performance

In a move that coincided with her marriage to Clark Gable, beginning in 1939 Carole Lombard embarked on a screwball comedy hiatus and turned her attention to dramatic films. What resulted were four melodramas filled with emotional intensity and pathos, and performances that were unlike anything Lombard had done before. Linda Williams describes melodrama as "the fundamental mode of popular American moving pictures" which "seeks dramatic revelation of moral and emotional truths through a dialectic of pathos and action."[1] In many instances, melodramatic action is motivated by "female desire and processes of spectator identification governed by a female point-of-view"[2] through what Williams calls the "feminized victimhood" of virtue or innocence.[3] The timing of Lombard's career shift strengthened her mature and domestic image. Melodrama's preoccupation with familial issues like childhood illness, love, and sacrifice may have been part of conscious decisions to make the genre's predominately female audience identify with Lombard, and to buttress her shifting off-screen star persona. Given that she made only four dramatic films and eventually returned to comedy by 1941, some may find that the phrase "dramatic period" overstates the importance of these titles in her oeuvre. I contend that they should be treated as a distinct temporal period unto themselves, especially when we consider that they were made at the same time Lombard's star persona was transitioning away from screwball

---

[1] Linda Williams, "Melodrama Revisited," in *Refiguring American Film Genres: History and Theory*, ed. Nick Browne (Berkeley: University of California Press, 1998), 42.
[2] Annette Kuhn, "Women's Genres," *Screen* 25 (1984): 18.
[3] Williams, 42–43.

comedy. The temporal coincidence of Lombard's career shift indicates that she had the chance to deviate from her comic performance style, and they echo Lombard's longing to be known as more than just a screwball star.

What follows is a textual analysis based assessment of Lombard's dramatic performances in: *Made for Each Other*, *In Name Only*, *Vigil in the Night*, and *They Knew What They Wanted*. As is the case with chapter 1, my methodology is predicated on the fact that these films have been rarely studied in scholarship on melodrama more broadly, or Lombard specifically. According to Andrew Klevan, performance scholarship can be useful in that it allows us to not only unpack movement, gestures, and tonality, but also the actor's presence within a space. Citing Stanley Cavell's work on the integration of a performer and the space of the *mise-en-scène*—which he describes as a combination of "projected visibility" and "ontological equality"[4]—Klevan explains that "the credibility of performance is created out of coherence and harmony with the film's environment—including the camera and other elements 'outside' the visible fictional world ..."[5] In that light, in what follows I will attempt to parse out reoccurring performance traits in order to formulate a long-overdue cohesive description of Lombard's dramatic style. Paying close attention to Lombard's presence on screen, I will explore how the cinematography, editing, and framing—particularly the close-up—captures her relationship with the objects and actors around her. This will also allow me to document the change in her performance style from comedy to melodrama. I argue that while Lombard's screwball performances are body-centric and lie primarily in her malleability and ease with physicality, in her dramatic performances she channels her understated actions inward and she reflects her characters' emotional variances through her face and in her voice.

Made for Each Other (*John Cromwell, 1939*)

Lombard's first melodramatic venture was in Selznick International Pictures' domestic comedy–drama, *Made for Each Other*. The film was touted as Lombard's "brilliant transition from comedienne to dramatic star," and was marketed around its intense familial storyline.[6] It tells the story of John and Jane Mason, a middle-class couple from Manhattan. John (James Stewart) is plagued by an almost crippling sense of inadequacy at his work in a law

---

[4]Stanley Cavell, *The World Viewed: Reflections on the Ontology of Film* (Boston: Harvard University Press, 1979), 37.
[5]Andrew Klevan, *Film Performance: From Achievement to Appreciation* (London: Wallflower Press, 2005), 5.
[6]*Made For Each Other* advertisement, *Photoplay*, April 1939, 11.

firm. His malaise trickles into his home life with Jane (Lombard) who, as the more headstrong and confident spouse, offers him continual encouragement. Momentary happiness arrives with the birth of their son, but John's feelings quickly return as he fears he is not a sufficient provider for his family, which causes marital tension. While at a New Year party, the couple are informed that their baby has been taken to a Catholic hospital and is being treated for a deadly respiratory infection and that his chance of survival is dependent upon a scarce serum that can only be located in Salt Lake City. Meanwhile, a severe storm has blanketed the entire country, making it difficult for the serum to reach the hospital in time to save their son's life. As the couple wait anxiously for the medicine, Jane keeps a bedside vigil.

The scene begins with a medium establishing shot of the Mason baby on his bed encased by an oxygen tent. The camera pans to a medium close-up of Lombard's face. She is wearing a black turtleneck, and in combination with the dark lighting and Sister Madeline's habit—who is standing behind her— Jane is swathed in black. As in the scene in *Love Before Breakfast,* the darkness juxtaposes Lombard's pale skin and the shadows cast by the low lights accentuate the scar on her cheek, adding a weariness to her face. While this may be a familiar angle from which to view Lombard's face, such an extended close-up was uncommon in Lombard's screwball comedies. Nor did Lombard usually rely on such understatement in her screwball performances: as was the case with the temper tantrum scene in *My Man Godfrey,* or Lily Garland's overdramatic outbursts in *Twentieth Century,* in keeping with the genre's light tone, Lombard's screwball character's emotions were more exaggerated, loud, and gesticulatory.

This scene from *Made for Each Other* demonstrates how Lombard was able to shift her performance style in a new genre. Christine Gledhill and Linda Williams explain that "melodrama employs the visceral language of embodiment, gesture, and vocal delivery" which is representative of the social and personal.[7] In particular, Lombard's performance is a reflection of the cinema actor's proximity with the spectator. Citing Carl Theodor Dreyer's rhetorical criticism on the differences between theatrical and cinematic melodrama, Klevan likens the former "with inauthentic, exaggerated representation at a distance" while the film camera is able to capture performance at a "micro level"[8] in such a way that gives audiences the feeling that they are in the midst of the narrative action. In this scene, Lombard's emotion is conveyed on her face, a performative technique that, as we have just seen, is typical of melodrama. Her eyes are focused on her baby off camera, and we see wrinkles around her eyebrows and bags under her eyes

---

[7] Christine Gledhill and Linda Williams, "Prologue: The Reach of Melodrama," in *Melodrama Unbound: Across History, Media, and National Cultures,* eds. Christine Gledhill and Linda Williams (New York: Columbia University Press, 2018), xxii.
[8] Ibid, 193–194.

that reveal Jane's worry. Her mouth is pursed open slightly, a reoccurring performative trait Lombard uses to convey her characters' anxiety or fear.

The film cuts to a slightly low angle shot of Jane's upper body and the Sister who stands behind her. Jane murmurs to herself, "I wish there was something I could do. If there was just something." Williams explains that melodrama "moves us to pathos for protagonists" by introducing forces out of their control, which allows them to be perceived as victims by the spectator.[9] Lombard's introspective performance signals Jane's despair and the dialog stresses that she is the victim of circumstances outside of her control—her son's illness—her universally relatable circumstances thus enable us to feel empathy for her. Each time Lombard says the word "something," her voice drops in an effort to emphasize Jane's feeling of complete helplessness and motherly worry, while her quiet, contemplative tone reveals her character's anxiety.

Sister Madeline encourages Jane to pray for her son, and takes her to the hospital chapel. In this scene, Jane is framed in an overhead shot at the altar, and though technically not a close-up, the dark lighting and Jane's kneeling position focuses our attention on her face. Lombard concentrates her gaze on the crucifix in order to show the scope of Jane's maternal anguish; though earlier in the scene Jane informed the Sister that she was not a Catholic, she turns to prayer in a desperate effort to ask for her son's recovery. She whispers to God that her son means so much to her and John, how they have "had him for such a little while." and how they want to "see him grow up to be a man. Please help my baby, we love him so." Throughout Lombard's performance, her lips tremble and her voice wavers to show how Jane is holding back her tears.

Crying, or other displays of emotion, are common in Lombard's comedies and melodramas, though her performance greatly differs depending on the genre. In her comedies, her characters are prone to exaggerated outbursts and fast-paced blustering such as the train scene from *Twentieth Century* or Irene's tantrum in *My Man Godfrey*. This scene from *Made for Each Other* is indicative of her dramatic style, as she offers a significantly softer, more introspective, and restrained performance that reflects the gravity of Jane's turmoil. Jane says very little in the scene, and instead Lombard relies primarily on her facial expressions and subtle changes in body language to convey the range of her character's emotions. For as much as Jane feels helpless as her son clings to his life, her silent pleading and desperate prayers indicate that she has not lost hope that her son will survive. Lombard's body position—facing upwards toward the crucifix—and her wide eyes suggest that Jane will fight for her son until the end and gives us a sense of hope that her son will pull through, which comes to fruition by the film's conclusion.

---

[9]Williams, 42.

FIGURES 5.1 & 5.2 *Carole Lombard appears as Jane Mason in* Made for Each Other *(John Cromwell, 1939). This was the first of a series of melodramatic roles Lombard played in the late 1930s and early 1940s in an effort to prove that she was not just a comedic actress.*

FIGURES 5.3 & 5.4 *Lombard's performance style in her dramatic films was often understated and introspective, as illustrated in these film stills from* Made for Each Other.

Lombard's performance simultaneously reflects Jane's anguish and private hope, and her restrained performance in this scene confirms that she was as adept at drama as she was with comedy.

Released on February 10, 1939 *Made for Each Other* was praised as "one of the finest pictures made in Hollywood in years,"[10] and both Lombard and Stewart received glowing reviews for two of "Hollywood's best" performances of the year.[11] One *Variety* review calls the picture noteworthy for being Lombard's "first straight dramatic role ... the serious Lombard is sure to cause comment."[12] The film made strong initial gains in mid-city markets like Seattle and Philadelphia—where the film garnered $9,000[13] and $15,000,[14] respectively—but *Variety* noted that Selznick International reported a total net loss of $292,000.[15] Despite the same *Variety* reviewer's prediction for "extended box-office strength,"[16] they suggest that perhaps it was "the serious Lombard" that kept moviegoers away.

Such a theory is within reason: this was Lombard's first non-comedy in nearly five years, and her presence on screen was a considerably understated version of the star persona that audiences had come to know in film and popular media. Charles Affron makes the case for the uniqueness of star acting, writing that "the shape of an individual performance is a paradigm for the shape of a career ... "[17] Using the example of Marlon Brando, he explains that we see a star's past performances in each of their roles: "if we do not see Brando's Stanley more than once, we see him again in his Terry Malloy, and even in his Fletcher Christian."[18] In Brando's case, however, his star persona was predicated on his versatility and Method style, so much so that physical and performative transformations became integral to his screen identity. Unlike Brando, throughout the latter half of the 1930s, Lombard's star persona had become grounded in screwball comedy and, as I have previously argued, her film performances and extratextual identity worked symbiotically to produce a cohesive star persona. In that way, it may have justifiably been more difficult for audiences to see Lily Garland, Irene Bullock, or Hazel Flagg in Lombard's *Made for Each Other* performance, since Jane is considerably more subdued in tone and demeanor than her previous roles.

---

[10]"The Shadow Stage: A Review of the New Pictures," *Photoplay*, April 1939, 53.
[11]"Reviews," *Photoplay*, July 1939, 91.
[12]"Film Reviews," *Variety*, Wednesday, February 1, 1939, 13.
[13]"Lombard-Stuart Preem Big $9000 in Seattle," *Variety*, Wednesday, February 8, 1939, 10.
[14]"Picture Grosses," *Variety*, Wednesday, February 15, 1939, 10.
[15]David Thomson, *Showman: The Life of David O. Selznick*. London: Abacus, 1993), 269.
[16]Ibid.
[17]Charles Affron, "Generous Stars," in *Star Texts: Image and Performance in Film and Television*, ed. Jeremy G. Butler (Detroit: Wayne State University Press, 1991), 97.
[18]Ibid.

In Name Only (*John Cromwell, 1939*)

Lombard's second dramatic film was RKO's romantic melodrama, *In Name Only*. Originally titled "Memory of Love," the film was renamed and completed in the spring of 1939 by director John Cromwell.[19] It follows the love triangle between a widowed artist named Julie Eden (Lombard), Alec Walker (Cary Grant), and his estranged wife, Maida (Kay Francis). In a situation that mirrors Lombard's own relationship with Gable and his second wife, Rhea—a similarity not likely lost on contemporaneous audiences—Julie is caught in a waiting game as Maida refuses to file for divorce despite the fact that her marriage is "in name only." Ignoring Alec's pressure to end the marriage, Maida stalls in fear of losing her social position and access to Alec's wealth. In despair, Alec gets drunk and after spending Christmas Eve in a hotel, falls gravely ill and is taken to hospital.

Having been barred from visiting Alec in his room by his parents, Mr. and Mrs. Walker (Charles Coburn and Nella Walker), Julie keeps a constant vigil in the hospital lobby. She is eventually summoned by Alec's physician, Dr. Gateson (Jonathan Hale), who warns her that Alec's life depends on her reassurance that Maida will no longer contest her divorce. In the penultimate scene, Julie must lie to Alec by telling him that Maida will no longer stand in the way of them being together. When Julie walks into the room toward Dr. Gateson, the camera tracks along with her in close-up. As a distinctly cinematic mode of expression, the close-up is a discursive technique that can reveal to the viewer the subtleties of a film performance. Béla Balázs describes it as a kind of "magnifying glass" which "brings us closer to the individual cells of life, it allows us to feel the texture and substance of life in its concrete details."[20] The close-up functions as "the art of emphasis,"[21] drawing attention to a specific, otherwise unidentifiable detail that heightens a film's mood and visual expression.

While not an inherently melodramatic mode of cinematic presentation,[22] the close-up lends itself to capturing what Hugo Munsterberg describes as the otherwise unnoticeable details and "emotional action of the face to sharpest relief."[23] Andrew Klevan builds upon Munsterberg's theory, and argues that character psychology in melodrama is "indirectly revealed by

---

[19]"Cromwell Calls 'Em On Grant-Lombard 'Memory'," *Variety*, Wednesday, February 8, 1939, 7.
[20]Béla Balázs, "Visible Man," in *Béla Balázs Early Film Theory: "Visible Man" and "The Spirit of Film*," eds. Erica Carter and Rodney Livingstone (New York: Berghahn Books, 2010), 38.
[21]Ibid, 39.
[22]Charles Affron, "Identifications," in *Imitations of Life: A Reader on Film & Television Melodrama*, ed. Marcia Landy (Detroit: Wayne State University, 1991), 110.
[23]Hugo Munsterberg *Hugo Munsterberg on Film: The Photoplay – a Psychological Study and Other Writings*, ed. Alan Langdale (New York: Routledge, 2002), 99.

the performer's relationship to other aspects of presentation" like editing and framing.[24] He explains that this relationship eliminates the need for the performer to "overtly or openly express their psychological states and betray their latent or covert aspects; instead, the performer remains faithful to the submerged quality of these emotions."[25] *In Name Only* offers a different perspective from which we typically view Lombard's performances: while many of her screwball films frame her in medium and long shots in order to display her proclivity for physical comedy, in dramatic films like *In Name Only*, she is predominately shown in close-up. The moments of physical "excess" that made her screwball performances so noteworthy are absent in this and other films from the period, resulting in a substantially tempered performance style. While I argue that in some films, Lombard's understated dramatic performance style is incongruent with the scope and severity of the narrative action—for example, see my discussion of *Vigil in the Night*— in this scene the reoccurring close-ups of Lombard's face capture the nuances of her facial expressions and body language, and allow her to convey the shades of Julie's grief over Alec's illness and the seemingly insurmountable barriers to her affair.

At the hospital, Alec's parents let Julie know that she is an unwanted presence in their son's life. Their initial protestations to accept Dr. Gateson's request to invite her into the hospital room show that, in spite of their son's happiness, they are still very much sympathetic to Maida. Lombard's performance makes it clear that Julie feels like an outsider. Julie tries in vain to hold her composure by maintaining her focus on Dr. Gateson, but Lombard's watery eyes and quivering mouth expose her character's feigned stoicism. She smiles faintly when she learns there is a chance Alec can recover. Given that audiences are meant to sympathize with Julie's character, we can assume her smile has less to do with her knowing that she is Alec's only savior—as Maida later remarks—and more that he has even the slightest chance at survival. Julie reassures Alec's father that they will not see each other any longer because "it's hopeless." Dr. Gateson asks if Alec thinks it is hopeless, and in the same over-the-shoulder shot, Julie looks down at the ground and nods her head slowly. Lombard's understated reaction indicates that Julie feels guilty about the precarious situation Alec is in, and that their love has inadvertently caused him so much heartache and physical turmoil.

Dr. Gateson instructs Julie to make Alec believe that there is hope, and to tell him "whatever he wants to hear," including that she still loves him. Lombard's chin trembles to show that Julie is still trying to keep her composure and be strong for Alec's sake, but that the situation is taking a toll on her. Lombard also bites her bottom and top lips to show that Julie is nervous about her task and is reluctant to give Alec false hope. However,

---

[24]Klevan, 14.
[25]Ibid.

FIGURES 5.5 & 5.6 *While audiences were likely more familiar with Lombard's high energy, full body screwball performance style, in dramatic roles like Julie Eden in* In Name Only *(John Cromwell, 1939), she conveys restrained emotion through her face and voice.*

in combination with her wide and slightly eager-looking eyes, Lombard's facial performance also reminds us that Julie will do whatever she can to save Alec's life, and that at that moment she is more worried about his well-being than her happiness.

Lombard's performance in this brief but telling close-up summarizes Julie's selflessness and love for Alec, and "pardons" her for her immoral actions. In a subsequent conversation Maida confesses that she would rather see Alec dead than with Julie. In a close-up reaction shot, Julie's eyes flash with a mix of astonishment and anger. Her eyebrows furrow and she tells Maida in a low, confident tone, "You don't love Alec. You don't love anybody but yourself." In combination with the earlier scene, this exchange asks audiences to consider the relative moral offenses by each woman; is Julie's emotional involvement with a legally married man more reprehensible than Maida's unscrupulous disregard for her estranged husband's life? Like Lombard's relationship with Gable where she was heralded as his "true love," Julie may be the "other woman" technically, but she is the one who holds Alec's heart and life in her hands. And like Rhea Gable, Maida is the scorned de facto wife that is standing in the way of Alec's happiness and, more urgently, his chance at a recovery.

In Name Only was released on August 18, 1939 to overwhelmingly positive critical reviews. Some praised the cast for their "good acting,"[26] including the *New York Times* who observed that Lombard "plays her poignant role with all the fragile intensity and contained passion that have lifted her to dramatic eminence."[27] John C. Flinn of *Variety* described the film as "an engrossing love story of today, at once plausible, deeply moving, tremendously stirring."[28] Though Flinn never explicitly makes the connection to Lombard's real-life love triangle, his observation that the film's love story was contemporaneously relevant suggests that, as Gehring argues, it "bore more than a passing resemblance to events in the actress's personal life."[29] *In Name Only* made a profit at the box office,[30] but not enough to be "commensurate with the glowing nature of the reviews."[31] RKO's national advertising and publicity tactics likely helped bolstered attendance in smaller markets: in upstate New York, for example, the studio offered moviegoers the chance to win a trip for two at an "attractive

---

[26]"The Shadow Stage: A Review of the New Pictures," *Photoplay*, October 1939, 64.
[27]"Alexander Korda Brings a Remake of 'Four Feathers' in Technicolor to the Capitol–'In Name Only,' a Romantic Drama, at the Music Hall," *New York Times*, August 4, 1939, L11.
[28]John C. Flinn, "Film Showmanship," *Variety*, August 9, 1939, 8.
[29]Gehring, 188. See also: David Bret, *Clark Gable: Tormented Star* (New York: Da Capo Press, 2008), 154.
[30]Richard Jewel, "RKO Film Grosses: 1931–1951," *Historical Journal of Film, Radio and Television*, vol. 14, no. 1 (1994): 56.
[31]Gehring, 189–190.

summer resort,"[32] while in Columbus, Ohio some theater owners gave away five pairs of tickets daily to the Ohio State Fair.[33] The film made a combined $173,000 during its second and third weeks at Radio City Music Hall alone, though it fell short of taking the top spot in the New York City market due to the August 21 release of MGM's *The Wizard of Oz* (Victor Fleming, 1939).[34]

Wes Gehring explains that despite Lombard's solid performance and the generally positive critical reviews, the box office receipts indicate that the public "preferred [her] in comedies."[35] He cites a review from *New York Sun* critic, Eileen Creelman, who writes that "Miss Lombard, far more effective in rollicking comedy, enjoys only a few laughs here."[36] *In Name Only* lacks many of the lighthearted moments found in *Made for Each Other,* and the film would have been considered a radical departure for the "Queen of Screwball Comedy." While Creelman's review does not justify the requirement for levity in Lombard's performance—particularly given the film's dark and tragic themes—it does speak to her familiarity as a comic actress. Similarly, a reader's letter from Dorothy Brooks Holcombe from Shorewood, Wisconsin published in the December 1939 issue of *Photoplay* provides us with an indication of public sentiment toward Lombard in her newly adopted genre. Holcombe cites Lombard's "lack of chic dress and make-up" as well as her "insufficient grasp of her role as the other woman" as the reasons for "the press and public's" criticisms.[37] She contends that Lombard "held her own in many a picture, but, given every advantage in star privileges, she was a poor second to Kay Francis."[38] Holcombe suggests that the film's producer, George Haight, should never have paired Lombard with Francis, who she praises as an "experienced actress with an innate sense of good showmanship."[39] Like Creelman, Holcombe's issue with Lombard in the film rests squarely on her alleged unconvincing dramatic performance style. We cannot overlook the fact that contemporaneous moviegoers like Holcombe would have likely been most familiar with Lombard in comedies. Unlike Lombard, Francis had previous experience in melodrama and was likely to be more accepted by the public in a dramatic role. These reviews, combined with the box office receipts, give us a glimpse into the public and critical moods toward Lombard's newly adopted genre.

---

[32] "Vacation Trip Prize in 'Name Only' Contest," *Variety*, August 28, 1939, 8.

[33] "'Name Only' Hook-Up With Ohio State Fair," *Variety*, September 6, 1939, 8.

[34] "'Oz'-Rooney-Garland Pep Up B'way, Standout $65,000, Boyer-Dunne 32G; Jessel Ups 'Andy' 25G, 'Name' 89G 3d," *Variety*, August 23, 1939, 7.

[35] Gehring, 190.

[36] Creelman quoted in Gehring, 190.

[37] "Boos and Bouquets," *Photoplay*, December 1939, 5.

[38] Ibid.

[39] Ibid.

Evidently, however, not everyone in Hollywood agreed with the critical consensus. At the same time that *In Name Only* was released, several newspaper articles were reporting that Lombard had been selected to play "the second Mrs. de Winter" in David O. Selznick's adaptation of Daphne du Maurier's novel, *Rebecca*. In a September 2, 1939 article written by gossip columnist Louella Parsons, she explains that the "plum [role] falls into the lap of Carole Lombard, who is the no. 1 femme star on the Selznick lot now ...,"[40] a reference to the fact that, just two years prior, Lombard had signed a three picture deal with Selznick International Pictures.[41] Presumably, Selznick's personal issues with Clark Gable[42] made it difficult for he and Lombard to work together on *Rebecca*, however this situation proves that he believed in Lombard's dramatic skills enough to consider casting her in such a prestigious adaptation.

Vigil in the Night (*George Stevens, 1940*)

On the heels of *Made for Each Other* and *In Name Only*, Lombard completed what was perhaps her most diverse and atypical role to date in *Vigil in the Night*. Based on a serialized novel by A.J. Cronin and directed by George Stevens, the film centers on an English nurse, Anne Lee (Lombard). Due to her sister and fellow nurse, Lucy's (Anne Shirley) carelessness, a child on their ward dies. In fear that Lucy will face prosecution because she has not yet completed her nursing certification, Anne takes the blame and is promptly fired from the hospital. Anne is relocated to Manchester City Hospital and quickly rises in the ranks to become a Sister. Shortly after Lucy joins Anne and the nursing team, a deadly respiratory epidemic strikes the city. Anne is put in charge of the children's isolation ward, which is drastically underfunded due to the negligence of the hospital's chair of the board, Matthew Bowley (Julien Mitchell). Through the tenacity of Anne

---

[40]Louella Parsons, "Carole Lombard Assigned Star Role in 'Rebecca'," *Los Angeles Examiner*, September 2, 1939, page unknown.
[41]Emily Carman, *Independent Stardom: Freelance Women in the Hollywood Studio System* (Austin: University of Texas Press, 2016), 158.
[42]Although Lombard was committed to a three-picture contract with Selznick, they only made two films together—*Nothing Sacred* and *Made for Each Other*. In a January 22, 1940 memo from Selznick to Lombard, he tells Lombard that due to his difficult working relationship with Gable on *Gone With the Wind*, he didn't want her to "suffer" the repercussions "in [her] personal life" should they make a third picture. It was widely reported that Gable did not like Selznick, despite what Selznick claims were his best efforts to make Gable happy during production. Selznick concludes his memo by stating that he relieves her of any contractual obligations for a third picture. See: *Memo from David O. Selznick*, ed. Rudy Behlmer (New York: Random House, 2000), 270.

and her confidant and supporter, Dr. Prescott (Brian Aherne), the hospital manages to curb the epidemic and improve the working conditions in the hospital.

When Bowley's son is stricken with the disease, Lucy decides to oversee his case in an effort to redeem her past mistakes, but quickly falls ill and dies. With little time to grieve due to the mounting severity of the outbreak, Anne leaves Lucy's deathbed and takes a moment of private reflection to mourn her loss. The scene begins with a long shot of Anne as she drifts lifelessly to the window of the isolation ward. Lombard moves slowly toward the camera, her eyes are looking at the ground to convey Ann's anguish. The camera tracks in to a close-up, and as it does, Anne takes off her nurse's jacket, collapses against the window and bursts into tears. Lombard's breathing is heavy and staggered, and she wrings the sleeve of the nurse jacket repeatedly to show how Anne is consumed by her emotions. Though half of her face is covered by the window frame in a composition that renders Anne's mourning in an intimate way, Lombard manages to convey the full effect of her character's private moment of despair.

Lombard's minimalist performance in this close-up is symptomatic of her understated dramatic acting style in contrast to her expansive comic performances, which may explain the limited public acceptance that this radically different style engendered. Overcome with the suddenness of her sister's death, Anne chokes on her tears. Lombard slows down her breathing and lets out a series of quick sighs to indicate Anne's pain. Her nose is pressed up against the frame, and she closes her eyes and begins to cry again, only this time her performance is much more pronounced. She makes a low crying noise while scrunching her mouth and draws in two loud breaths as if Anne's crying has made it difficult to breathe. Lombard opens her eyes and lifts her head away from the window. With a heavy gaze fixed just out of sight below the camera, Anne quietly murmurs, "Oh, my baby." Lombard inhales a deep breath to show that Anne is trying to regain her composure, indicating to the audience that this brief burst of emotion was a cathartic release in her otherwise controlled demeanor. Anne slowly turns away from the window with her lips pursed together in the way Lombard typically does to indicate that her character is holding back their tears. She turns her back to the camera and walks slowly toward the door she originally entered.

Although melodrama has often been criticized for its "moments of excess which provoke disbelief, irony, laughter,"[43] Jane Feuer argues that, in fact, the so-called "overblown bad acting" in such iconic melodramas as *The Bad and the Beautiful* (Vincente Minnelli, 1953), *Magnificent Obsession*

---

[43] John Mercer and Martin Shingler, *Melodrama: Genre, Style, Sensibility* (London: Wallflower Press, 2004), 21.

(Douglas Sirk, 1954), and *Written on the Wind* (Douglas Sirk, 1956) "are in keeping with related conventions for distilling and intensifying emotion."[44] The core component of melodramatic acting is the juxtaposition between intensely emotive—what some might call overindulgent—performance signs and controlled, understated expression. Similarly, Jeremy Butler argues that in the context of television melodrama, "stylized 'over-acting' is certainly appropriate for the intensity of emotions that are portrayed."[45] Butler's idea is also relevant to cinematic melodrama and, in this case, Lombard's performance in *Vigil in the Night*. For an actress who was identified by her expressive and gesticulative comedic performance style, in the context of the traumatic events that have unfolded in the narrative—Lucy's death, the magnitude of the respiratory epidemic, the dismal working conditions in the isolation ward—her performance in this scene seems underplayed. The shot that I described rests on Lombard's emotive abilities and how she conveys her character's feelings almost without any dialog and barely any movement. Besides her initial—and very brief—hysterics, the depths of Anne's emotional torment are kept hidden just below the surface, and there is no dramatic tension in her performance between over-expression and constraint. Lombard consciously over-performs in her screwball comedies for comic or narrative effect; in this scene, it is almost as if she holds back from offering the type of emotional outburst one would expect a "Carole Lombard character" to express. While in screwball she typically uses her entire body, this is perhaps her most understated and psychologically-driven performance. Interestingly, Lombard does not actually shed any tears in this scene, and instead relies solely on varying facial expressions in this close-up shot to convey the range of Anne's torment. She offers a performance that is somewhat underwhelming given the emotional gravity of the scene and the intense expressivity that is resonant with her more recognizable comic acting style.

Aesthetically, too, the film is an outlier among Lombard's body of work. Fitting with the sterility of the hospital, all of the glamorous markers of Lombard's stardom have been stripped away. This is arguably the most "natural" of Lombard's on-screen looks, likely done in an effort to underscore the film's somber narrative and Anne's working-class milieu. She appears to wear almost no makeup—most noticeably no lipstick—and her costumes consist of either a stark black and white nurse's uniform or a conservative tweed skirt suit. Lombard's lack of makeup reveals her under-eye bags and laugh lines around her mouth, imbuing her image with a mature weariness. They also add a fatigued look to Lombard's face that complements her character's emotional distress. Meanwhile, Lombard's costumes desexualize

---

[44]Jane Feuer, "Melodrama, Serial Form and Television Today," *Screen* Vol. 25, No. 1 (January–February 1984): 10.
[45]Jeremy G. Butler, *Television Style* (New York: Routledge, 2010), 42.

FIGURES 5.7 & 5.8 *In* Vigil in the Night *(George Stevens, 1940) Lombard plays an English nurse named Anne Lee, who faces a smallpox epidemic in her underfunded hospital. This is arguably Lombard's most unglamorous and complex role, allowing her to demonstrate her performative versatility.*

her body: they are functional rather than beautiful or chic, and are in keeping with the rigors of Anne's profession. The whiteness of the nurse's jacket in this scene could represent Anne's purity and tireless determination, for she does whatever she can to save the ailing children. The simplicity of Lombard's appearance here is a considerable departure from her previous films, but it mirrors the minimalism of her dramatic performance.

Released in February 1940, *Vigil in the Night* received mixed reviews including one from *Variety* that claimed the film "lacks buildup of essential punches in dramatic scenes."[46] The same reviewer suggests that the film is "too sombre and depressing in dramatic content for general audiences," but praises its attention to factual detail regarding the nursing profession.[47] Today, the film is now considered "one of the most realistic hospital movies ever made."[48] Reviews for Lombard were generally positive, with one *Photoplay* critic praising her performance as evidence of "how versatile an actress she is."[49] RKO's publicity focused on the film's realism and the three main leads' dramatic performances,[50] but despite the pre-release buildup and good reviews for Lombard and the cast, box office returns were dismal and RKO recorded a profit of merely $82,000.[51] According to Wes Gehring, this was further proof that "the movie-going public would support Lombard only in comedy."[52] For a public who was familiar with seeing Lombard partake in rousing physical comedy scenes in breezy screwball films, her subdued performance in *Vigil in the Night* likely proved too anomalous to accept; Anne Lee is the opposite of the sassy, lighthearted persona Lombard established both on and off screen, and the criticisms that the film "lacked" the essential dramatic punches gives rise to the idea that Lombard underperformed Anne's grief in a way that is often atypical of the melodramatic genre.

They Knew What They Wanted (*Garson Kanin, 1940*)

Carole Lombard's last dramatic venture was in the 1940 adaptation of the 1924 Pulitzer Prize winning Sidney Howard play, *They Knew What They Wanted*. She plays Amy Peters, a San Francisco waitress who begins

---

[46]"Vigil In The Night," *Variety*, Wednesday, February 7, 1940, 14.
[47]"Vigil In The Night," 14.
[48]Gehring, 200.
[49]"The Shadow Stage: A Review of The New Pictures," *Photoplay*, April 1940, 95.
[50]For an example of this, see: *Vigil in the Night* advertisement, *Variety*, Wednesday, February 5, 1940, 12–13; *Vigil in the Night* advertisement, *Photoplay*, March 1940, 1.
[51]Jewel, 57.
[52]Gehring, 200.

a correspondence courtship with an Italian Napa Valley vineyard owner named Tony Patucci (Charles Laughton). Tony is illiterate and has asked his playboy farm hand, Joe (William Gargan), to write the letters on his behalf. Tony sends Amy a photo of Joe in fear she would not find him attractive. When he sends a letter asking Amy to marry him, she half-heartedly accepts because she believes it is a way for her to escape her menial life. After arriving at the Patucci vineyard, Amy soon discovers the real Tony and reluctantly decides to stay. In a drunken display of overconfidence and machismo during a celebration on the eve of their wedding, Tony falls off the roof of their house while playing a game with his friends, and breaks both legs. The couple decides to postpone their nuptials until he recovers. Joe and Amy help to nurse Tony back to health, but growing sexual tension gets the better of them and they sleep together. When Amy discovers she is pregnant, she decides to leave Tony and have the baby on her own.

Amy is a more hardened, cynical, and psychologically complex character than Lombard's other dramatic or comic heroines. In Amy and Joe's final confrontation scene, Lombard's performance skillfully captures the depths of her character's vulnerability. The scene begins with a long shot of Joe quietly walking into Amy's bedroom. She is in the foreground packing her bag, determined to leave Tony while he is asleep in the next room. The film cuts to a medium close-up of Lombard's face. Her glaring eyes reveal the resentment Amy feels toward Joe, and with a snarl to indicate Amy's distain she says, "What'd you come back for, I don't want nothin' from you!" Joe reminds Amy that she has no place to go, and she replies in an affirmative yet sarcastic whisper, "I bet that makes you feel real bad, you being so noble." Lombard spits out her words and draws out "bad," emphasizing the flat "a" noise to give the word its full effect. It should be noted that throughout her performance Lombard speaks with a casual speech pattern, drops the ends of words and uses slang, all of which reminds us of Amy's working-class background. Lombard played working-class characters earlier in her career—for example, Regi in *Hands Across the Table* and Maggie King in *Swing High, Swing Low*—however, for these performances she never significantly changed her speaking voice. Instead, Lombard only alters her accent and vocal intonation when she plays upper class characters—or characters pretending to be of the upper class—such as her self-consciously exaggerated Garbo impersonation in *The Princess Comes Across* or her reoccurring clipped, posh accent in *No More Orchids* and *Lady by Choice*. Lombard's decision to modify Amy's vocal pattern adds depth to her characterization and shows just how essential her voice was to her multilayered dramatic performance.

The venom dripping in Lombard's voice conveys Amy's bitterness and frustration with Joe for getting in the way of her future. In a reverse shot of Joe, he flippantly comments that he came back to marry Amy. Cutting back to Amy, her face softens. Lombard's eyes widen and mouth gapes open slightly—a reoccurring Lombard performance trait in emotionally tense scenes—and her shoulders—previously tensely hunched—drop down in relief. Her watery eyes twinkle as if she is about to cry and in a softer, breathy voice Amy quietly asks, "You'd [sigh] honest to goodness marry me?" In the same over-the-shoulder close-up of Amy, we hear Joe say, "I gotta do what's right. You got nothin' to worry about. Me? Well, I'm satisfied I'm doing the right thing." As he says the line, Lombard's face hardens and her eyes narrow to show Amy's rage. Amy grimaces to reveal her clenched teeth, reaches her right arm up and slaps Joe's face.

Amy whispers incredulously "I'd marry you?" through gritted teeth. Lombard's low voice cracks as she continues, "A few minutes I lose my head, I do something I'll be ashamed for the rest of my life." She says the line quickly with a quivering voice similar to the scene in *In Name Only*. However, while in that scene Lombard was emoting Julie's hopelessness, here she couples the quivering with a clipped delivery to indicate Amy's embarrassment. In two very different scenes, the same vocal effect is modified by the speed and tone of her delivery to convey contrasting emotions. Amy repeats, "I'd marry you. You think I sunk so low where I can't get insulted?" Lombard says the "I'd marry you" line with the same disbelief as she did before. The mirroring provides a roundness to her outburst but also confirms Amy's impassioned bitterness toward Joe's insincere proposal.

In what is arguably the climax of the film, Lombard vacillates her emotional range to convey a mix of frustration and indignation. Her performance suggests that Amy's resentment is partially self-inflicted because she admits that in a moment of weakness, she threw away her stable future with Tony. She has not yet been reconciled with her own actions, a fact that she admits when she says she will have to live with her shame for the rest of her life. But Amy's anger is also clearly directed at Joe, whose line "I'm doing the right thing" reveals he will marry her not out of genuine desire, but to save her from the humiliation of having to raise a child out of wedlock. Amy realizes that Joe never loved her, and that his proposal was a half-hearted gesture out of duty. Lombard's performance imbues Amy with a hard edge and sense of lethargy that reflects her exasperation with life. And while I do not mistake her as being a cold character, Lombard's performance radiates a raw weariness that is in keeping with the deprivation of Amy's social and economic conditions.

Critical reviews of *They Knew What They Wanted* were generally positive, and it was celebrated as a "class picture … guaranteed to delight the emotionally inclined."[53] The same reviewer praised Lombard, calling her performance "perhaps the best dramatic bit she has done."[54] However,

---

[53] "Film Reviews," *Variety*, Wednesday, October 9, 1940, 16.
[54] Ibid.

another early *Variety* review predicted that most of the film's box office business would derive only from the immense publicity attention given to the film by RKO.[55] In keeping with the vineyard setting, the studio hired young women dressed in Italian style costumes to stomp on grapes at the San Francisco premiere.[56] Additionally, during the filming Lombard and Laughton were invited to tour Berringer Vineyards in St. Helena, California, a visit that was publicized by studio publicity. RKO's efforts were modestly rewarded, and the studio recorded a profit of $291,000.[57] Likely disappointed by the string of box office failures—and considering that Lombard had invested in several of her dramatic projects—*They Knew What They Wanted* marked the last of her dramatic films. Less than a month after the film's release in October 1940, *Variety* reported that Lombard's next film would be a return to screwball comedy in Alfred Hitchcock's *Mr. & Mrs. Smith*.[58]

Conclusion

Through these textual analyses it becomes clear that Lombard consistently modifies several basic facial and vocal performance tactics in each of her dramatic films, all of which are aided by the habitual use of the close-up. In contrast to screwball comedy, which relies on wide shots to frame an actor's physical performance, melodrama uses close-ups to convey subtle facial expressions. These close-ups allowed Lombard to draw upon acting techniques that were seldom part of her screwball repertoire. Though none of these dramatic films were ultimately successful at the box office, they gave her a chance to act in non-comedy genres and to extend her skills beyond the realm of screwball comedy.

At a time when Lombard's own personal life was changing, these films had a different pace and gave her career a new direction. The mixed critical praise and lukewarm box office returns suggest that Lombard's star persona was far too synonymous with screwball comedy for the public to accept her in anything other than a comic role. This, of course, is significant because it is another example that confirms the "star-character" symbiosis that Dyer outlines as being central to Hollywood stardom. With the press and the studios positioning Lombard's stardom in relation to screwball—compounded by references to her early career in slapstick

---

[55]"Lombard–Laughton Find Good Preem," *Variety*, Wednesday, October 16, 1940, 10.

[56]"Grape-Crushing Stunt For Lombard-Laughton," *Variety*, Wednesday, October 9, 1940, 8.

[57]Richard B. Jewell, *RKO Pictures: A Titan is Born* (Los Angeles: University of California Press, 2012), 211.

[58]"Time For Comedy," *Variety*, Wednesday, November 6, 1940, 3.

as a way to validate her screwball proficiency—it is no wonder that the public was reluctant to accept Lombard as a dramatic actress. Her dramatic image fundamentally betrayed everything that, for years, they had been told Lombard represented: she was no longer the kooky, free spirit, but instead, a more serious and sober woman. Given the fact that other classical Hollywood stars transitioned from genre to genre, one could reasonably argue that had she lived and continued to work in drama, perhaps over time the public and critical consensus would have shifted—but such a theory is merely conjecture. What can be stated more definitely is that these dramatic films are tremendously important to Lombard's career as a whole, and to a broader understanding of the evolution of her performance style. The study of Lombard's facial and vocal performances confirms that she was just as proficient a dramatic actress as she was a comedian, and that these films should be considered alongside her screwball comedies when assessing the breadth of her career.

6

"If women ruled the world": Lombard as protofeminist

Throughout her career, Carole Lombard was consistently outspoken about contemporaneous political and social issues. As a staunch progressive and vocal supporter of President Franklin Delano Roosevelt's New Deal policies, Lombard was someone whose politics were central to public discourse about her star image, and she personified the protofeminist ideology of the prewar and wartime periods. I define her as a protofeminist because many of her political and social statements predate the second-wave feminist movement yet were very much in line with the second wave's focus; Lombard did not have a larger social movement in which to couch her feminist ideology. And yet, there was an obvious ideological contradiction in Lombard's protofeminism, largely due to the trappings of traditional femininity and glamour that were essential for a Hollywood actress, and the extent to which her stardom was contained by the cultural framework and ideological apparatus of the Hollywood studio system. This chapter therefore outlines Lombard's political and social activism, making note where her politics overlapped with her status as a Hollywood movie star.

Lombard's social and political engagement can be seen within a broader context of Hollywood activism, a topic which has become the center of renewed scholarly attention. Hollywood stars have been embedded in politics since the early days of cinema, and their influence both on policy and public opinion has, in many cases, been profound. As Stephen J. Ross explains, movie stars not only "show us how to dress, look, or love. They teach us how to think and act politically."[1] The ten

---

[1] Steven J. Ross, *Hollywood Left and Right: How Movie Stars Shaped American Politics* (New York: Oxford University Press, 2011), 5.

Hollywood stars that Ross profiles in his book, including individuals with such diverging ideologies as Ronald Reagan and Jane Fonda, all held the belief that as public figures, they had an obligation to take part in political life, and use their platform to further political and social causes.[2] Lombard also shared this sentiment, advocating at different times in her career for women's rights in the workplace, increased representation of women in politics, and economic independence as a solution to gender inequality.

On the other side of the spectrum, there are cases of Hollywood stars who have suffered career ending repercussions for their activism, the most well known being the directors, writers, and actors that were targets of the red-baiting House Un-American Activities Committee (HUAC) investigations in 1947.[3] Ross offers the example of Charlie Chaplin, whose left leaning politics of the 1920s through the 1940s resulted in him being investigated by the FBI for allegedly promoting Communist causes in his films,[4] eventually leading to the actor's exile from the United States in 1952. Unlike Chaplin, whose politics were seen as a threat to the very fabric of American life and social values, Lombard did not face such a backlash. Although she was vocal about her politics, Lombard's views were made to appear "safe" by her screen persona and the gender politics of screwball comedy. To that end, I argue that her activism was framed—if not, exploited—by the Hollywood system to reaffirm Lombard's screwball image. If, as I have argued in earlier chapters, the screwball woman is defined by her rejection of patriarchal order and gender conventions, then Lombard's political activism makes sense; her outspoken and progressive nature "fit" the unruly screwball mold. Couching Lombard's star persona against the political continued even in death. On January 16, 1942, less than a month after the deadly attack on Pearl Harbor and the U.S.'s formal declaration of war, Lombard died in a plane crash while returning to Los Angeles from a war bonds tour in her home state of Indiana. The timing of her premature death inspired patriotic fervor across the nation and imbued her star persona a deep-rooted tragic patriotism that recontextualizes some posthumous interpretations of her career and star image in relation to her death.

---

[2] Ibid.

[3] Most notably, the Hollywood Ten, a group of ten directors and writers who were brought before the House Un-American Activities Committee because of their alleged affiliations with the Communist party. After collectively refusing to testify, these men were cited for contempt of Congress, fined and jailed. They, along with others, also found themselves on what is known as the "Hollywood blacklist," which prevented them from working at any of the major studios in an official capacity.

[4] Ross, 12.

Lombard the protofeminist

I have previously argued that Carole Lombard was "ahead of her time" in terms of her projection of a modern type of femininity. In many of her films including the majority of her screwball comedies, her characters address gender and female equality in terms that pushed the boundaries, particularly for the way they use physical comedy—a form of comic expression typically reserved for male performers—to react against a social or personal injustice or to rebel against equally dominant male characters.[5] As I have discussed in chapters 3 and 4, off the screen Lombard represented the 1930s modern woman, someone who cultivated a balance between her "masculine" and "feminine" characteristics. She was outspoken on a variety of feminist issues such as women's role in the home and workplace, equal pay, and increased representation of women in politics. In the 1930s and early 1940s, Lombard was one of the few Hollywood stars to promote these progressive—for their time—ideas, and I would argue that Lombard existed in this space between the first and second-wave feminist movements—many of her views are a natural extension of the suffrage of the nineteenth and early twentieth centuries while predating the concerns of sexual, political, and reproductive rights of the second wave. As such, I identify her, to a certain extent, as a protofeminist: someone whose feminist ideology was anomalous to the historical time in which she lived. While there are very contradictory aspects to Lombard's feminist impulses, on the whole her stardom represented an ideology that was generally progressive.

We cannot separate Lombard's protofeminism from the material and industrial context of the 1930s Hollywood studio system. Lombard was an independent and business-savvy star, and someone who ultimately changed the nature of star labor within Hollywood. In her groundbreaking study of freelance labor and gender, Emily Carman identifies Lombard as one of several actresses of the 1930s including Janet Gaynor, Miriam Hopkins, Irene Dunne, and Constance Bennett who "chose to leave their 'parent' studios when their contracts were up for renewal by mid decade, seeking independence and greater control over their careers."[6] These women "worked with independent producers, signed non-exclusive and non-option contracts, made a limited number of

---

[5] For example, in both *Mr. & Mrs. Smith* and *True Confession* (Ruggles, 1937), her characters are told they cannot work because they are married. In the former film, Ann's termination from a department store stems from a "company policy not to employ married women" in an effort to "aid the unemployment crisis." In the latter film, Helen's husband, Ken, forbids her from accepting a job and tells her that it is a husband's duty to take care of his wife.

[6] Emily Carman, "Independent Stardom: Female Film Stars and the Studio System of the 1930s," *Women's Studies* Vol. 37, No. 6 (2008): 585.

pictures at a time, or negotiated for a percentage of their film's profits."[7] Lombard's stardom was cultivated by the studio system, but by the late 1930s Carman notes that she "leveraged her popularity"[8] and rejected institutionalized contractual labor to become one of the first Hollywood stars to work as a freelance actor. Freelancing proved advantageous for Lombard because it gave her more authority over her image and the types of roles she played and enabled her to articulate the conditions of her labor in front of and behind the camera. Her decision foregrounded the "independent stardom movement of 1930s Hollywood" that "broke new ground to help establish practices that have been commonplace for A-list stars" in today's film industry.[9] She was also the first star to propose profit participation, and in 1938 renegotiated her 1937 three-picture "percentage deal" contract with Selznick International Pictures which gave her a reduced salary of $100,000 in exchange for a 20 percent cut of the distributor's gross of $1.6 to $1.7 million, and subsequent smaller percentages as the gross increased. This contract also included a "no loan-out" clause, the right to employ the costume designer of her choice—Travis Banton—and all legal rights to her image including those used in advertisements and other promotions. Similarly, her three-picture contract with RKO in 1938 gave her a reduced salary of $75,000 plus a net percentage deal of an additional $75,000 from domestic and international box office profits,[10] as well as any "speciality" road-show screenings and an "arbitrated share of the studio block-booking packages of her films."[11] It also contained other terms including a billing clause, story and co-star approval, and the right to employ her personal publicist, Russell Birdwell.[12] Lombard's shrewd business sense and collaborative relationship with producers and studios[13] became a major component of her independent star persona, and the unprecedented degree of control she retained over her career challenged the "hierarchical and paternalistic structure" of the industry, as well as the historical narrative and periodization about freelance labor in the Hollywood studio system.[14]

Fundamental to Lombard's independent star persona is the idea of a female star with what Carman calls "male business sense."[15] *Photoplay*

---

[7] Ibid, 585.
[8] Carman, 2016, 39.
[9] Ibid, 24.
[10] Ibid, 158.
[11] Ibid, 2.
[12] Ibid, 158.
[13] Ibid, 3.
[14] Ibid, 4.
[15] Carman, 2008, 609.

columnist Hart Seymore dubbed her as the "perfect example of a modern Career Girl,"[16] which Carman explains was based on Lombard's capability to "live by the logical premise that women have equal rights with men."[17] As I briefly discussed earlier, the evocative 1937 *Photoplay* article "How I Live By A Man's Code" considers Lombard's independent female star persona by publishing her "rules" for how to be successful in business and at home. Lombard advises women to "play fair [with men] ... don't burn over criticism—stand up to it like a man" and "be consistent" in work and play,[18] statements that simultaneously champion equality and maintain gender difference. She goes on to explain that she "doesn't believe in a man's world," and encourages women to "work—and like it." She adds, "All women should have something worthwhile to do, and cultivate efficiency at it, whether it be housekeeping or raising chickens. Working women are interesting women ..."[19] Carman writes that such advice "implies that women would be wise to adapt Lombard's strategy" if they too want to succeed in the business world.[20]

According to Carman, Lombard's independent female star persona emerged when she "attained greater professional autonomy in the mid-1930s."[21] The gender implications of physical comedy and the screwball genre strategically fit Lombard's star persona because she was able to perform female independence on screen in a way that complemented her off-screen personality. There was, therefore, an ideological imperative for the studios to promote Lombard as an independent star by the mid 1930s, for it symbiotically brought together the "real" and "reel" sides of her star persona. We cannot ignore the fact that the *Photoplay* article was published in 1937; having just made *My Man Godfrey* (1936) and *Nothing Sacred* (1937), Lombard was at the height of her screwball fame. Although Carman notes that Lombard was the "ultimate publicity hound" who "actively courted various studio publicists to keep her name constantly appearing in fan discourse,"[22] it was likely no coincidence that such an article was published when it was. As Anthony Slide reminds us, it was the studios that determined which stories got published,[23] so we must view the "How I Live by a Man's Code" article with the understanding that it

---

[16] Hart Seymore, "Carole Lombard tells: 'How I Live By A Man's Code'," *Photoplay*, June 1937, 12.
[17] Carman, 608.
[18] Seymore, 78.
[19] Ibid.
[20] Carman, 609.
[21] Ibid, 598.
[22] Ibid, 113.
[23] Anthony Slide, *Inside the Hollywood Fan Magazine: A History of Star Makers, Fabricators, and Gossip Mongers* (Jackson: University Press of Mississippi, 2010), 8.

FIGURE 6.1 *In this June 1937* Photoplay *article, Carole Lombard offers her "rules" for women to be successful at work and home. These types of publicity materials worked in tandem with her screen image to reinforce her independent star persona. (Copyright holder unknown.)*

was published for a particular reason—to reaffirm Lombard's independent, screwball persona—and designed to elicit a specific response from the fan magazine readers—to view Lombard's independent star as indistinguishable from the Lombard heroines they saw on screen. Ultimately, this article rationalized Lombard's on-screen screwball persona as a natural extension of the private, "real" Carole Lombard.

From the perspective of today's feminist awareness, the *Photoplay* article is not without issues, the most glaring being that it overlooks the fact that Lombard's independence was achieved in privileged circumstances out of reach for the majority of American women. During the 1930s, countries such as the U.S., Canada, and Sweden threatened to limit married women's rights to work, arguing that "working married women not only robbed men of jobs but also created unfair competition by accepting low wages."[24] Married or widowed women like Ann Smith in *Mr. & Mrs. Smith* often faced "outright hostility" when trying to enter the labor force, and "discrimination against married women forced single women to delay marriage ... in order to keep their jobs."[25] Lombard's advice—though in principle sounds well meaning—was impractical and economically unfeasible for the average American woman. By 1937 Lombard had garnered considerable star power in Hollywood, and as Carman's book makes clear, she was in the advantageous position to articulate the conditions of her labor and to demand a high salary. The *Photoplay* article also ignores the years of contractual labor and studio control that Lombard endured to achieve her lucrative position. It depicts Lombard as an inspirational yet fundamentally unattainable figure for the average female reader who also strives to become financially independent and thus exposes the ordinary/extraordinary dichotomy that Dyer argues mobilizes public fascination with stars.[26]

Moreover, while the article advocates equality, it does so only to a point. Paradoxically, Lombard's star persona also upheld conservative gender ideology through her glamorous and overtly feminine physical appearance, as well as her widely publicized acceptance of domesticity and motherhood in the late 1930s and early 1940s.[27] In this case, Lombard's effort at championing gender equality gets called into question by the injunction to "be feminine." This strategy was likely conceived by Lombard's publicist[28] and the fan magazines to contextualize and make palatable her atypical business expertise by arguing that she also demonstrates what Jane Gaines calls "correct female sexual behavior."[29] Seymore reveals how Lombard adopted an assertive tone and confident business sense, but explains that

---

[24] Barbara Hobson, "Women's Collective Agency, Power Resources and the Framing of Citizenship," in *Extending Citizenship, Reconfiguring States*, eds. Michael P. Hanagan and Charles Tilly (Oxford: Rowman & Littlefield Publishers, Inc., 1999), 157.

[25] Melanie Buddle, *The Business of Women: Marriage, Family, and Entrepreneurship in British Columbia, 1901–51* (Vancouver: UBC Press, 2010), 39. See also: Leslie J. Reagan, "When Abortion Was a Crime: Reproduction and the Economy in the Great Depression," in *Women's America: Refocusing The Past*, eds. Linda K. Kerber, Jane Sharon De Hart, Cornelia Hughes Dayton, Judy Tzu-Chun Wu (Oxford: Oxford University Press, 2016), 451.

[26] Richard Dyer, *Stars* (London: BFI Publishing, 1998), 47.

[27] In an interview given shortly after her marriage to Gable, Lombard famously said that she was eager to retire and "let Pa be the star. I'll stay home and darn the socks and look after the kids." See: "Two Happy People: Part IV," *Movie and Radio Guide*, May 1940, page unknown.

[28] When the *Photoplay* article was published, Lombard was already working as a freelance actress, and her publicity was handled by the Myron Selznick's talent agency, Joyce-Selznick Ltd. See: Carman, 70.

[29] Jane Gaines, "War, Women, and Lipstick: Fan Mags in the Forties," *Heresies* Vol. 5, No. 2 (1985): 44.

she was only able to become an independent "career girl" by consciously maintaining her feminine proclivities and appearance. The article points to the ideological contradictions that Lombard was operating in: it is reflective of her profession, because maintaining a traditionally "feminine" and glamorous image was essential for a Hollywood actress. One can therefore understand that the limits of her protofeminism and her advocacy of gender difference stems from the material reality of her career and the ideological constraints of the period. And while Lombard was consistently outspoken in articulating her social politics, it is important not to be anachronistic: she was not a feminist theoretician but a movie star, and her feminism was necessarily restricted to the available discourses of the time and thus appears somewhat contradictory.

Comparing Lombard to contemporary feminist comedians exposes further the limits of Lombard's rhetoric. Linda Mizejewski explains that by the early 2000s "women were increasingly visible in the comedy scene" and that the distinction between being a pretty comic and being funny became less culturally irrelevant.[30] Comic transgression has always been a challenge for female comedians, but those working in the post 2000s period like Tina Fey, Amy Poehler, Samantha Bee, and Hannah Gadsby more often than not write their own material, which bestows them with agency over their work that actresses from the classical period like Lombard or Lucille Ball could not claim.[31] Lombard differs from these comediennes primarily because she had no large-scale existent societal movement to frame her feminist rhetoric and, more importantly, because she was rarely the author of her own publicity. She may have cooperated with publicists and studio press departments, but ultimately her ideology was mediated and contextualized by the columnists, press outlets, and studio publicity departments that were in control of shaping the discourse around her star persona. The *Photoplay* article goes to great lengths to downplay the potentially radical and transgressive undertones of her ideological stance, and Lombard's "feminine" appearance redeems the threat of her "masculine" mindset. Her rules may run counter to conservative gender ideology, but they are safely contained by the warning that women should not forget their "natural" femininity, which she defines as a woman's privilege to "choose the right shade of lipstick" and be "insane about a certain brand of perfume."[32] This advice foregrounds outward displays of beauty and the consumption of makeup and fashion products as barometers of a woman's feminine worth. The logic of the article suggests that a woman's "masculine" business sense will best serve her as a consumer and in the way that she conforms to conservative expectations of physical beauty.

---

[30] Linda Mizejewski, *Pretty/Funny: Women Comedians and Body Politics* (Austin: University of Texas Press, 2014), 2.
[31] Ibid, 5.
[32] Seymore, 78.

The tension between Lombard's transgressive and conventional gender politics can also be seen in the discourse surrounding other female stars of the period. For example, Lies Lanckman explains that while fan magazines of the mid to late 1920s focused on Norma Shearer's "well-bred" and respectable middle-class background, Shearer's star image was later complicated by her roles in Pre-Code films like *The Divorcee* (Robert Z. Leonard, 1930), *A Free Soul* (Clarence Brown, 1931), and *Strangers May Kiss* (George Fitzmaurice, 1931) in which she played sexually active unmarried women.[33] However, Shearer avoided condemnation because her ideology and on-screen sexually liberated image were outweighed by her "stable" marriage to MGM executive, Irving Thalberg,[34] and familial background.[35] Like the balance between the progressive discourse surrounding Shearer's screen persona and star image, Lombard's contradictory statements "Be feminine" and "be a man about it" exposes the delicate compromise between gender identity and female self-sufficiency, and delineates the possibility that women in the 1930s could be as knowledgeable and successful in the workforce as men in their own right.

As I have demonstrated, the transgressive nature of her protofeminist ideology were often safely contained within a larger patriarchal discourse, a fact that becomes even clearer when we examine the structure, content, and reaction to Lombard's speech in an episode of her 1939 ill-fated radio show, *The Circle*. Touted as the radio version of the famed Algonquin Round Table of the 1920s, *The Circle*, a Kellogg sponsored program, was an hour-long variety radio show that aired on Sundays nights on the NBC-Red network from January to June of 1939.[36] Lombard starred alongside other notable Hollywood stars such as Cary Grant, Ronald Colman, and Groucho and Chico Marx. The show was heavily publicized in the months prior to its January 15, 1939 premiere as a "roundtable discussion" show where "participants will mull over choice bits of poetry, philosophy, anecdotes, and general conversation in an atmosphere of informal and impromptu discussion and music."[37] Despite the enthusiastic media hype, including one *Radio Mirror* magazine spread that described it as "the season's most star-studded show,"[38] *The Circle* was an immediate flop, with critics citing poor scripts and internal conflicts as reasons for its failure.[39]

---

[33] Lies Lanckman, "'What Price Widowhood?': The Faded Stardom of Norma Shearer," in *Lasting Screen Stars: Images that Fade and Personas that Endure*, eds. Lucy Bolton and Julie Lobalzo-Wright (London: Palgrave Macmillan, 2016), 76.
[34] Given Thalberg's power and influence across Hollywood, it is unlikely that fan magazines would ever dare to publish stories that portrayed his wife in a negative or compromised light.
[35] Ibid, 78.
[36] "Join the Kellogg Show," *Broadcast*, January 11, 1939, pg. 51.
[37] "Roundtable Discussion Marks Kellogg Program," *Broadcast*, January 11, 1939, 11.
[38] "Colossal is the word for it," *Radio Mirror*, March 1939, 24–25.
[39] *Broadcast*, March 11, 1939, 49.

Just a month after its premiere, on February 15, 1939 *Variety* reported that Colman had walked out and that both Grant and Lombard[40] would follow suit because "the material being written for them ain't what it should be."[41]

On the only surviving episode, originally broadcast on January 22, 1939, Lombard delivered her most radical diatribe entitled "If Women Ruled." The segment begins with Colman asking Lombard for a "feminine point of view," to which she initially resists, saying "I know what you're after, you want me to say what I think so you and your henchmen can sit back and sneer ... You always do when women try to be intelligent." Then, Lombard adds "Because all men are women-haters at heart," a line that is both excessive in sentiment and a superficial interpretation of Lombard's gender politics, and which also exposes the heavily scripted and unnatural tone of the program. The division between Lombard—whom the cast playfully called "Our Nell"[42]—and her male co-stars' gender politics is clearly defined as being playfully adversarial.

Lombard begins with the prediction that "one day we'll have a woman President, what do you say about that?" Grant quips, "She'll never be the father of our country!", a remark that garners a loud laugh from the studio audience. Lombard sighs and replies, "Tut tut, nothing but a technicality. You're deliberately trying to belittle the idea and be-muddle the issue." She continues in a softer tone, "I know how you feel about it, you're scared. A woman will only get to be President over your dead body," to which she jokingly adds, "which might be a very good idea." Grant concedes that he would probably vote for Lombard's "hypothetical woman President." Lombard replies, "Yes, come to think of it, I guess you would. You'd want her to get elected so you could take your dimples down to Washington and profile your way into the cabinet."

Colman asks Lombard what would happen if a woman were in the White House. Lombard answers,

> I'll tell you what would happen. If women ran this world it would be a better world, if you really want to know ... It wouldn't be the kind of a

---

[40] Lombard terminated her contract in March, 1939. See: *Broadcast*, March 11, 1939, 49.

[41] "Reber Exercises Tongue and Temper; Now Kellogg 'Circle' Has No Prez," *Variety*, February 15, 1939, 27. It should be noted that neither Groucho nor Chico Marx had no such similar complaints. The same article mentions that they had their own exclusive writers. Both stayed on the program until its cancellation.

[42] "Our Nell" is a reference to the George Gershwin musical satire of the same title, which ran at the Nora Bayes Theater in New York from December 4, 1922 to January 6, 1923. It tells the story of a New England farm family involving ill-fated romance and larceny. See: Howard Pollack, *George Gershwin: His Life and Work* (Los Angeles: University of California Press, 2006), 275–278.

world that bombs kids in the streets and taxes their parents to pay for the bombs. It wouldn't be a world where people starve with a surplus of food to eat all around them.[43]

She continues to explain that the difference between men and women is that the latter are "realists," and attributes the causes of war and poverty to "male stupidity, male sentiment and male greed."[44] She concedes that "women are greedy too, but they know how to get what they want. They don't let stupid sentimental considerations get in their way." Lombard's speech ends with the simplistic assertion that "Men are children, women are realists. Take it or leave it, gents, take it or leave it!"[45]

Lombard's speech had the potential to be a radical critique of the gender inequality in national and international politics. However, *The Circle*'s writers fail to engage in any sort of fruitful debate and instead, the segment is marred by both the content of Lombard's speech and the dismissive discourse preceding and immediately following it. Given Lombard's progressive ideology, it is within reason to suggest she would have agreed with her scripted prediction of a future female president. However, identifying women's greatness by their emotional and psychological superiority over men rings hollow, and on the whole, the speech reduces what could have been a fruitful discussion about the future of women in politics to a series of corny jokes and stereotypes. Even more problematic is that the speech was not written by Lombard herself, but by the show's—presumably male—writers. Lombard was simply the messenger of simplistic gendered rhetoric. Therefore, Lombard's gender politics once again get muddled, this time by a script that attempts to reproduce and extend her protofeminist persona while not actually taking into account the details of such a position.

The male stars' reactions to Lombard's speech safely contain her feminist message with a pejorative and dismissive tone. Immediately following Lombard's last line, Grant sighs and says "Phew, my my, what an orator our little Nell turned out to be!" Groucho quips, "Anybody wanna play a game of rummy?" to which Lombard replies indignantly, "Goodnight!" Grant continues, "Tsk tsk tsk, well well our Nell has gone off in a huff." His line is immediately followed by a barbershop quartet singing a jazzy song called "Our Nell," whose lyrics playfully plead with Lombard to return to the microphone. Their collective half-mocking tone, coupled with Grant's later line, "There, there little one, we really appreciated your speech" infantilizes Lombard and removes any threat of active feminist impulses from an already watered down push for gender equality. Like Lombard's screwball characters, whose transgressive physical comedy is almost always

---

[43] "If Women Ruled," *Radio Mirror*, May 1939, 31.
[44] Ibid.
[45] Ibid.

undermined by her own glamorous femininity, Lombard's speech—itself not particularly convincing—is challenged by dismissive rhetoric and misogyny masked as comedy.

Higher taxes, please!

While Lombard's activism primarily focused on issues related to gender and the advancement of women's roles in the public and private spheres, she also entered into contemporaneous political debates. Her most successful and explicitly political demonstration came in 1938 when she made an impassioned statement in support of President Franklin Delano Roosevelt's Revenue Act of 1935 and subsequent Revenue Act of 1937. The former, dubbed by critics as the Wealth Tax, "hoisted the top personal income-tax rate from 63 to 79 percent ..." while the latter "closed tax loopholes for individuals."[46] These bills allowed Roosevelt to keep his campaign promise of "more equitable income distribution."[47] Higher taxation for the wealthy also upheld the illusion that the "forgotten men"—veterans from the First World War—and working-class Americans would reap the benefits of New Deal economic reforms; in reality, however, the federal government collected too little revenue to offer any substantial financial assistance to those worst hit by the Depression.[48] Lombard's progressive, pro-America statement came just a year after she earned $465,000 in annual income—$150,000 per picture plus $5,000 for radio appearances[49]—a sum that made her the highest paid actress in Hollywood.[50] Although Lombard paid over $350,000 in personal income taxes in 1938, she happily confessed that after deducting various business fees and other expenses, she was left with a mere $20,000.[51] Not one to complain, she admitted:

> I have no kicks at all. Fact is I'm pretty happy about the whole thing. Twenty thousand a year is plenty for me and as for giving the government most of my income, I think that's fine. I enjoy this country. I like the parks and highways and the good schools and everything that this government does. After all, every cent anybody pays in taxes is spent to benefit him. I

---

[46] Mark Leff, *The Limits of Symbolic Reform: The New Deal and Taxation, 1933–1939* (New York: Cambridge University Press, 1984), 91–92.
[47] Ibid, 92.
[48] Ibid, 93.
[49] Adjusted for inflation, this is roughly $8 million USD in today's dollar value.
[50] Wes Gehring, *Carole Lombard: The Hoosier Tornado* (Indianapolis: Indiana Historical Society Press, 2003), 188.
[51] Frederick C. Othman, "Carole Lombard 'Glad to pay' $445,000 taxes, said," *San Jose News*, August 26, 1938, 6.

don't need $465,000 a year for myself, so why not give what I don't need to the government for improvement of this country? There's no better place to spend it."[52]

Her pro-tax stance made headlines across the country, and as Eric Hoyt explains, her attitude "anticipated the sense of patriotic tax-paying the U.S. government tried to foster among the public" when the country entered the Second World War.[53]

Lombard's unusual and unpopular support for higher taxes gave a boost to her public image.[54] Recalling Lombard's comments in an article for the *New Yorker*, Alva Johnston wrote "probably no other news item ever did so much to increase the popularity of a star."[55] It likely bolstered her popularity precisely because of the selfless patriotic stance she took regarding her extraordinarily high income. At a time when the Depression-weary public was looking for any sign of an economic reprieve, here was a star who not only celebrated reinvesting her salary into the national infrastructure, but who was admitting that the wages for Hollywood's top earners were out of sync with the rest of the population. Lombard's remaining $20,000 was still far and above the average American household income which stood at $2,116 per annum,[56] but her pleasure at seeing her country reap the benefits of her labor softened the still sizable disparity. Her "share the wealth" mentality authenticated her characteristic down-to-earth "un-Hollywood" star persona,[57] and made her a public champion of FDR's progressive domestic policies.

Patriotism and an untimely death

Lombard's final demonstration of political activism, a war bonds tour to her home state of Indiana, also turned out to be the most tragic, and one for which she paid the ultimate sacrifice. Shortly after the United States officially declared war on Japan on December 8, 1941, the Hollywood

---

[52] Ibid.
[53] Eric Hoyt, "Hollywood and the Income Tax, 1929–1955," *Film History* Vol. 22 (2010): 12.
[54] Ibid.
[55] Alva Johnston, "Public Relations – IV," *New Yorker*, September 9, 1942, 31.
[56] Cal West Med "Average U.S. Income Told," *Western Journal of Medicine* Vol. 50 (May 1939): 389.
[57] Aside from her fateful war bond rally and her championing of federal income tax, Lombard's charitable nature extended to her local community. In the late 1930s, she set up scholarships for three girls to attend the University of Southern California, and privately funded several other students' college tuitions in the Los Angeles area. See: Marian Rhea, "Lombard Unlimited," *Radio Mirror*, April 1939, 19.

community began to organize their own war effort; Lombard was one of the first Hollywood stars to offer her services. In late 1941 the Gables wrote to President Roosevelt—whom they had visited in Washington, D.C. the year prior—to "offer their services wherever needed." In a letter reply, Roosevelt expressed his gratitude but urged them to continue producing entertainment in order to upkeep wartime morale.[58] On December 10, 1941, the Hollywood Victory Committee was formed in order to provide "stage, screen, and radio performers that were not in military service a means to contribute to the war effort."[59] Clark Gable was rumored to have been feeling unsatisfied with simply continuing with his work in Hollywood,[60] and was appointed chairman of the Screen Actors Division. The first meeting was held in mid December at the Hollywood Roosevelt Hotel, where Gable expressed his hope that "every star would pledge his services."[61] Among the list of duties were war bond tours, repeating the highly successful efforts led by Hollywood stars like Mary Pickford, Douglas Fairbanks, and Charlie Chaplin during the First World War.[62]

Exactly how Lombard got involved with her fateful Midwest war bond tour is unclear. Lombard left Los Angeles on the morning of January 12 along with her mother, Bess Peters, and MGM publicity agent, Otto Winkler, heading first to Salt Lake City. The party arrived in Indianapolis on the evening of the 14th, and on the 15th proceeded to the State House Central Rotunda to sell bonds.[63] After selling an impressive $2 million worth of war bonds in a few hours, Lombard headed to the Cadle Tabernacle for a patriotic evening rally where she led the crowd in singing the national anthem. On the morning of the 16th, Lombard was said to have persuaded a reluctant Bess to fly home instead of taking their scheduled train journey. Legend has it that Bess Peters was an avid numerologist who believed that the number three was bad luck for her daughter; the combination of Carole's age (33), the flight number (TWA 3), the flight's arrival time in Los Angeles (3:00 a.m.), and their party size (3) were signs to avoid air travel.[64]

---

[58] Garceau, 140.

[59] Terry Rowan, *World War II Goes to the Movies & Television Guide* (Raleigh, NC: Lulu, 2012), 227.

[60] I am doubtful as to the veracity of this rumor. Gable was a lifelong conservative Republican and member of the Motion Picture Alliance for the Preservation of American Ideals. He stayed out of politics throughout his career—the exception of which was in 1952 when he attended a televised rally in support of General Dwight D. Eisenhower's presidential primary campaign. Gable's political activism in the late 1930s and early 1940s and his support of Roosevelt would most likely have been at the behest of Lombard.

[61] Garceau, 141.

[62] Jennifer Frost, "Dissent and Consent in the 'Good War': Hedda Hopper, Hollywood Gossip, and World War II Isolationism," *Film History* Vol. 22 (2010): 175.

[63] Matzen, 163.

[64] Swindell, 298–299.

After Bess unsuccessfully tried to talk her daughter out of taking a plane, it is rumored that the trio left their fate to a flip of a coin—a "bad luck" detail later found in the stories of tragic stars like Buddy Holly, the Big Bopper, and Richie Valens. I am suspicious as to the veracity of this story because no evidence has ever surfaced, but its continued retelling in Lombard biographies remains a persistent reminder of the tragedy and mythologizing of the final few hours before her death.

After making stops in St. Louis, Kansas City, and Albuquerque the group was informed that military personnel were given priority status and that all civilian passengers would be required to disembark.[65] According to former TWA agent Ed Knudsen, in an uncharacteristic move Lombard threw her weight around and demanded that her party should be given seats because she too was on a government appointed trip; Lombard's wishes were accommodated.[66] Already three hours late departing from Albuquerque due to poor visibility, the plane stopped in Las Vegas to refuel due to the extra weight of the passengers and cargo.[67]

Later that evening, Clark Gable received word that Lombard's plane was down just outside of Las Vegas. Gable, Carole's brother, Stuart, and Otto Winkler's wife, Jill, left immediately for Las Vegas on a flight chartered by MGM.[68] When the party arrived, Gable was escorted to the local sheriff's office where he was met by deputies and military police from the nearby McCarren Field.[69] The plane had crashed in the foothills of Table Rock Mountain just after takeoff around 7:00 p.m. Gable was eager to go up to the mountain to find Lombard but his friends and MGM publicity agents, Howard Strickling, Ralph Wheelwright, and Eddie Mannix persuaded him to remain behind. Mannix and Wheelwright made the treacherous seven-mile trek to the base of the crash site where they discovered the charred wreckage. They identified what was remaining of Lombard's severely burned and decapitated body, and sent a cable to Gable which read "No survivors. All killed instantly."[70] The sheer scope of the destruction, heavy snow, and the impassable terrain of Mt. Potosi made recovery efforts difficult, and even to this day hikers find artifacts and bodily remains strewn across

---

[65] Matzen, 189.
[66] Ibid, 191.
[67] "January 16, 1942: Transcontinental and Western Air (TWA), Douglas DC-3 (NC1946) Potosi Mountain, NV," Lost Flights: Historical Aviation Studies and Research, accessed May 9, 2015, http://www.lostflights.com/Commercial-Aviation/11642-TWA-TWA-Douglas-DC-3/5007934_mqCvFr.
[68] Michelle Morgan, *Carole Lombard: Twentieth-Century Star* (Gloucestershire: The History Press, 2016), 221.
[69] Garceau, 146.
[70] Ibid, 147.

the mountainside.⁷¹ The 1942 Civil Aeronautics Board's investigation into the crash cited the cause as pilot error,⁷² though various theories have continued to circulate including poor visibility due to government issued blackout air space,⁷³ and even a preposterous rumor that the plane was shot down by undercover Nazi agents.⁷⁴

Larry Swindell and Robert Matzen write that publicity-shy Gable had declined a war bonds tour request from New York Head of Publicity, Howard Dietz.⁷⁵ According to Swindell, Gable claimed he would be starting work on his upcoming picture, *Somewhere I'll Find You* (Wesley Ruggles, 1942) and despite offers from studio head, Louis B. Mayer, to rearrange his schedule, he refused to commit to the tour and persuaded Lombard to take his place.⁷⁶ Meanwhile Jean Garceau insists that Lombard, not Gable, was asked to lead the first national war bond tour.⁷⁷ While this may seem like an incidental detail, the former version is often used as evidence to support Gable's guilt over allegedly arguing with Lombard before her departure,⁷⁸ and the widely cited rumor that Lombard decided to take a plane rather than a train home because she discovered that Gable was having an affair with his co-star, Lana Turner⁷⁹—a claim that Turner emphatically denied.⁸⁰ This theory has been reinforced by a January 13, 1942 newspaper article that claims Lombard was to continue on to Cleveland—in Gable's home state of Ohio—from Indianapolis as part of an East Coast war bond tour.⁸¹

This article adds credence to the claim that Lombard's decision to fly home was not part of her original tour schedule, the logic being that there must have been a significant reason why she would change her plans at the last minute. It strengthens the tragic love narrative underpinning their star couple image; Gable as the heartbroken and guilt-ridden widower and

---

⁷¹Alan Bennett, "At long last, a soldier is laid to rest," *The Journal Tribune*, August 13, 2016, accessed August 20, 2016, http://m.journaltribune.com/news/2016-08-13/Front_Page/At_long_last_a_soldier_is_laid_to_rest.html#.V7hp2JMrKHp.

⁷² "Final report of January 16, 1942 accident involving NC1946, Docket No. SA-58, File No. 119-42," Adopted July 16, 1942, accessed July 26, 2016, http://ntl1.specialcollection.net/scripts/ws.dll?file&fn=8&name=*S%3A\DOT_56GB\airplane%20accidents\websearch\011642.pdf.

⁷³ "January 16, 1942: Transcontinental and Western Air (TWA), Douglas DC-3 (NC1946) Potosi Mountain, NV."

⁷⁴Henry Jaglom *My Lunches with Orson: Conversations between Henry Jaglom and Orson Welles*, ed. Peter Biskind (New York: Metropolitan Books, 2013), 62.

⁷⁵ Matzen, 145–146.

⁷⁶ Swindell, 294.

⁷⁷ Garceau, 142.

⁷⁸ Matzen, 244.

⁷⁹ Swindell, 298.

⁸⁰Lana Turner, *Lana – the Lady, the Legend, the Truth* (Boston: Dutton, 1982), 73.

⁸¹ Gladys Hobbs, "Carole is Quitting Films to Sell War Bonds," *The Desert News*, January 13, 1942, 5.

Lombard as the dutiful wife who sacrificed her life while simultaneously supporting her country and attempting to save her marriage. I am hesitant to believe this story or that she was ever scheduled to continue on to the East Coast. This war bonds trip was arranged so that Lombard could specifically visit Indiana[82] as a sort of patriotic homecoming, with only whistle stops in Salt Lake City, Ogden, Utah, and Chicago before reaching Indianapolis.[83] Furthermore, Lombard was due back in Los Angeles on Monday, January 19 for a preview screening of *To Be or Not To Be*;[84] a further East Coast trip would therefore not have been possible given that it would have taken at least three days for Lombard to return to Los Angeles by train. More generally, it is hard to accept that a person as unwaveringly patriotic and professional as Lombard would rush home because of an unsubstantiated rumor, the likes of which she would have undoubtedly been used to given her status as a public figure and Gable's reputation as a womanizer. While I do not doubt that she altered the mode of her return transportation, I do not believe that her decision to take a plane was to squash an alleged affair. Rather, as she allegedly explained to *Life* photographer Myron Davis, she wanted to return home as quickly as possible after a tiring but successful trip.[85] My opinion may be in the minority among Gable and Lombard fans, and the legend of Lombard rushing home on a plane to confront Gable persists today. It is a perspective that paints Gable in a negative light and cements the tragic twist to the romantic fable that is the Gable–Lombard marriage by leaving many questions unanswered. Because we will never know for certain why she decided to take a plane home, these largely unconfirmed stories have been allowed to fester and have blossomed into a constitutive part of the Lombard legend.

With Lombard's death fresh in the public consciousness, in the 1940s her posthumous star persona was further cemented in a discourse of patriotism through three national honors. The first was the Presidential Medal of Freedom, bestowed posthumously by Roosevelt for being the first woman killed in the line of duty.[86] Accompanying the medal sent to Gable was a note from the president saying, "She gave unselfishly of her time and talent to serve her government in peace and in war. She loved her country …"[87] The second, occurring on January 15, 1944—almost two years to the day of Lombard's death—was a solemn ceremony given by the California Shipbuilding

---

[82] Garceau, 143.
[83] Matzen, 147.
[84] Ibid, 146.
[85] "Carole Lombard Dies in Crash After Aiding U.S. Defense Bond Campaign," *LIFE*, January 26, 1942, 25.
[86] Benjamin F. Shearer, ed. *Home Front Heroes: a biographical dictionary of Americans during wartime* (Westport, CT: Greenwood Press, 2007), 533.
[87] Garceau, 151.

Corporation where over 15,000 guests watched as Clark Gable, Louis B. Mayer, Irene Dunne, and Lombard's best friend, Madalynne (Field) Lang, christened a Liberty ship as the *S.S. Carole Lombard*. The final honor came in 1946 when Clark Gable received the Silver Medal Award from the U.S. Treasury Department celebrating Lombard's "contribution of exceptional value to the great national success of the War and Victory Loans ..."[88]

Another layer of patriotism was added to Lombard's posthumous stardom thanks to Gable's highly publicized service in the Army Air Force. In 1942 on August 11, 41-year-old Gable was officially sworn in as a private at the federal building in Los Angeles. After completing basic training at Officer Candidate School in Miami, Gable served as an aerial gunner, flying five combat missions with the 8th Air Force 351st Bombardment Group.[89] He also served as a cameraman, filming footage in the United Kingdom that was used in the Army Air Force film *Combat America* (1945), which he also narrated. Although he was far older than the average army recruit, it was reported that Gable was eager to enlist because Lombard had encouraged him to do so prior to her death,[90] having allegedly sent him a telegram while on her way home from her war bonds tour that read "Pappy, you'd better get in this man's army."[91] Whether true or not, Gable's service was contextualized as being the ultimate tribute to Lombard. With each award and, in combination with the circumstances of her death and suspected motives behind Gable's wartime service, Lombard's posthumous star persona in the immediate post war period evolved from her being merely an actress who died too young, to a celebrated heroine whose patriotic actions came at the most costly sacrifice.

Conclusion

Lombard's political and social activism was often used as a marketing tool designed to carve out the contours of her independent star persona. Positioning her off-screen stardom in relation to a feminist agenda made sense in the 1930s, as such an ideology reaffirmed the unconventional characteristic attributed to her on-screen screwball persona. This analysis is not intended to dismiss Lombard's gender politics, nor am I aiming to downplay the progress she made as a business woman in Hollywood. Lombard made tremendous strides in creating a space for Hollywood actors

---

[88] Vernon L. Clark to Clark Gable, correspondence, June 18, 1946.
[89] Chrystopher J. Spicer, *Clark Gable: Biography, Filmography, Bibliography* (Jefferson, NC: McFarland & Co., Inc., 2002), 217.
[90] Ibid 66.
[91] Gabe Essoe, *The Films of Clark Gable* (New York: Citadel Press, 1970), 49.

to articulate the conditions of their labor in front of and behind the camera, and for that she should be celebrated. Overwhelmingly, however, Lombard's feminist ideology was contained by patriarchal tactics that deemed her social activism secondary to her glamorous star persona. Lombard was, first and foremost, a Hollywood star. Her politics, though progressive for their time, ultimately served a specific purpose in Hollywood and should be considered within the wider framework of the system in which she worked.

Similarly, Lombard's interest in national politics and, in particular, the war effort, were also used to contextualize her star persona in the prewar and wartime periods. Hollywood used Lombard's tragic death as an impetus to promote the war effort, encouraging the public to invest in war bonds as a way to "Buy a share in America."[92] With the creation of Roosevelt's propaganda agency, the Office of War Information, in June 1942, the federal government "was able to exercise considerable influence over the content of wartime Hollywood movies"[93] through script consultations and the ability to grant or withhold seals for international film exhibition. As such, Lombard's war bonds tour and her death became a persistent reminder of Hollywood's role in the Allied war effort, and her patriotism thus became the ultimate symbol of personal sacrifice for the preservation of democracy and freedom. As these examples demonstrate, Lombard's politics were co-opted at both an industrial and national level as a matter of economics—to sell movies—and national interest—to encourage public support for the war effort. Such instances demonstrate the role of political ideology to Hollywood stardom, and how a star's politics can inform our reading of their public persona.

---

[92] *Carole Lombard's Life Story*, 1942, 35.
[93] Clayton R. Koppes and Gregory D. Black, *Hollywood Goes to War: Patriotism, Movies and the Second World War from 'Ninotchka' to 'Mrs. Miniver'*. (London: Tauris Parke Paperback, 2000), viii.

Conclusion

Lombard's legacy (1942–present)

Throughout this book I have made the case that screwball comedy was a significant, but not singular, influence on Carole Lombard's star persona. From the beginning of her career in the mid 1920s to her death in 1942, her performances spanned various genres and her accompanying star persona evolved in tandem with her on-screen image. By expanding my analysis to encompass the breadth of Lombard's filmography as well as the progression of her star persona, I have challenged the temptation to contextualize her stardom in relation only to screwball comedy. In doing so, I have also highlighted Lombard's talents in other genres such as slapstick comedy and melodrama. Traits most associated with her screwball heroines like physical comedy, feisty comic timing, and confidence are but a fraction—albeit an important one—of her performance idiolect. Lombard's characters are tenacious, determined, and expressive, but are also prone to emotional vulnerability and occasional stubbornness—a humanizing combination that, in turn, made Lombard an endearing and likable cultural figure.

The larger goal of this book is to challenge the prevailing discourse about Lombard as a performer and star, and to try to understand why she resonated—and still resonates—so profoundly as a screwball comedian. Approaching Lombard's stardom from a temporal and historical distance means that I have access to the evolving discourse surrounding her public and private persona. During Lombard's lifetime, her career and star persona evolved much more significantly than previously thought, and I have made the case that her rise to screwball stardom by the mid 1930s was born out of circumstance, luck, and trial and error. In chapter 1 I demonstrated how Lombard first gained attention in Hollywood in the late 1920s as a slapstick comedian. Her tenure as a Paramount Studios starlet in the early 1930s, the focus of chapter 2, resulted in a series of generically diverse film roles, and a largely unsuccessful attempt at evoking sophistication as one of Hollywood's most glamorous stars. In chapter 3 I explored her screwball comedies, and argued that despite making her first screwball film, *Twentieth Century*, in 1934, Lombard did not achieve success or notoriety as a screwball comedian until the release of *My Man Godfrey* in 1936, the year the genre gained national popularity. In chapters 4 and 5, I argued that by 1939, Lombard's personal and professional life were changing, beginning with her long-anticipated marriage to Clark Gable, which prompted a shift in the discourse about her star persona that included motherhood and domesticity. Her decision to become a freelance actress in 1937 allowed Lombard to take control of her career, and by 1939 she turned her attention away from screwball to melodrama in an effort to demonstrate her diversity as a performer. Lombard's melodramas were critical successes, though her change of pace did not resonate with audiences, who instead preferred her feisty and vibrant screwball persona. Finally, chapter 6 takes a deeper look at the intersection of Lombard's feminism and patriotism, and how her politics was used to contextualize her star persona in life and in death. This brief summation reiterates what my book has already identified at length, namely that Carole Lombard's professional accomplishments and varied star persona prove her value beyond the context of screwball comedy.

The central questions that have driven my research are as follows: in light of Carole Lombard's work in several genres and transformative star persona, why did she resonate so distinctly with audiences as a screwball comedian and what impact does this have on our understanding of her career and star persona? In a performance context, the incongruity between Lombard's desire to work in genres other than comedy and the public's lack of acceptance of her dramatic work speaks to the extent to which recognizability is an important factor in Hollywood stardom.[1] Siegfried Kracauer writes:

> The typical Hollywood star resembles the non-actor in that he acts out a standing character identical with his own or at least developed from it, frequently with the aid of make-up and publicity experts. As with any real-life figure on the screen, his presence in a film points beyond the film ... he uses his acting talents, if any, exclusively to feature the individual he is or appears to be, no matter for the rest whether his self-portrayal

---

[1] Pamela Robertson Wojcik, "Typecasting," in *Movie Acting, the Film Reader*, ed. Pamela Robertson Wojcik (New York: Routledge, 2004), 170.

exhausts itself of a few stereotypical characteristics or brings out various potentialities of his underlying nature.[2]

Stardom occurs through the actor's reappearance in films and recognition in different roles, in which he creates a character "identical with his own" off-screen persona. In each performance, the Hollywood star draws upon "stereotypical characteristics" and "various potentialities of his underlying nature" that are also attributed to their off-screen studio-engineered image. This creates a "double identification" in which we simultaneously see both the character and the star—a process which is key to the commodification of stardom.[3]

Gaylyn Studlar explains that when an actor "disappears" into a role, there can be a disconnection in terms of audience recognition. She writes, "it is generally acknowledged that making your star unrecognizable is dangerous … because the value of stardom is most frequently measured in audience anticipation seeing—and recognizing—their favorite box-office attraction."[4] In Lombard's case, the verisimilitude of her screwball performances was buttressed by fan magazine stories and publicity materials that emphasized the similarities between star and character. She was a "believable" screwball comedian, in part, because of the volume of publicity discourse that was published over a several year span that framed the down-to-earth, vibrant and "party girl" iterations of her Hollywood star persona in direct relation to her on-screen characters. Collectively, these sources perpetuated the myth that by watching Lombard's screwball films, audiences would be brought closer to her "true" or "authentic" self. By contrast to her glamour girl or dramatic/domestic star personas, there was no apparent critical or public gap between Lombard's comic on- and off-screen personalities; her screwball heroines were thought to be extensions of the "real" Carole Lombard. Screwball comedy may have brought Lombard immense fame and is the genre for which she is best remembered—but screwball alone does not sum up her star persona. In fact, I would argue that Lombard's screwball comedy linkage has, in many ways, been a paralyzing force in posthumous receptions which, in part, explain why Lombard's stardom has not been fully explored.

I would therefore like to return to this particular conundrum and offer a final reflection on Lombard's status as a faded star in contemporary film studies. In the introduction to their book *Lasting Screen Stars*, Lucy Bolton and Julie Lobalzo Wright point out that the question of a star's longevity is

---

[2]Siegfried Kracauer, *Theory of Film: The Redemption of Physical Reality* (Princeton: Princeton University Press, 1960), 99–100.
[3]Robertson Wocjik, 174.
[4]Gaylyn Studlar, *This Mad Masquerade: Stardom and Masculinity in the Jazz Age* (New York: Columbia University Press, 1996), 237–238.

shaped by a number of factors, including, among others, "race, nationality, age, gender, and sexuality."[5] There is not one singular reason why some stars remain popular into old age and death while others do not, which is why longevity is such a difficult topic to study. To be clear: Lombard is not a "forgotten" star in the sense that she is absent from popular media or film scholarship. As I have outlined throughout the book, for example, there have been several biographical studies about Lombard published since 1970s, but virtually all—in either title, content, or a combination of the two—emphasize her screwball comedy associations. Happily too, in recent years there have been several excellent books, chapters, and journal articles by the likes of Emily Carman, Michael Hammond, and Christina Lane that probe into various aspects of Lombard's stardom beyond screwball comedy, touching upon topics as wide ranging as star labor to her relationship with Clark Gable. Their research has made exceptional strides in "correcting" the Lombard record, but in light of the fact that her screwball comedy persona has been promulgated for nearly eighty years in contemporaneous popular media, such a task takes time and a multitude of voices.

Several lines of inquiry must be considered in order to understand the "mystery" of why Lombard has faded, and an important one that I will turn to first is, rather surprisingly, her close association with screwball comedy and the effects of her screwball persona. Lombard's screwball star–character symbiosis has had a profound effect on how we make sense of and write about her stardom today. Lombard's screwball reputation being a factor in hindering further studies into her work outside of the genre is, in part, related to the critical standing of screwball comedy. Screwball is a genre with a strong scholarly status, yet relatively lesser popular appeal. This becomes clearer if we compare it to film noir. The interest in the latter spans scholarly works and popular cinephilia, including academic books, film studies courses, film festivals and the annual worldwide celebration of film noir appropriately called "Noirvember." Stars like Humphrey Bogart and Robert Mitchum can therefore give rise to important academic studies and be popular "icons" for their links to noir, but noir alone does not solely define either star's persona. By contrast, interest in screwball comedy is more specialized. The genre has a longstanding presence in film history and genre studies, and is often included with other subgenres in romantic comedy scholarship, beginning primarily with Stanley Cavell's *Pursuits of Happiness* and continuing through to the works of contemporary scholars such as Tamar Jeffers McDonald,[6] Steve Neal and

---

[5]Lucy Bolton and Julie Lobalzo Wright, "Introduction," in *Lasting Screen Stars: Images that Fade and Personas that Endure*, eds. Lucy Bolton and Julie Lobalzo Wright (London: Palgrave Macmillan, 2016), 3.

[6]Tamar Jeffers McDonald, *Romantic Comedy: Boy Meets Girl Meets Genre* (London: Wallflower Press, 2007).

Frank Krutnik,[7] Tina Olsin Lent,[8] and Kathrina Glitre.[9] For the erudite cinephile, screwball comedy remains a well-loved genre, and has inspired recent retrospectives such as Turner Classic Movies' "Friday Night Spotlight" series in November 2013[10] and a BFI Southbank film season in April 2014.[11] However outside of these specialist circles, screwball comedy has not crossed over to popular media attention in the same way as film noir. This is one reason why Lombard's stardom, which is mostly associated with screwball, has faded.

Contributing to Lombard's relative narrow popularity is her lack of canonical films and the nature of her work with auteurs. Curiously, she worked with several noted auteurs of the classical Hollywood period such as Alfred Hitchcock, Howard Hawks, and Ernst Lubitsch, but few of these films have garnered canonical status in the director's respective filmographies—with the exception of *To Be or Not to Be*. Although the unflattering reviews and accusations of "poor taste" Lubitsch's satire received upon its initial release in 1942[12] reflected the fresh sensitivity many Americans felt about the war, in the years since it has steadily gained critical and popular prestige, and is now considered a classic wartime comedy and an example of the infamously hard-to-define "Lubitsch touch."

In a different category than *To Be or Not to Be* are *Twentieth Century* (1934) and *Mr. & Mrs. Smith* (1941); both made by notable auteurs, but they are not considered canonical within their oeuvres. Lombard first worked with Howard Hawks in *The Road to Glory* (1926) and again in her first screwball comedy, *Twentieth Century*. Given the generic significance of the latter film, it is surprisingly underrepresented in auteurist studies of Hawks. Robin Wood describes Hawks's films as being without a clearly identifiable visual style, writing that he "has never been afflicted with this disease of self-consciousness."[13] Wood further explains that "all of his best films are examples of established Hollywood genres" but that Hawks has arguably

---

[7]Frank Krutnik and Steve Neal, *Popular Film and Television Comedy* (London: Taylor & Francis, 2002).
[8]Tina Olsin Lent, "Romantic Love and Friendship: The Redefinition of Gender Relations in Screwball Comedy," in *Classical Hollywood Comedy*, eds. Kristine Brunovska Karnik and Henry Jenkins (New York: Routledge, 1995): 314–331.
[9]Kathrina Glitre, *Hollywood Romantic Comedy: States of the Union, 1934–65* (Manchester: Manchester University Press, 2006).
[10]"Introduction to Screwball Comedies," *Turner Classic Movies*, accessed June 20, 2016, http://www.tcm.com/this-month/article/770283%7C0/Friday-Night-Spotlight-Screwball-Comedies.html.
[11]"Flirting with screwball," *British Film Institute*, April 3, 2014, accessed June 20, 2016, http://www.bfi.org.uk/news-opinion/bfi-news/flirting-screwball.
[12]Bosley Crowther, "The Screen – *To Be or Not to Be*." *New York Times*, March 7, 1942, L13.
[13]Robin Wood, *Howard Hawks*, new edition (Detroit: Wayne State University Press, 2006), 5.

"produced probably the best works within each genre he has tackled."[14] Hawks's method arises from his "collaboration with actors and cameras that constitute mise-en-scene"[15] and perhaps what one might call his exploratory approach toward his stories and characters. Peter Bogdanovich identifies "professionalism" as being a reoccurring theme in several of Hawks's films, and points out that in several love sequences—such as those in *Only Angels Have Wings* (1939), *To Have and Have Not* (1944), *The Big Sleep* (1946), and *Red River* (1948)—the "woman is the aggressive one" in his romantic narratives.[16]

If one accepts auteur theory as being a valid method of consolidating the thematic and stylistic consistencies in a director's body of work, then *Twentieth Century* justifiably fits as a "Hawksian" film. First, its narrative is centered around theatrical professionalism and, as I have argued in chapter 3, Lily Garland's transformation into a celebrated Broadway and film actress incites a level of confidence and self-assurance in her character that she does not possess at the beginning of the film. She could be considered one of Hawks's "aggressive" women precisely in her feigned indifference and staunch revulsion toward Oscar throughout most of the narrative. Second, regarding Wood's theory of Hawks's films being emblematic of genres, *Twentieth Century* is often cited as one of the first films that fueled American audiences' fascination with screwball comedy in the 1930s.[17] Finally, in several interviews about its production Hawks emphasized the collaborative environment he cultivated for Barrymore and Lombard, including the well-known rumor that Hawks threatened to fire Lombard if she "acted." She was allegedly instructed to "do anything that comes into [her] mind,"[18] which resulted in her rapid-fire delivery that eventually became synonymous with her screwball style. The conditions for *Twentieth Century* to be a celebrated Howard Hawks film are therefore present. Yet compared to his most notable screwball film, *Bringing Up Baby* (1938), it has been markedly understudied. This state of affairs might be a simple case of mis-timing; Hawks later admitted that when the film was released "the public wasn't ready for seeing two stars act like comedians the way those two did."[19] His rationale may be correct, but I do not think it fully justifies *Twentieth Century*'s minor standing.

---

[14]Ibid, 6.
[15]Ibid, 8.
[16]Peter Bogdanovich, *The Cinema of Howard Hawks* (New York: Film Library of the Museum of Modern Art, 1962), 18–19.
[17]Wes D. Gehring, *Carole Lombard: The Hoosier Tornado* (Indianapolis: Indiana Historical Society Press, 2002), 11.
[18]Joseph McBride, *Hawks on Hawks* (Lexington: The University Press of Kentucky, 2003), 65.
[19]Ibid.

I point to my earlier argument about the established screwball canon as a possible reason why *Twentieth Century* is not considered a canonical Howard Hawks film. Stanley Cavell's *Pursuits of Happiness* has an unmatched reputation within screwball scholarship, particularly through the way he engages with the themes of marriage and remarriage. The film examples in his book have in turn benefited from his book's iconicity and many of them, including *Bringing Up Baby,* have become benchmark examples of screwball comedy. In his book-length study of *Bringing Up Baby,* Gerald Mast introduces the film via Cavell's work, and how it "fits into a rich tradition of romantic comedy that stretches from Rome to Shakespeare to Hollywood."[20] He offers his opinion that *Baby* "is the essence of thirties screwball comedy. It is also quintessential Howard Hawks ..."[21] Borrowing his rationale, I argue that *Bringing Up Baby* is "quintessential Howard Hawks" because of the extensive academic and popular attention it has received since the 1970s, especially in comparison to the lesser studied *Twentieth Century.* Both Katharine Hepburn and Cary Grant's enduring star popularity and long film careers have also contributed to *Bringing Up Baby*'s staying power. Conversely, while Lombard and Barrymore were major Hollywood stars in the 1930s, they both arguably fall into a "specialist cinephile" league in terms of the long-term popularity of their personae. Finally, *Bringing Up Baby* was made in 1938 at the height of the classical screwball period and when screwball comedy was already a well defined film genre. By contrast, *Twentieth Century* was not advertised as a screwball comedy upon its release in 1934, and the designation was applied retroactively after the genre came into vogue in 1936, which further explains the film's lesser critical standing.

Lombard's last screwball comedy, *Mr. & Mrs. Smith* has the distinction of being Hitchcock's only straight comedy film, which in itself would seem noteworthy. However, because it is anomalous among his suspenseful, psychologically-driven narratives it is often overlooked, particularly in comparison to his better-known titles such as *Vertigo* (1958), *Psycho* (1960), and *The Birds* (1963). In his book-length interview with the director, François Truffaut describes Hitchcock's style as one of immense control "over all the elements of his film," and it is through his authorial command that his "screen signature can be identified as soon as the picture begins."[22] According to Truffaut, the quality of instant recognizability is precisely what is missing from *Mr. & Mrs. Smith,* which he considers to be "out of line with the rest of [Hitchcock's] work."[23] However, I would argue that the marriage-driven

---

[20]Gerald Mast *Bringing Up Baby*, ed. Gerald Mast (New Brunswick: Rutgers University Press, 1994), 3.
[21]Ibid, 330.
[22]François Truffaut, *Hitchcock: A Definitive Study of Alfred Hitchcock*, revised edition (New York: Simon & Schuster, 1986), 18.
[23]Truffaut, 139.

narrative and the plethora of sexual innuendoes woven throughout the film fit thematically within his oeuvre.[24] Hitchcock claims that he only agreed to make *Mr. & Mrs. Smith* as "a friendly gesture to Carole Lombard," and that since he "didn't understand the type of people who were portrayed in the film, all I did was to photograph the scenes as written."[25] He defers authorial status to screenplay writer Norman Krasna and compares his experience on the film with that of a studio-contract director,[26] whose personal vision is barely identifiable in the finished product. Both of these authorial "oddities" within the Hawks and Hitchcock canon have hindered Carole Lombard's long-term visibility as a star.

A final, brief reason to explain Lombard's narrow popularity is the iconicity of the Gable–Lombard star couple. In chapter 4, I documented the impact of her marriage to Gable, noting how her independent persona was situated in direct contrast to her role as an allegedly contented housewife. In chapter 6, I also explained how in the years immediately following Lombard's tragic death, Lombard's patriotism was bolstered by Gable's military service. Following his military discharge in 1944, Gable resumed his acting career in Hollywood, making another twenty-one films before his death from a heart attack in November 1960. In the eighteen years between Lombard's death and his own, Gable dated several Hollywood stars including Ann Sheridan, Virginia Grey, Paulette Goddard and Nancy Davis, and remarried twice, first to Sylvia Ashley then, finally, to Kathleen (Kay) Williams. Although Gable moved on personally and professionally, fan magazine discourse habitually made reference to Lombard. These outlets often took note of the physical similarities between Lombard and Gable's girlfriends and wives, implying that he was searching for another Carole. For example, about Williams, *Photoplay* columnist Elza Schallert wrote: "… with her light coloring, she is particularly stunning in black and pure white gowns, which, strangely enough, was also true of Carole Lombard. She seems just the type that a Gable would approve and appreciate …"[27]

Additionally, fans read about Gable's alleged loneliness, with stories such as "Is Gable's Love Life Jinxed?,"[28] "Clark Gable: The Lonely Man"[29] and "Live Alone and Like It?"[30] making the case that no woman

---

[24]For example, the final close-up shot of Ann's skis crossing—a visual metaphor for the couple's imminent sexual reconciliation—or the heated, innuendo-laden exchange between Ann and David in their apartment on the night of their anniversary.
[25]Truffaut, 139.
[26]Ibid.
[27]Elza Schallert, "The Girl in Clark Gable's Life," *Photoplay* (June 1944), 93.
[28]Jack Wade, "Is Gable's Love Life Jinxed?" *Modern Screen* (February 1952), 40–41; 64; 66.
[29]"Clark Gable: The Lonely Man, His Life Story in Pictures" *Look* (September 7, 1954), 60–65.
[30]Nate Edwards, "Live Alone and Like It?" *Modern Screen* (April 1955), 30.

could live up to Lombard. Such a perspective was bolstered by rumors that claimed Gable left the couple's Encino ranch decor virtually unchanged,[31] as well as alleged quotes from him about their marriage, including one in which he reminisced that his life with Lombard was "a perfect thing. I never expect to find it again."[32] Gable seemingly did find happiness with Williams, whom he married in 1955 and with whom he had a son, John.[33] Yet comparisons between Lombard and Williams continued,[34] so much so that Kay addressed Carole's presence in her memoirs, writing: "Carole was a part of Clark's life before I ever met him. Why should I be jealous or resent that?"[35] In short, Gable's star persona was tethered to the memory of Carole Lombard.

Of course, this popular discourse has also had an effect on Lombard's stardom. Her posthumous star persona has been recontextualized in various media texts in relation to Gable's, and in many ways their star couple image has become a defining feature of their individual public identities. In the years since Gable's death, he and Lombard have been the subject of books, movies, TV specials, DVD special features, and even contemporary magazine articles. As I have previously discussed, many of these texts perpetuate the "true love" myth, including, for example, a 1996 *People* special issue about "The Greatest Love Stories of the Century." The magazine quotes Gable's friend, Esther Williams, who stated, "They had an ineffable quality of romance, the ability to have fun together. They were soulmates who thought life was delicious, and they made everyone's life delicious around them."[36] With each reference, the mythology of Gable and Lombard's star coupledom grows deeper roots, and becomes a more constitutive part of Lombard's stardom that, at least in a popular context, has overshadowed her professional accomplishments.

The Lombard effect

In reality, Carole Lombard was more than just a screwball comedian, and not simply Clark Gable's wife. Far from being a one-dimensional star, Lombard encapsulated in her persona a series of ideological and social

---

[31] Kay Gable, *Clark Gable: A Personal Portrait* (New York: Prentice-Hall, 1961), 25.
[32] Janet Franklin, "Which Girl Has the Gable?" *Modern Screen* (July 1948), 52.
[33] Born in March 1961, four months after Gable's death.
[34] See: Frances Kish, "She Calls him 'Pappy,' But She Calls him 'Darling'," *Photoplay* (February 1957), 86.
[35] Gable, 66.
[36] "Clark Gable and Carole Lombard," *People*, February 12, 1996, 124.

binaries that speak not only to the multifaceted nature of her public image, but also the complex and contradictory construction of screen femininity within the 1930s and 1940s Hollywood studio system. At different times in her career she represented both sophisticated Hollywood glamour and earthy pastoralism; screwball "Queen" and serious melodramatic actress; a vivacious party girl and contented homebody. She was also considered a patriotic American who consistently tried to extend her influence beyond Hollywood at a time of darkening global politics and economic instability.

To focus solely on Lombard's contributions to screwball comedy or her romantic relationships ignores the consequential advancements she made as a protofeminist, actor, and businesswoman, and the extent to which she made it possible for other female stars in the studio era and beyond to "cultivate and maintain their own independent stardom in American cinema."[37] Although the cultural and industrial conditions in Hollywood have evolved substantially since Lombard's death, it is not hard to identify her influence on female comedians over the past eighty years. From Lucille Ball, who cited Lombard's mentorship and comedic style as inspiration for her character Lucy Ricardo in *I Love Lucy* (1951–1957);[38] to Mary Tyler Moore, whose TV persona responded to the social and cultural changes of the second-wave feminist movement, and who offered female viewers an example of 1970s independent womanhood; to contemporary comedians like Tina Fey and Amy Poehler, who have established themselves as performers, creators, and businesswomen across different media platforms. As women in Hollywood continue to fight for representational and pay equity, we can take inspiration from people like Lombard, who leveraged her power and influence to change the conditions of performative labor in the studio system. This and other achievements should not be overlooked, and it is my hope that this book constitutes the much-needed first steps into deeper scholarly work on, and wider academic recognition of Carole Lombard as an actress and star.

In a 1939 interview with *Radio Mirror*, Lombard was asked about the future of her career beyond the screen. She was quoted as saying, "I'll never retire. I'll always want to be doing something ... Maybe advertising, maybe publicity. Maybe I'd like to manage a theater. I don't know. I just know that when pictures turn thumbs down on me as one day they must, and radio, too, I'll try something else. I'd go crazy just sitting around."[39] It is futile to speculate what Lombard would have done had she lived. However, her

---

[37]Emily Carman, *Independent Stardom: Freelance Women in the Hollywood Studio System* (Austin: University of Texas Press, 2016), 147.
[38]Lucille Ball, *Love, Lucy* (New York: Berkeley Boulevard Books, 1997), 168.
[39]Rhea, 19.

diverse accomplishments across nearly twenty years as a Hollywood actress and businesswoman justifiably warrant further studies into other aspects of her stardom. Less than a decade before she made this comment, Lombard had successfully transitioned from silent to sound film, and after a long period of trial and error was able to find her niche with the studios and film audiences in screwball comedy. Lombard's lengthy and varied filmography confirms that she possessed serious acting talents, and when coupled with her outspoken politics, proclivity for national and community activism, and transformative star image, it is easy to demonstrate that she was much more than just "the Screwball Girl."

BIBLIOGRAPHY

"20th Century." *Variety*. Tuesday, May 8, 1934, 14.
"$94700 for 'Lightnin', Roxy; 'Morocco' and 'Blue Angel' Only Other Standout Films on B'way." *Variety*. December 10, 1930, 9.
Abrams, Brett L. *Hollywood Bohemians: Transgressive Sexuality and the Selling of the Movie Dreamland*. Jefferson: McFarland & Co. Inc., 2008.
"Actress demands damages for cut." *Los Angeles Times*. October 13, 1927, A9.
Addison, Heather. "Transcending Time: Jean Harlow and Hollywood's Narrative of Decline." *Journal of Film and Video* 57.4 (Winter 2005): 32–46.
"'Adverse' $22,000, 'Hussy' $20,000, Both Terrif on Raised Pittsburgh Sales." *Variety*. September 9, 1936, 10.
Affron, Charles. "Generous Stars." In *Star Texts: Image and Performance in Film and Television,*. Ed. Jeremy G. Butler, 90–101. Detroit: Wayne State University Press, 1991.
Affron, Charles. "Identifications." In *Imitations of Life: A Reader on Film & Television Melodrama*. Ed. Marcia Landy, 98–117. Detroit: Wayne State University Press, 1991.
Ager, Cecilia. "Going Places." *Variety*. May 8, 1934, 57.
Agnes O'Malley to John A. Waldron. April 29, 1927. Correspondence. General Files, MSC.
"Alexander Korda Brings a Remake of 'Four Feathers' in Technicolor to the Capitol – 'In Name Only,' a Romantic Drama, at the Music Hall." *New York Times*. August 4, 1939, L11.
Alexander, Paul. *Boulevard of Broken Dreams: The Life, Times, and Legend of James Dean*. New York: Plume Publishing, 1997.
"Among the Idle Rich." *Picture Play*. March 1931, page unknown.
Anderson Wagner, Kristen. "Have Women a Sense of Humor?": Comedy and Femininity in Early Twentieth-Century Film." *The Velvet Light Trap* Number 68 (Fall 2011): 35–46.
Andrin, Muriel. "Back to the Slap: Slapstick's Hyperbolic Gesture and the Rhetoric of Violence." In *Slapstick Comedy*. Eds. Tom Paulus and Rob King, 226–235. New York: Routledge, 2010.
Arnaz, Desi. *A Book*. New York: Warner Books, 1977.
Arnold, Rebecca. *Fashion, Desire and Anxiety: Image and Morality in the 20th Century*. New Brunswick, NJ: Rutgers University Press, 2001.
Arnold, Rebecca. *The American Look: Fashion, Sportswear, and the Image of Women in the 1930s and 1940s*. New York: I.B. Tauris, 2009.
"'Asking' With Spitalny Gals $26,000, Mich." *Variety*. September 16, 1936, 9.
"Astor Influence." *Variety*. September 9, 1936, 25.
Bakhtin, Mikhail. *Rabelais and his World*, first Midland books edition. Trans. Helene Iswolsky. Bloomington: Indiana University Press, 1984.

Balázs, Béla. "The Spirit of Film" In *Béla Balázs Early Film Theory:"Visible Man" and "The Spirit of Film."* Eds. Erica Carter and Rodney Livingstone, 91–211. New York: Berghahn Books, 2010.

Balázs, Béla. "Visible Man." In *Béla Balázs Early Film Theory:"Visible Man" and "The Spirit of Film."* Eds. Erica Carter and Rodney Livingstone, 1–89. New York: Berghahn Books, 2010.

Baldwin, Faith. "Do Hollywood Women Spoil Their Men?" *Photoplay*. May 1939.

Balio, Tino. "Selling Stars: The Economic Imperative." In *The Classical Hollywood Reader*. Ed. Steve Neale, 209–226. New York: Routledge, 2012.

Balio, Tino. "Selling Stars." In *Grand Design: Hollywood as a Modern Business Enterprise, 1930–1939*. Ed. Tino Balio, 143–176. Berkeley: University of California Press, 1995.

Ball, Lucille. *Love, Lucy*. New York: Berkeley Boulevard Books, 1997.

Barrios, Richard. *A Song In The Dark: The Birth of the Musical Film*. Oxford: Oxford University Press, 2010.

Barton, Sabrina. "'Crisscross': Paranoia and Projection in *Strangers on a Train*." *Camera Obscura* Vol. 9, Nos. 1–2 (1991): 74–100.

Barthes, Roland. "The Face of Garbo." In *Stardom and Celebrity: A Reader*. Eds. Sean Redmond and Su Holmes, 261–262. London: SAGE Publications, 2007.

Baskette, Kirtley. "Hollywood's Unmarried Husbands and Wives." *Photoplay*. December 1938.

Batkin, Jane. *Identity in Animation: A Journey into Self, Difference, Culture and the Body*. London: Routledge, 2017.

Becker, Christine. "Clark Gable: The King of Hollywood." In *Glamour in a Golden Age: Movie Stars of the 1930s*. Ed. Adrienne L. McLean, 245–266. New Brunswick: Rutgers University Press, 2011.

Belton, John. *American Cinema/American Culture*. 4th ed. New York: McGraw-Hill Education, 2012.

Bennett, Allen. "At long last, a soldier is laid to rest." *The Journal Tribune*. August 13, 2016. Accessed August 20, 2016. http://m.journaltribune.com/news/2016-08-13/Front_Page/At_long_last_a_soldier_is_laid_to_rest.html#.V7hp2JMrKHp.

Bergson, Henri. *Laughter: An Essay on the Meaning of the Comic*. Trans. Cloudesley Brereton and Fred Rothwell. Los Angeles: Green Integer, 1999.

Biery, Ruth. "Why Carole Changed Her Mind." *Screenland*. September, 1931, 104.

Black, Ford. "Will Clark Gable Ever Marry Carole Lombard?" *Motion Picture*. February, 1939.

Bogdanovich, Peter. *The Cinema of Howard Hawks*. New York: Film Library of the Museum of Modern Art, 1962.

Bogdanovich, Peter and Orson Welles. *This Is Orson Welles*. New York: Da Capo Press, 1994.

Bolton, Lucy and Julie Lobalzo Wright. "Introduction." In *Lasting Screen Stars: Images that Fade and Personas that Endure*. Eds. Lucy Bolton and Julie Lobalzo Wright, 1–8. London: Palgrave Macmillan, 2016.

"Boos and Bouquets." *Photoplay*. December 1939, 5.

Boone, Betty. "What About Carole Lombard?" *Screenland*. June 1931.

Breen, Joseph to David O. Selznick. October 21, 1937. History of Cinema: Hollywood and the Production Code, Reel 13. Motion Picture Association of

America: Production Code Administration Records, 1927–1967. Margaret Herrick Library Special Collection, Los Angeles.
Bret, David. *Clark Gable: Tormented Star*. New York: Da Capo Press, 2008.
Bringing Up Baby. Ed. Gerald Mast. New Brunswick: Rutgers University Press, 1994.
Broadcast. March 11, 1939, 49.
Brooks, Peter. *The Melodramatic Imagination: Balzac, Henry James, Melodrama, and the Mode of Excess*. New Haven: Yale University Press, 1976.
Brown, Tom. *Spectacles in "Classical" Cinema: Musicality and Historicity in the 1930s*. New York: Routledge, 2016.
Brunovska Karnick, Kristine. "Community of Unruly Women: Female Comedy Teams in the Early Sound Era." *Continuum: Journal of Media & Cultural Studies* Vol. 13, No. 1 (1999): 77–95.
Brunovska Karnick, Kristine and Henry Jenkins. "Comedy and the Social World." In *Classical Hollywood Comedy*. Eds. Kristine Brunovska Karnick and Henry Jenkins, 265–281. New York: Routledge, 1995.
Bryant, Roger. *William Powell: The Life and Films*. Jefferson: McFarland & Co., Inc., 2006.
Buddle, Melanie. *The Business of Women: Marriage, Family, and Entrepreneurship in British Columbia, 1901–51*. Vancouver: UBC Press, 2010.
Busch, Noel F. "A Loud Cheer for the Screwball Girl." *Life*. October 17, 1938.
Byrge, Duane and Robert Milton Miller. *The Screwball Comedy Films: A History and Filmography, 1934–1942*. Jefferson: McFarland & Co. Inc., 1991.
Cal West Med "Average U.S. Income Told." *Western Journal of Medicine* Vol. 50 (May 1939).
"Cal York Announcing." *Photoplay*. March 1933.
Callahan, Dan. *Barbara Stanwyck: The Miracle Woman*. Jackson: The University Press of Mississippi, 2012.
"Calloway Puts L.A. Par Out Front With Smacko $22,000, 'Live' Clicks Off 21G, 'Dream' Okay, 'Kids' Skids." *Variety*. October 30, 1935, 8.
Carman, Emily. "Independent Stardom: Female Film Stars and the Studio System in the 1930s." *Women's Studies: An Interdisciplinary Journal* Vol. 37, No. 6 (2008): 583–615.
Carman, Emily. *Independent Stardom: Freelance Women in the Hollywood Studio System*. Austin: University of Texas Press, 2016.
"Carole Lombard." *Dear Mr. Gable*. Accessed November 17, 2015. http://dearmrgable.com/?page_id=3216.
"Carole Lombard Dies in Crash After Aiding U.S. Defense Bond Campaign." *LIFE*. January 26, 1942, 25.
"Carole Lombard: Is She Man-Proof Now?" *True Confessions*. August 1934, 16–19.
Carole Lombard's Life Story, 1942.
Carruthers, Daphne. "Goodbye Carole!" *Modern Screen*. April 1942.
Castonguay, James. "Myrna Loy and William Powell: The Perfect Screen Couple." In *Glamour in the Golden Age: Movie Stars of the 1930s*. Ed. Adrienne McLean, 220–244. New Brunswick: Rutgers University Press, 2011.
Cavell, Stanley. *Pursuits of Happiness: The Hollywood Comedy of Remarriage*. Boston: Harvard University Press, 1984.

Cavell, Stanley. *The World Viewed: Reflections on the Ontology of Film*. Boston: Harvard University Press, 1979.
Chivers, Sally. *The Silvering Screen: Old Age and Disability in Cinema*. Toronto: University of Toronto Press, 2011.
Crichton, Kyle. "Fun in Flickers." *Colliers*. February 24, 1940, 11.
Churchhill, Douglas W. "Lunacy Hath Charms at the box office. " *New York Times*. July 11, 1937, L10.
Churchill, Douglas. "The Year in Hollywood; 1934 May Be Remembered as the Beginning of the Sweetness-and-Light Era." *The New York Times*. December 30, 1934, X5.
Churchwell, Sarah. "'The Most Envied Couple in America in 1921': Making the Social Register in the Scrapbooks of F. Scott and Zelda Fitzgerald." In *First Comes Love: Power Couples, Celebrity Kinship and Cultural Politics*. Eds. Shelley Cobb and Neil Ewen, 29–54. New York: Bloomsbury Publishing Inc., 2015.
Clark, Danae. "Acting in Hollywood's Best Interest: Representations of Actor's Labor during the National Recovery Administration." *Journal of Film and Video* Vol. 42, No. 4 (Winter 1990): 3–19.
"Clark Gable and Carole Lombard." *People*. February 12, 1996, 124.
"Clark Gable: The Lonely Man, His Life Story in Pictures" *Look*. September 7, 1954, 60–65.
Clark Gable: Tall, Dark and Handsome. Dir. Susan F. Walker. Turner Network Television, 1996.
Clayton, Alex. *The Body in Hollywood Slapstick Comedy*. Jefferson, NC: McFarland & Company, Inc., 2007.
Clayton, Alex. "Play-Acting: A Theory of Comedic Performance." In *Theorizing Film Acting*. Ed. Aaron Taylor, 47–61. New York: Routledge, 2012.
Cobb Shelley and Neil Ewen. "Golden Couples." In *First Comes Love: Power Couples, Celebrity Kinship and Cultural Politics*. Eds. Shelley Cobb and Neil Ewen, 9–12. New York: Bloomsbury, 2015.
Cogan, Frances B. *All-American Girl: The Ideal of Real Womanhood in Mid-Nineteenth Century America*. Athens: University of Georgia Press, 1989.
Cohan, Steve. *Masked Men: Masculinity and the Movies in the Fifties*. Bloomington: Indiana University Press, 1997.
Colman, Ronald, Cary Grant, Carole Lombard, Groucho Marx, Lawrence Tibbett. "The Circle." NBC-Red. Hollywood: January 22, 1939.
"Coming and Going." *Film Daily*. June 24, 1930, page unknown.
Coulson, Victoria. *Henry James, Women and Realism*. Cambridge: Cambridge University Press, 2007.
Crafton, Donald. "Pie and Chase: Gag, Spectacle, and Narrative in Slapstick Comedy." In *Classical Hollywood Comedy*. Eds. Kristine Brunovska Karnick and Henry Jenkins, 106–119. New York: Routledge, 1995.
Creelman, Eileen. "Some Gay Light Comedy in *Hands Across The Table* with Carole Lombard," *The New York Sun*, November 2, 1935.
Cripps, Thomas. *Slow Fade to Black: The Negro in American Film, 1900–1942*. New York: Oxford University Press, 1993.
"Cromwell Calls 'Em On Grant–Lombard 'Memory'." *Variety*. Wednesday, February 8, 1939, 7.

Crowther, Bosley. "Females of the Species." *New York Times*. January 16, 1938, X5.
Crowther, Bosley. "The Screen – *To Be or Not To Be*." *New York Times*. March 7, 1942, L13.
Cruikshank, Herbert. "Three-In-One Girl." *Motion Picture*. November 1930, 74.
Dallek, Robert. *Franklin D. Roosevelt and American Foreign Policy: 1932–1945*. New York: Oxford University Press, 1979.
Davidson, Bill. *The Real and Unreal*. New York: Lacer Books, 1962.
DeCordova, Richard. *Picture Personalities: The Emergence of the Star System in America*. Champaign: University of Illinois Press, 2001.
DeCordova, Richard. "The Emergence of the Star System in America." In *Stardom: Industry of Desire*. Ed. Christine Gledhill, 17–29. London: Routledge, 1991.
D'Haeyere, Hilde. "Splashes of Fun and Beauty: Mack Sennett's Bathing Beauties." In *Slapstick Comedy*. Eds. Tom Paulus and Rob King, 207–225. New York: Routledge, 2010.
Desjardins, Mary. "'Fan Magazine Trouble': The AMPP, Studio Publicity Directors, and the Hollywood Press, 1945–1952." *Film History* Vol. 26, No. 3 (2014): 29–56.
Dietz, Edith. "She Scoffs at the Terrors of Filmland." *Screen & Radio Weekly*. December 1934: 4–5.
Dixon Mann, Margaret. "Happiness Ahead for Clark and Carole." *Picture Play*. August 1938, page unknown.
Doane, Mary Ann. "The Moving Image: Pathos and the Maternal." In *Imitations of Life: A Reader on Film & Television Melodrama*. Ed. Marcia Landy, 283–306. Detroit: Wayne State University Press, 1991.
Doherty, Edward. "Can the Gable–Lombard Love Story Have a Happy Ending?" *Photoplay*. May 1938.
Doherty, Thomas. *Hollywood's Censor: Joseph I. Breen and the Production Code Administration*. New York: Columbia University Press, 2007.
Dorgan, Dick. "A Song of Hate." *Photoplay*, July 1922.
Downing, Lisa and Sue Harris. *From Perversion to Purity: The Stardom of Catherine Deneuve*. Manchester: Manchester University Press, 2007.
Dyer, Richard. *Heavenly Bodies: Film Stars and Society*. New York: Routledge, 2004.
Dyer, Richard. *Stars*. London: BFI Publishing, 1998.
Dyer, Richard. "Stars." In *Stardom and Celebrity: A Reader*. Eds. Sean Redmond and Su Holmes, 78–84. London: SAGE Publications, 2007.
Dyer, Richard. *White: Essays on Race and Culture*. New York: Routledge, 1997.
Eckert, Charles. "The Carole Lombard in Macy's Window." In *Movies and Mass Culture*. Ed. John Belton, 95–118. London: The Athlone Press, 1999.
Edwards, Nate. "Live Alone and Like It?" *Modern Screen*. April 1955, 30.
Ellenberger, Alan E. *The Valentino Mystique: The Death and Afterlife of the Silent Film Idol*. Jefferson: McFarland & Co., Inc., 2005.
Ellis, John. "Stars as Cinematic Phenomenon." In *Star Texts: Image and Performance in Film and Television*. Ed. Jeremy Butler, 300–315. Detroit: Wayne State University Press, 1991.
Essoe, Gabe. *The Films of Clark Gable*. New York: Citadel Press, 1970.

Evans, Delight. "Your Guide at a Glance to the Best Current Pictures." *Screenland.* May 1942, 52.
Eyman, Scott. *Ernst Lubitsch: Laughter in Paradise.* Baltimore: Johns Hopkins University Press, 2000.
"Fast and Loose." *The Film Daily.* November 30, 1930, page unknown.
Feuer, Jane. "Melodrama, Serial Form and Television Today." *Screen* Vol. 25, No. 1 (January–February 1984): 4–17.
"Film Reviews – 20th Century," *Variety*, May 8, 1934, 14.
"Film Reviews." *Variety.* March 18, 1936, 17.
"Film Reviews." *Variety.* Wednesday, February 1, 1939, 13.
"Film Reviews," *Variety*, Wednesday, October 9, 1940, 16.
"Final report of January 16, 1942 accident involving NC1946, Docket No. SA-58, File No. 119–42." Adopted July 16, 1942. Accessed July 26, 2016. http://ntl1.specialcollection.net/scripts/ws.dll?file f 8 &name=*S%3A\ DOT_56GB\airplane%20accidents\websearch\011642.pdf.
Fischer, Lucy. "Greta Garbo and Silent Cinema: The Actress as Art Deco Icon." *Camera Obscura* 48, Vol. 16, No. 3 (2001): 82–111.
Fischer, Lucy. "Introduction: Movies of the 1920s." In *American Cinema of the 1920s: Themes and Variations.* Ed. Lucy Fischer, 1–22. New Brunswick: Rutgers University Press, 2009.
Flinn, John C. "Film Showmanship." *Variety.* August 9, 1939, 8.
"Flirting with screwball." *British Film Institute.* April 3, 2014. Accessed June 20, 2016. http://www.bfi.org.uk/news-opinion/bfi-news/flirting-screwball.
"Former Fort Wayne Star Asks $35,000 Damages." *Garrett Clipper.* October 31, 1927, 3.*The Fort Wayne Journal-Gazette*, morning edition. Thursday October 8, 1908, 7.
Fox News. "Charlie Kirk: Taylor Swift should stay away from politics." Filmed October 2018. YouTube video, 3: 19. October 8, 2018. https://www.youtube.com/watch?v=bALPzuQcqHA.
Framke, Caroline. "Who is Taylor Swift voting for? She'll never tell. *Vox.* November 8, 2016, https://www.vox.com/culture/2016/11/8/13565144/who-is-taylor-swift-voting-for-clinton-trump-election.
Francisco, Charles. *Gentleman: The William Powell Story.* London: St. Martin's Press, 1985.
Franklin, Janet. "Which Girl Has the Gable?" *Modern Screen.* July 1948, 52.
"From Vamp to 'Oomph.'" *Photoplay.* August 1939, 32.
Frost, Jennifer. "Dissent and Consent in the 'Good War': Hedda Hopper, Hollywood Gossip, and World War II Isolationism." *Film History* Vol. 22 (2010): 170–181.
Gable, Clark. 1955. Last Will and Testament. Los Angeles, California: http://dearmrgable.com/Will1.jpg.
Gable, Kathleen. *Clark Gable: A Personal Portrait.* New Jersey: Prentice-Hall, 1961.
Gaines, Jane. "War, Women, and Lipstick: Fan Mags in the Forties." *Heresies* Vol. 5, No. 2 (1985): 42–47.
Gaines, William P. "Hollywood Snubs Paris." *Photoplay.* April 1934, 79.
Garceau, Jean. *Dear Mr. G-.* Boston: Little, Brown and Company, 1961.

Gehring, Wes D. *Carole Lombard: The Hoosier Tornado*. Indianapolis: Indiana Historical Society Press, 2003.
Gehring, Wes D. *Romantic vs. Screwball Comedy: Charting the Difference*. Lanham: Scarecrow Press, 2002.
Gehring, Wes D. "Screwball Comedy: An Overview." *Journal of Popular Film and Television* Vol. 13, No. 4 (Winter 1986): 178–185.
Glancy, Mark. "*Picturegoer:*The Fan Magazine and Popular Film Culture in Britain During the Second World War." *Historical Journal of Film, Radio and Television* Vol. 31, No. 4 (December 2011): 453–478.
Gledhill, Christine and Linda Williams. "Prologue: The Reach of Melodrama." In *Melodrama Unbound: Across History, Media, and National Cultures*. Eds. Christine Gledhill and Linda Williams, ix–xxvi. New York: Columbia University Press, 2018.
Glenn, Susan A. *Female Spectacle: The Theatrical Roots of Modern Feminism*. Cambridge: Harvard University Press, 2000.
Glitre, Kathrina. *Hollywood Romantic Comedy: States of the Union, 1934–65*. Manchester: Manchester University Press, 2006.
Goffman, Erving. *The Presentation of Self in Everyday Life*. Edinburgh: University of Edinburgh, 1956.
Goldstein, Patti. "Garbo Walks." *New York Magazine*, December 12, 1977.
"Grape-Crushing Stunt For Lombard-Laughton." *Variety*. Wednesday, October 9, 1940, 8.
Gray, Gary. "The New Mr. and Mrs." *Screenland*. October 1931, 27.
Greene, Jane M. "Manners Before Morals: Sophisticated Comedy and the Production Code, 1930–1934." *Quarterly Review of Film and Video* Vol. 23, No. 3 (2011): 239–256.
Greene, Jane M. "A Proper Dash of Spice: Screwball Comedy and the Production Code." *Journal of Film and Video* Vol. 63, No. 3 (Fall 2011): 45–63.
Grogan, Sarah. *Body Image: Understanding Body Dissatisfaction in Men, Women and Children*. New York: Routledge, 2017.
Grossman, Julie. "Film Noir's 'Femme Fatale' Hard Boiled Women: Moving Beyond Gender Fantasies." *Quarterly Review of Film and Video*. Vol. 24 (2007): 19–30.
"Guilders Vote Cagney's 'Bottom' Best in November." *Variety*. December 11, 1935, 3.
Gundle, Stephen. *Glamour: A History*. Oxford: Oxford University Press, 2008.
Gunning, Tom. "Buster Keaton, or the Work of Comedy in the Age of Mechanical Reproduction." In *Hollywood Comedians, the Film Reader*. Ed. Frank Krutnik, 73–78. London: Routledge, 2003.
Gunning, Tom. "Crazy Machines in the Garden of Forking Paths: Mischief Gags and the Origins of American Film Comedy." In *Classical Hollywood Comedy*. Eds. Kristine Brunovska Karnick and Henry Jenkins, 87–105. New York: Routledge, 1995.
Gunning, Tom. "Mechanisms of Laughter: The Devices of Slapstick." In *Slapstick Comedy*. Eds. Tom Paulus and Rob King, 137–151. New York: Routledge, 2010.
Hall, Gladys. "Lombard – As She Sees Herself." *Motion Picture*. November 1938, 35.
Hall, Mordaunt. "John Barrymore in '20th Century'; Actor Revels in Role of Egomaniac Producer – 'Double Door' – The Murderer and the Governor – A Molnar Novel." *The New York Times*. May 13, 1934, X3.

Hands Across the Table advertisement. *Variety*. October 16, 1935, 72.
Hansen, Miriam. "Pleasure, Ambivalence, Identification: Valentino and Female Spectatorship," *Cinema Journal* Vol. 25, No. 4 (Summer 1986): 6–32.
Hammond, Michael. "Good Fellowship': Carole Lombard and Clark Gable." In *First Comes Love: Power Couples, Celebrity Kinship and Cultural Politics*. Eds. Shelley Cobb and Neil Ewen, 53–72. London: Bloomsbury, 2015.
Haralovich, Mary Beth. "The Proletarian Woman's Film of the 1930s: Contending with Censorship and Entertainment." *Screen* 31:2 (Summer 1990): 172–187.
Harris, Eleanor. "She Knew What She Wanted." *Screen Life*. March 1941, 22–24.
Harris, Warren G. *Clark Gable: A Biography*. New York: Three Rivers Press, 2002.
Harris, Warren G. *Gable and Lombard*. New York: Simon & Schuster, 1974.
Hartley, Katharine. "What's Become of the Good Scout?" *Modern Screen*. August 1938, 26–27; 86.
Harvey, James. *Romantic Comedy in Hollywood: From Lubitsch to Sturges*. New York: Da Capo Press, 1998.
Haskell, Molly. *From Reverence to Rape: The Treatment of Women in the Movies*. Chicago: University of Chicago Press, 1987.
Hastings, Dennison. "Clark Gable's Romantic Plight." *Photoplay*. September 1937, 12–13, 77.
Hill, Donna L. *Rudolph Valentino, the Silent Idol: His Life in Photographs*. Blurb Publishing, 2010.
Hobbs, Gladys. "Carole Is Quitting Films to Sell War Bonds." *The Desert News*. January 13, 1942. 5.
Hobson, Barbara. "Women's Collective Agency, Power Resources and the Framing of Citizenship." In *Extending Citizenship, Reconfiguring States*. Eds. Michael P. Hanagan and Charles Tilly, 149–178. Oxford: Rowman & Littlefield Publishers, Inc., 1999.
Holden, Stephen. "She Wanted To Be Alone, But Not Always." *New York Times*, August 21, 1994.
Hollinger, Karen. *The Actress: Hollywood Acting and the Female Star*. New York: Routledge, 2006.
Home Front Heroes: A Biographical Dictionary of Americans During Wartime. Ed. Benjamin F. Shearer. Westport, CT: Greenwood Press, 2007.
Hook, S.R. "How To Get Your Own Clark Gable." *Movie Mirror*. June 1939, 36.
Horowitz, Susan. *Queens of Comedy: Lucille Ball, Phyllis Diller, Carol Burnett, Joan Rivers and the New Generation of Funny Women*. Amsterdam: OPA, 1997.
Horton, Robert. "The Mysterious Lady." *Film Comment*. Vol. 26, No. 4 (July–August 1990): 30–32.
"How Do You Like These Newcomers?" *Los Angeles Times*. March 25, 1925, C4.
"How Sylvia Changed 'Carole of the Curves' to Svelte Carole Lombard!" *Photoplay*. April 1933, 50–51.
Hoyt, Caroline S. "Can the Gable-Lombard Romance Last?" *Modern Screen*. May 1939, 24–25.
Hoyt, Eric. "Hollywood and the Income Tax, 1929–1955." *Film History* Vol. 22 (2010): 5–21.
Hugo Munsterberg on Film: The Photoplay – a Psychological Study and Other Writings. Ed. Alan Langdale. New York: Routledge, 2002.
"Inside Facts Concerning a Popular Star." *Washington Post*. June 1, 1930, A4.

"Introduction to Screwball Comedies." *Turner Classic Movies*. Accessed June 20, 2016. http://www.tcm.com/this-month/article/770283%7C0/Friday-Night-Spotlight-Screwball-Comedies.html.
Jacobs, Lea. "Industry Self-Regulation and the Problem of Textual Determination." In *Controlling Hollywood: Censorship and Regulation in the Studio Era*. Ed. Matthew Bernstein, 87–101. New Brunswick: Rutgers University Press, 1999.
"January 16, 1942: Transcontinental and Western Air (TWA), Douglas DC-3 (NC1946) Potosi Mountain, NV." *Lost Flights: Historical Aviation Studies and Research*. Accessed May 9, 2015. http://www.lostflights.com/Commercial-Aviation/11642-TWA-TWA-Douglas-DC-3/5007934_mqCvFr.
Jeffers McDonald, Tamar. *Doris Day Confidential: Hollywood, Sex and Stardom*. New York: Palgrave Macmillan, 2013.
Jeffers McDonald, Tamar. "Reviewing Reviewing the Fan Mags." *Film History* Vol. 28, No. 4 (2016): 29–57.
Jeffers McDonald, Tamar. *Romantic Comedy: Boy Meets Girl Meets Genre*. New York: Columbia University Press, 2007.
Jenkins, Henry. "'A High-Class Job of Carpentry': Towards a Typography of Early Sound Comedy." In *Movie Acting, the Film Reader*. Ed. Pamela Robertson Wojcik, 111–126. London: Routledge, 2004.
Jenkins, Henry. *What Made Pistachio Nuts?: Early Sound Comedy and the Vaudeville Aesthetic*. New York: Columbia University Press, 1992.
Jermyn, Deborah. "'Introduction: Get a life, ladies. Your old one is not coming back': ageing, ageism and the lifespan of female celebrity." In *Female Celebrity and Ageing: Back in the Spotlight*. Ed. Deborah Jermyn, 1–14. New York: Routledge, 2014.
Jewel, Richard. "RKO Film Grosses: 1931–1951." *Historical Journal of Film, Radio and Television*. Vol. 14, No. 1 (1994): 56.
Jewell, Richard B. *RKO Pictures: A Titan is Born*. Los Angeles: University of California Press, 2012.
Johnston, Alva. "Public Relations – IV." *New Yorker*. September 9, 1942.
"Kaleidoscope!" *Los Angeles Times*. September 18, 1927, page unknown.
"Keeping the Home Fires Burning." *Talking Screen*. June 1930, 68.
Kelly, Gillian. "Robert Taylor: The 'Lost' Star with the Long Career." In *Lasting Screen Stars: Images that Fade and Personas that Endure*. Eds. Lucy Bolton and Julie Lobalzo Wright, 85–98. London: Palgrave Macmillan, 2016.
Kellow, Brian. *The Bennetts: An Acting Family*. Lexington: The University Press of Kentucky, 2004.
Kendall, Elizabeth. *The Runaway Bride: Hollywood Romantic Comedy of the 1930s*. New York: Cooper Square Press, 1990.
King, Barry. "Articulating Stardom." In *Stardom: Industry of Desire*. Ed. Christine Gledhill, 169–185. London: Routledge, 1991.
King, Barry. "Articulating Stardom." In *Star Texts: Image and Performance in Film and Television*. Ed. Jeremy Butler, 125–154. Detroit: Wayne State University Press, 1991.
King, Barry. "Stardom, Celebrity, and the Money Form." *The Velvet Light Trap* No. 65 (Spring 2010): 7–19.
King, Rob. *The Fun Factory: The Keystone Film Company and the Emergence of Mass Culture*. Los Angeles: University of California Press, 2009.

King, Rob. "'Uproarious Inventions:' The Keystone Film Company, Modernity, and The Art of the Motor." In *Slapstick Comedy*. Eds. Tom Paulus and Rob King, 114–136. New York: Routledge, 2010.

Kingsley, Grace. "Actress Returns to Pathe." *Los Angeles Times*. January 22, 1929, A10.

Kirk, Charlie. "Taylor Swift endorses Bredesen …" October 12, 2018, 8:02 a.m. https://twitter.com/charliekirk11/status/1050763713467297793.

Kish, Frances. "She Calls him 'Pappy,' But She Calls him 'Darling'." *Photoplay*. February 1957, 86.

Klein, Amanda Ann. *American Film Cycles: Reframing Genre, Screening Social Problems, and Defining Subcultures*. Austin: University of Texas Press, 2011.

Klevan, Andrew. *Film Performance: From Achievement to Appreciation*. London: Wallflower Press, 2005.

Koppes, Clayton R. and Gregory D. Black. *Hollywood Goes To War: Patriotism, Movies and the Second World War from 'Ninotchka' to 'Mrs. Miniver.'* Berkeley: University of California Press, 1990.

"Korda not in on 'To Be'." *Variety*. Wednesday, February 11, 1942, 4.

Kotsilibas-Davis, James and Myrna Loy. *Myrna Loy: Being and Becoming*. New York: Knopf, 1987.

Kracauer, Siegfried. *Theory of Film: The Redemption of Physical Reality*. Princeton: Princeton University Press, 1960.

Kugler, Dorothy. "How Carole Lombard Became the Best-Dressed Star." *Movie Classic*. May 1935, 28.

Kuhn, Annette. "Women's Genres." *Screen* 25 (1984): 18–28.

Lahue, Kalton C. *Mack Sennett's Keystone: The Man, the Myth, and the Comedies*. New York: A.S. Barnes, 1971.

Lanckman, Lies. "'What Price Widowhood?': The Faded Stardom of Norma Shearer." In *Lasting Screen Stars: Images that Fade and Personas that Endure*. Eds. Lucy Bolton and Julie Lobalzo Wright, 71–84. London: Palgrave Macmillan, 2016.

Lane, Christina. "A Modern Marriage for the Masses: Carole Lombard, Clark Gable, and the Cultural Front." *Quarterly Review of Film and Video* Vol. 33, No. 5 (January 2016): 401–436.

Lang, Harry. "The Utterly Balmy Home Life of Carole Lombard." *Motion Picture*. February 1937, 36.

Lang Hunt, Julie. "How Carole Lombard plans a party." *Photoplay*. February 1935.

Leaming, Barbara. *Marilyn Monroe*. New York: Three Rivers Press, 1998.

Leff, Mark. *The Limits of Symbolic Reform: The New Deal and Taxation, 1933–1939*. New York: Cambridge University Press, 1984.

Leffner, Timothy Dean. *Mabel Normand: The Life and Career of a Hollywood Madcap*. Jefferson, NC: McFarland & Co., Inc., 2016.

Leider, Emily. *Dark Lover: The Life and Death of Rudolph Valentino*. London: Faber, 2004.

Letter from John Hammell to Joseph L. Breen, September 21, 1936. Motion Picture Association of America. Production Code Administration records, Margaret Herrick Library, Academy of Motion Picture Arts and Sciences.

Lewis, Frederick. "Is Carole Lombard in Love at Last?" *Liberty magazine*. November 14, 1936, 46–47.

Lewis, Judy. *Uncommon Knowledge*. New York: Simon & Schuster, 1994. *Life*, October 17, 1938.
"Lombard-Benny Fine $14 000 in Kansas C." *Variety*. Wednesday March 11, 1942, 10.
"Lombard Laughton Find Good Preem." *Variety*. Wednesday, October 16, 1940, 10.
"Lombard-Stuart Preem Big $9000 in Seattle." *Variety*. Wednesday, February 8, 1939, 10.
Lubitsch, Ernst. "Mr. Lubitsch Takes The Floor For Rebuttal." *New York Times*. Sunday, March 29, 1942, 3.
Lumenick, Lou. "Why did Carole Lombard die?" *New York Post*. January 19, 2014. Accessed May 8, 2015. http://nypost.com/2014/01/19/why-did-carole-lombard-die/.
Madame Sylvia. "Fat? Thin? You Can Be Just Right!" *Modern Screen*. April 1935, 92.
Maddox, Ben. "The Real Down-Low on Lombard." *Photoplay*. January 1937, 16.
Made For Each Other advertisement. *Photoplay*. April 1939, 11.
Mann, May. "A Date with Clark Gable." *Screenland*. May 1937.
Manners, Dorothy. "She Won't Put On An Act!" *Modern Screen*. October 1934.
"The Marital Mixup of Carole and Clark." *Modern Screen*. March 1939, 58–59.
Marshall, P. David. "The Cinematic Apparatus and the Construction of the Film Celebrity." In *The Film Cultures Reader*. Ed. Graeme Turner, 228–239. New York: Routledge, 2002.
Masek, Mark J. *Hollywood Remains to be Seen: A Guide to the Movie Stars' Final Homes*. Nashville: Cumberland House, 2001.
Matthews, Glenna. *"Just A Housewife": The Rise and Fall of Domesticity in America*. New York: Oxford University Press, 1987.
Matzen, Robert. *Carole Lombard: A Bio-bibliography*. Westport: Greenwood Press, 1988.
Matzen, Robert. *Fireball: Carole Lombard and the Mystery of Flight 3*. Pittsburgh: GoodKnight Books, 2014.
Matzen, Robert. "Party Girl." *Thoughts about life in general and old Hollywood in particular*. Date unknown. http://robertmatzen.com/tag/carole-lombard-party-house/.
McBride, Joseph. *Frank Capra: The Catastrophe of Success*. Jackson: The University Press of Mississippi, 1992.
McBride, Joseph. *Hawks on Hawks*. Lexington: The University Press of Kentucky, 2003.
McCarthy, Todd. *Howard Hawks: The Grey Fox of Hollywood*. New York: Grove Press, 1997.
McCracken, Ellen. *Decoding Women's Magazines: From Mademoiselle to Ms.* London: MacMillan Press Ltd., 1993.
McDonald, Paul. *The Star System: Hollywood's Production of Popular Identities*. New York: Wallflower Press, 2000.
McLean, Adrienne. *Being Rita Hayworth: Labor, Identity, and Hollywood Stardom*. New Brunswick, NJ: Rutgers University Press, 2005.
McLean, Adrienne. "The Cinderella Princess and the Instrument of Evil: Surveying the Limits of Female Transgression in Two Postwar Hollywood Scandals." *Cinema Journal* Vol. 34, No. 3 (Spring 1995): 36–56.

McLean, Adrienne. "'New Films in Story Form': Movie Story Magazine and Spectatorship," *Cinema Journal* Vol. 42, No. 3 (Spring 2003): 3–26.

McRobbie, Angela. *The Aftermath of Feminism: Gender, Culture and Social Change*. London: SAGE Publications, 2009.

McRobbie, Angela. "Postfeminism and Popular Culture: Bridget Jones and the New Gender Regime." In *Interrogating Postfeminism: Gender and the Politics of Popular Culture*. Eds. Yvonne Tasker and Diane Negra, 27–39. Durham: Duke University Press, 2007.

Memo from David O. Selznick. Ed. Rudy Behlmer. New York: Random House.

Mercer, John and Martin Shingler. *Melodrama: Genre, Style, Sensibility*. London: Wallflower, 2004.

Milberg, Doris. *The Art of the Screwball Comedy: Madcap Entertainment from the 1930s to Today*. Jefferson: McFarland & Co., Inc., 2013.

Mills, Brett. *Television Sitcom*. London: British Film Institute, 2006.

Mizejewski, Linda. *Pretty/Funny: Women Comedians and Body Politics*. Austin: University of Texas Press, 2014.

Moorhead, Jim. "'Gable, Lombard' A Lie." *The Evening Independent*. March 5, 1976, 28.

Morgan, Michelle. *Carole Lombard: Twentieth-Century Star*. Gloucestershire: The History Press, 2016.

Moser, Laura. *Bette Davis*. London: Haus Publishing, 2004.

Moses, Robert. "Carole Lombard: Hollywood's Leading Hostess." *American Movie Classic*. June 1992, 4–6.

"Movie of the Week: *True Confession*." *Life*. December 13, 1937, 70.

"Movie Reviews: *Love Before Breakfast*." March 14, 1935, K18.

Mulvey, Laura. "Visual Pleasure and Narrative Cinema." *Screen* Vol. 16, No. 3 (1975): 6–18.

Musser, Charles. "Divorce, DeMille and the Comedy of Remarriage." In *Classical Hollywood Comedy*, eds. Kristine Brunkova Karnick and Henry Jenkins, 282–313. New York: Routledge, 1995.

My Lunches With Orson: Conversations between Henry Jaglom and Orson Welles. Ed. Peter Biskind. New York: Metropolitan Books, 2013.

"My Man Godfrey." *Variety*. Wednesday, September 23, 1936, 16.

"'Name Only' Hook-Up With Ohio State Fair." *Variety*. September 6, 1939, 8.

Naremore, James. *Acting in the Cinema*. Los Angeles: University of California Press, 1988.

"National Box Office Survey." *Variety*. Wednesday, February 25, 1942, 11.

Neale, Steve and Frank Krutnik. *Popular Film and Television Comedy*. London: Taylor & Francis, 2002.

Neupert, Richard. *The End: Narration and Closure in the Cinema*. Detroit: Wayne State University Press, 1995.

"N'York Critics Echo Fan Mag Raves!" *Variety*. May 8, 1934, 26.

Newquist, Roy. *Conversations with Joan Crawford*. New York: Citadel Press, 1980.

Neyer, Rob. "The Screwball: Fading Away." In *The Neyer/James Guide to Pitchers: An Historical Compendium of Pitching, Pitchers, and Pitches*. Eds. Rob Neyer and Bill James, 52–55. New York: Simon & Schuster, Inc., 2004.

Nochimson, Martha P. *Screen Couple Chemistry: The Power of 2*. Austin: The University of Texas Press, 2002.

Oettinger, Malcolm H. "Another Three Cheers!" *Picture Play*. December 1930, 34.
Ohmann, Richard. *Selling Culture: Magazines, Markets, and Class at the Turn of the Century*. London: Verso, 1996.
Olsin Lent, Tina. "Romantic Love and Friendship: The Redefinition of Gender Relations in Screwball Comedy." In *Classical Hollywood Comedy*. Eds. Kristine Brunovska Karnick and Henry Jenkins, 314–331. New York: Routledge, 1995.
Orgeron, Marsha. "'You Are Invited to Participate': Interactive Fandom in the Age of the Movie Magazine," *Journal of Film and Video* Vol. 61, No. 3 (Fall 2009): 3–23.
Othman, Frederick C. "Carole Lombard 'Glad to pay' $445,000 taxes, said." *San Jose News*. August 26, 1938, 6.
Ott, Frederick W. *The Films of Carole Lombard*. New York: Citadel Press, 1972.
"'Oz'-Rooney-Garland Pep Up B'way, Standout $65,000, Boyer-Dunne 32G; Jessel Ups 'Andy' 25G, 'Name' 89G 3d." *Variety*. August 23, 1939, 7.
Paterno, Vincent. "Going exotic with the orchid lady." *Carole & Co*. November 15, 2011. Accessed March 29, 2017. http://carole-and-co.livejournal.com/741699.html.
Paterno, Vincent. "January 21, 1942 – a sad farewell …" *Carole & Co*. January 20, 2011. Accessed March 27, 2016. http://carole-and-co.livejournal.com/375145.html.
Paterno, Vincent. "'Motion Picture,' May 1932: They also served for Sennett." *Carole and Co*. May 27, 2013. Accessed October 6, 2015. http://carole-and-co.livejournal.com/604533.html.
Paterno, Vincent. "One more party pic." *Carole and Co*. October 23, 2008. Accessed November 14, 2015. http://carole-and-co.livejournal.com/147855.html.
Paterno, Vincent. "Prepare for a Sennett September." *Carole and Co*. July 15, 2012. Accessed Accessed August 25, 2015. http://carole-and-co.livejournal.com/527662.html.
Paterno, Vincent. "Where Lombard rests and why … " *Carole & Co*. October 30, 2009. Accessed March 29, 2017. http://carole-and-co.livejournal.com/251265.html.
"Philly Grid Mobs No Pix Help; 'Fathers,' Flesh 21G, 'Sacred' 17G." *Variety*. December 1, 1937, 10.
"Picture Grosses." *Variety*. Wednesday, February 15, 1939, 10.
Pokorny, Michael and John Sedgwick. "Stardom and the Profitability of Film Making: Warner Bros. in the 1930s." *Journal of Cultural Economics* 25 (2001): 157–184.
"Pre-X-Mas Drops B'way H.O. Pix Sharply; 'Sacred' $77,000 2nd Wk., 'Zola' 2nd $30,000, 'Damsel' $16,000." *Variety*. December 8, 1937, 7.
Rafferty, Terrence. "Forever Screwball, Forever Fearless." *New York Times*. November 20, 2008, 18.
Ramsaye, Terry. *A Million and One Nights: A History of the Motion Picture Industry*. New York: Simon & Schuster, 1964.
Reagan, Leslie J. "When Abortion Was a Crime: Reproduction and the Economy in the Great Depression." In *Women's America: Refocusing The Past*. Eds. Linda K. Kerber, Jane Sherron De Hart, Wu, 415–456. Oxford: Oxford University Press, 2016.

Real, Evan. "Taylor Swift's Political Post Sparks Voter Registration Surge." *The Hollywood Reporter*. October 9, 2018. https://www.hollywoodreporter.com/news/taylor-swifts-political-instagram-post-sparks-voter-registration-surge-1150521.

Renzi, Thomas C. *Screwball Comedy and Film Noir: Unexpected Connections*. North Carolina: McFarland & Company, Inc., 2012.

"Review: *Mr. & Mrs. Smith*." *Variety*. January 22, 1941, 16.

"Review of *Ned McCobb's Daughter* (Pathé)." *Film Spectator*. November 10, 1928, page unknown.

"Review of *Show Folks* (Pathé)." *Picture Play*. March 1929, page unknown.

"Reviews." *Photoplay*. July 1939, 91.

"Reviews – To Be or Not To Be." *Motion Picture Daily*. Thursday, February 5, 1942, 5.

Rhea, Marian. "Lombard Unlimited." *Radio Mirror*. April 1939, 18.

Riviere, Joan. "Womanliness as Masquerade." In *Formations of Fantasy*. Eds. Victor Burgin, James Donald, Cora Kaplan, 33–58. London: Routledge, 1987.

Robertson Wojcik, Pamela. "Typecasting." *Criticism* Vol. 45, No. 2 (Spring 2003): 223–249.

Robertson Wojcik, Pamela. "Typecasting." In *Movie Acting, the Film Reader*. Ed. Pamela Robertson Wojcik, 169–190. New York: Routledge, 2004.

Robinson, Eugene. "Taylor, Kanye and the bad blood of politics." *The Washington Post*. October 6, 2018. https://www.washingtonpost.com/opinions/taylor-kanye-and-the-bad-blood-of-politics/2018/10/11/2bb03d8a-cd90-11e8-a360-85875bac0b1f_story.html?noredirect=on&utm_term=.3474e22b6464.

Rogers St. Johns, Adela. "Pursuit of the Hollywood He-Man." *Photoplay*, June 1936.

Ross, Sara. "'Good Little Bad Girls': Controversy and the Flapper Comedienne." *Film History* Vol. 13, (2001): 409–423.

Ross, Steven J. *Hollywood Left and Right: How Movie Stars Shaped American Politics*. New York: Oxford University Press, 2011.

Rowan, Terry. *World War II Goes to the Movies & Television Guide*. Raleigh: Lulu, 2012.

Rowe, Kathleen. *The Unruly Woman: Gender and the Genres of Laughter*. Austin: University of Texas Press, 1995.

Russell, Frederick. "The Life Story of Carole Lombard – part one." *Film Pictorial*. June 27, 1936.

Russell, Frederick. "The Life Story of Carole Lombard – part two." *Film Pictoral*. July 4, 1936.

"'Sacred' $19,000, 'Damsel' 12G, Cincy." *Variety*. December 9, 1937, 9.

Sarris, Andrew. "The Sex Comedy Without Sex." *American Film* Vol. 3, No. 5 (March 1978): 8–15.

Sarris, Andrew. *You Ain't Heard Nothin' Yet: The American Talking Film, History & Memory, 1927–1949*. New York: Oxford University Press, 1998.

Schallert, Elza. "The Girl in Clark Gable's Life." *Photoplay*. June 1944, 93.

Schatz, Thomas. *Hollywood Genres: Formulas, Filmmaking, and The Studio System*. New York: McGraw-Hill, 1981.

"The Screen in Review." *Picture Play*. April 1933, 60.

"Screen News." *Screenland*. December 1931, 128.

Seidman, Steve. "Performance, Enunciation, and Self-reference in Hollywood's Comedian Comedy." In *Hollywood Comedians, the Film Reader*. Ed. Frank Krutnik, 21–42. London: Routledge, 2003.
Sennett, Mack and Cameron Shipp. *King of Comedy*. Lincoln: iUniverse.com, Inc., 2000.
Seymore, Hart. "Carole Lombard tells: 'How I Live By A Man's Code.'" *Photoplay*, June 1937.
"The Shadow Stage: A Review of the New Pictures." *Photoplay*. April 1939, 53.
"The Shadow Stage: A Review of the New Pictures." *Photoplay*. October 1939, 64.
"The Shadow Stage: A Review of the New Pictures." *Photoplay*. April 1940, 95.
Sharot, Stephen. "The 'New Woman,' Star Personas, and Cross-class Romance Films in 1920s America." In *Journal of Gender Studies* Vol. 19 (2010): 73–86.
Shingler, Martin. *Star Studies: A Critical Guide*. London: Palgrave Macmillan, 2012.
Shumway, David. "Constructing Romance, Mystifying Marriage." *Cinema Journal* Vol. 30, No. 4 (Summer 1991): 7–23.
Sikov, Ed. *Screwball: Hollywood's Madcap Romantic Comedies*. New York: Crown Publishers, 1989.
Slide, Anthony. *Inside the Hollywood Fan Magazine: A History of Star Makers, Fabricators, and Gossip Mongers*. Jackson: University Press of Mississippi, 2010.
Smits, Ted. "Hollywood Stars Drop Dignity To Romp at Amusement Resort; Carole Lombard Sets Hot Pace." *St. Petersburg Evening Independent*. June 17, 1935, 8.
"Society Girl Goes Into Drama." *Los Angeles Times*. February 4, 1925, A9.
Spensley, Dorothy. "The Last Will and Testament of Carole Lombard …" *Modern Screen*. April 1942.
Spensley, Dorothy. "The Orchid Bids Farewell to the Screen." *Talking Screen*. June 1930.
Spicer, Andrew. *Historical Dictionary of Film Noir*. Lanham: Scarecrow Press, Inc., 2010.
Spicer, Christopher J. *Clark Gable: Biography, Filmography, Bibliography*. Jefferson, NC: McFarland & Co., Inc., 2002.
Spigel, Lynn. *Welcome to the Dreamhouse: Popular Media and Postwar Suburbs*. Durham, NC: Duke University Press, 2001.
"Spring Temp. Cuts Down N.Y. B.O.: 'To Be' Strong $37 000, 'Invaders,' 40G, Fine, A.&C. Ride for $24 000." *Variety*. Wednesday, March 11, 1942, 9.
Squire, Marian. "The Girl's Eye View." *Variety*. December 1, 1937, 6.
Staggs, Sam. *Close-Up on Sunset Boulevard: Billy Wilder, Norma Desmond, and the Dark Hollywood Dream*. New York: St. Martin's Press, 2002.
Street, James. "Two Happy People – Part 1." *Movie and Radio Guide*. May 1940, page unknown.
Stone, Mary. "Mr. Hitchcock Meets The Smiths." *Mr. and Mrs. Smith*. DVD. Directed by Alfred Hitchcock. Burbank Warner Home Video, 2004.
"Strike Over, Weather Better, B'way OK; Dionnes Nice $85,000 1st Week, 'Klondike Annie' 50G, 'Breakfast' 40G." *Variety*. March 18, 1936, 9.
"Suit Over Scar on Girl Settled." *Los Angeles Times*. October 15, 1927, page unknown.

Sunderland, Mitchell. "Can't Shake it Off: How Taylor Swift Became a Nazi Idol." *Broadly*. May 23, 2016. https://broadly.vice.com/en_us/article/ae5x8a/cant-shake-it-off-how-taylor-swift-became-a-nazi-idol.
Swift, Taylor. "I'm writing this post …" Instagram post. October 8, 2018. https://www.instagram.com/p/BopoXpYnCes/?hl=en&taken-by=taylorswift.
Swindell, Larry. *Screwball: The Life of Carole Lombard*. New York: William Morrow & Company, Inc., 1975.
Symmons, Tom. *The New Hollywood Historical Film: 1967–78*. London: Palgrave Macmillan, 2016.
The Talkies. Ed. Richard Griffith. New York: Dover, 1971.
Thomson, David. *Showman: The Life of David O. Selznick*. London: Abacus, 1993.
"Time For Comedy." *Variety*. Wednesday, November 6, 1940, 3.
"To Be or Not To Be (1942)." TCM. Accessed September 1, 2015. http://www.tcm.com/tcmdb/title/93439/To-Be-or-Not-to-Be/articles.html.
"To Be or Not To Be advertisement." *Variety*. Wednesday, March 11, 1942, 26.
"'To Be or Not To Be' Release on March 6." *Motion Picture Daily*. Wednesday, February 4, 1942, 1.
Tornabene, Lyn. *Long Live the King: A Biography of Clark Gable*. New York: Pocket Books, 1976.
Townsend, Leo. "Good News," *Modern Screen*. March 1936, 12–13.
Tremper, Ellen. *I'm No Angel: The Blonde in Fiction and Film*. Charlottesville: University of Virginia Press, 2006.
Truffaut, François. *Hitchcock*, revised edition. New York: Simon & Schuster, 1985.
Turner, Lana. *Lana – the Lady, the Legend, the Truth*. Boston: Dutton, 1982.
"UA Delays Release of Lombard Picture." *Motion Picture Daily*. Tuesday, January 27, 1942, 4.
Unknown. *Carole Lombard's Life Story*. 1942.
Unknown. "Good News," *Modern Screen*. August 1939.
Unknown. "How Will the Gable-Lombard Romance End?" *Hollywood magazine*. June 1937.
Unknown. "These Are Not Poison at the Box Office." *Look*. July 5, 1938.
"United Artists advertisement." *Variety*. December 1, 1937, 32–33.
"Vacation Trip Prize In 'Name Only' Contest." *Variety*. August 28, 1939, 8.
"Valentino Loses Battle With Death: Greatest of Screen Lovers Fought Valiantly For Life." *Plattsburgh Sentinel*, August 24, 1926.
Variety. July 15, 1925, 35.
Vermilion, Billy Budd. "The Remarriage plot in the 1910s." *Film History*, Vol. 13 (2001): 359–371.
Vernon L. Clark to Clark Gable. Correspondence. June 18, 1946.
Vigil In the Night advertisement. *Variety*. Wednesday, February 5, 1940, 12–13.
Vigil In the Night advertisement. *Photoplay*. March 1940, 1.
"Vigil In The Night." *Variety*. Wednesday, February 7, 1940, 14.
'Villa' Balto's Big One at $19,500; '20th' 15G, Mild." *Variety*. May 8, 1934, 9.
Wade, Jack. "Is Gable's Love Life Jinxed?" *Modern Screen*. February 1952, 40–41; 64; 66.
Walker, Brent E. *Mack Sennett's Fun Factory: A History and Filmography of His Studio and His Keystone and Mack Sennett Comedies, with Biographies of Players and Personnel*. Jefferson: McFarland and Co., 2010.

Walker, Nancy A. *A Very Serious Thing: Women's Humor and American Culture*. Minneapolis: University of Minnesota Press, 1988.
Ware, Susan. *Beyond Suffrage: Women in the New Deal*. Boston: Harvard University Press, 1981.
Ware, Susan. *Holding Their Own: American Women in the 1930s*. Michigan: Twayne Publishers, 1984.
Waterbury, Ruth. "How Clark Gable is Conquering Loneliness." *Photoplay*. August 1942, 34.
Waterbury, Ruth. "Our Home, Our Work – And Children." *Movie Mirror*. November 1939, 45.
Waterbury, Ruth. "What the Loss of Carole Lombard means to Clark Gable." *Photoplay*. April 1942, 30.
Weaver, William R. "The Money-Making Stars of a Quarter of a Century." *Motion Picture Herald*. September 28 1940, 123–124.
White, Pamela. *Uninvited: Classical Hollywood Cinema and Lesbian Representability*. Bloomington: Indiana University Press, 1999.
Whiteley Fletcher, Adele. "A Heart to Heart Letter to Carole Lombard and Clark Gable." *Screen Guide*. November 1936, 5.
"The Wife Clark Gable Forgot." *Confidential*, July 1955.
"'Wife' 25G, Quins $20,000, Give Lent Trimmin' in Cleve." *Variety*. March 11, 1936, 11.
Wilk, Ralph. "A Little from Lots." *The Film Daily*. August 13, 1934, 8.
"William Powell is a Man of Many Vivid Contrasts." *Washington Post*. February 15, 1931, A4.
Williams, Linda. "Melodrama Revisited." In *Refiguring American Film Genres: History and Theory*. Ed. Nick Browne, 42–88. Berkeley: University of California Press, 1998.
Wilson, Elizabeth. "It Looked Good for a Laugh at the Time." *Silver Screen*. January 1941, page unknown.
Wilson, Victoria. *A Life of Barbara Stanwyck: Steel-True, 1907–1940*. New York: Simon & Schuster, 2013.
Within Our Gates: Ethnicity in American Feature Films, 1911–1960. Ed. Alan Gevinson. Los Angeles: University of California Press, 1997.
"Wives – Carole Lombard." *Dear Mr. Gable*. Accessed July 11, 2015. http://dearmrgable.com/?page_id=3216.
Wood, Robin. *Howard Hawks*, new edition. Detroit: Wayne State University Press, 2006.
Worth, Don. "Will Carole Lombard's Marriage End Her Career?" *Motion Picture Magazine*. July 1939.
York, Cal. "30 Girls in a Race for Stardom." *Photoplay*. April 1932, 75.
Young, Kay. *Ordinary Pleasures: Couples, Conversation, and Comedy*. Columbus: The Ohio State University Press, 2001.
Zeitz, Joshua. *Flapper: A Madcap Story of Sex, Style, Celebrity and the Women Who Made America Modern*. New York: Three Rivers Press, 2006.
Zemon Davis, Natalie. *Society and Culture in Early Modern France: Eight Essays*. Stanford: Stanford University Press, 1975.
"'Zieggy' $23,000, 'Swing Time' $17,500, 'Godfrey' $18,000, St. Louis' Big Week." *Variety*. September 9, 1936, 8.

INDEX

Activism 12, 177–8, 188–9, 194–5, 207
Advertisements
    movie poster 24, 27, 95–6, 115
    promotional material 17, 100–3, 115, 137, 140, 145–6, 181–4
    publicity photo 8, 18, 19, 65, 104, 146
Affron, Charles 161–2
Athleticism
    The Campus Vamp (1928) 34–6
    childhood- 15, 61
    The Princess Comes Across (1936) 90–2
    Run, Girl, Run (1928) 28, 30–1
    star persona 10, 14, 21, 23, 64, 106, 134
    The Swim Princess (1928) 41–3, 48
    See also female body

Bakhtin, Mikhail 80, 86, 92
Ball, Lucille 184, 206
Barrymore, John 79, 80, 85–6, 88, 96, 202–3
Bathing Beauties 9, 17, 20, 21, 25–6, 27, 36, 45, 46
    See also Sennett Girl Comedies
Beauty
    glamour girl 50–1, 59–60, 63–4
    juxtaposed with physical comedy 10, 26, 73, 89, 91–2, 94–6
    star image 19, 59–60, 63–4
    See also female body; femininity
Bennett, Constance 55, 66–7, 179,
Body politics 6, 10, 38, 74, 90–2, 94–6
    See also female body; femininity
Bogdanovich, Peter 15, 202
Box office 6, 50, 55, 62, 78, 96, 97, 105, 116, 132–3, 147, 151, 161, 165–6, 171, 174, 180, 199

Breen, Joseph 108, 111, 138
Bringing Up Baby (1938) 10–11, 77, 202–3
Busch, Noel F. 1–4, 20, 53–4

The Campus Carmen (1928) 14, 37–9, 43
The Campus Vamp (1928) 14, 32–7, 43, 44, 45–6
Car accident 18–19, 27, 53, 91
Carman, Emily 6, 13, 50, 179, 200
"Carole of the Curves" 19, 60–2
Cavell, Stanley 10, 71, 156, 200, 203
Celebrity 8, 136, 147–8
Chaplin, Charlie 15–16, 26, 178, 190
The Circle (1939) 3, 185–8
Clayton, Alex 10, 26, 38, 43, 111, 131–2
Close-up shot 19, 24, 37, 41, 45, 47, 63, 82, 89, 98–100, 109, 113, 123–4, 156, 157–8, 162–3, 165, 168, 169, 172–3, 174, 204
Colman, Ronald 56–7, 185, 186
Columbo, Russ 66
Consumerism 8, 25–6, 34, 36, 48, 51, 64, 77, 184
Crowther, Bosley 112–14, 133

Domesticity
    in film 118–19
    marriage 11, 126, 148
    star couple 134, 136, 150–1, 183, 198
Dwan, Allan 15, 73
Dyer, Richard
    ordinary/extraordinary paradox 61, 103, 183
    stardom 104, 129, 174
    whiteness 94

Eilers, Sally 33, 44

Fan magazine
  methodology 7–9, 11
  Photoplay 7, 8, 30–31, 61–2, 66–7, 68, 88, 115
  relationship with Clark Gable 137, 138, 140, 141–2, 143, 148, 204
  Screenland 7, 15, 57, 64, 132
  star persona 15, 50, 56–7, 60, 64, 66, 68, 102–3, 104, 149, 182–3, 199
  Fashion
  Bathing Beauties 25, 36
  star persona 50, 60, 62–3, 64–5, 68, 184
Female body
  appearance 19, 25, 60–2, 90–2, 106, 116,
  conventions 38–9
  gaze 23
  performance 31, 73–4, 94–5, 106–12, 119, 121
  See also athleticism; beauty; body politics; female comedy
Female comedy 10–11, 26, 28, 38, 51, 73–4, 76, 90–2, 94–5, 106–16
Feminism
  second-wave 12, 177–9, 193, 206
  See also proto-feminism
Femininity
  ideology 9, 11, 12, 38, 65, 94, 177, 179, 181–4
  performance 12, 25, 30–2, 39–40, 48, 90–2, 95, 106–16, 117, 127–9, 132
  star image 2–3, 26, 48, 90, 95, 112–14, 152–3, 177, 179, 181–4, 188, 206
  See also beauty; body politics
Field, Madalynne 28, 37, 194
Film noir 200–1
Film reviews
  In Name Only 165–7
  Love Before Breakfast 96
  Made for Each Other 161
  My Man Godfrey 105
  Nothing Sacred 116

They Knew What They Wanted 173–4
To Be or Not to Be 132–4
Twentieth Century 78–9, 88
Vigil in the Night 171
Flapper 31–2, 61, 76-7
Francis, Kay 50, 59, 62–3, 162, 166
Freelance labor 10, 11, 106, 179–81, 197

Gable, Clark
  affair 57, 104, 136, 137–9, 140, 142, 143, 144
  Gone With the Wind (1939) 140, 153
  John Clark Gable 205
  Josephine Dillon 142, 144
  Judy Lewis 138
  Kathleen Gable 204–5
  "The King of Hollywood" 137, 147
  Rhea Gable 104, 138, 139, 142–3, 144
  star persona 11, 139, 140–1, 143, 146, 147–8, 153
  Sylvia Ashley 204
  World War II 190, 194, 204–5
  See also marriage; *No Man of Her Own* (1932); plane crash; star couple
Gable and Lombard (1976) 4, 135
Gags 42, 51, 95, 137
Garceau, Jean 145, 150
Gaze
  female gaze 32, 37, 43, 45, 46, 95, 131, 158
  male gaze 23, 36, 43, 45, 46, 47, 130
  See also Laura Mulvey
Gehring, Wes 4, 16, 20, 34, 59, 71, 165, 166, 171
Gender
  ideology 12, 32, 38, 79, 86, 90, 94, 107, 112–16, 135, 148–50, 152, 153, 179, 181–8
  star persona 11, 12, 73, 115, 148–50, 178, 179, 181–8, 194
  transgression 3, 26, 31, 36, 37, 38–9, 40, 76, 80, 90, 92, 112–16, 178, 181–8

See also body politics; independent stardom

Genre
  conventions and ideology 51–4, 111, 119, 120, 181
  star persona 5–6, 9, 10, 34, 49, 50–1, 72, 73, 148, 157, 166, 174–5, 181, 197, 198–9, 200–4
  See also film noir; melodrama; screwball comedy; slapstick comedy

The Girl From Everywhere (1927) 14, 23–7, 32, 39

Glamour
  marriage with William Powell 58, 59–60
  star persona 5, 12, 43, 50–1, 54, 59–60, 61–9, 91, 95, 103–4, 177, 199, 206
  See also fashion

Glitre, Kathrina 72, 120, 201
Grant, Cary 77, 90, 162, 185–7, 203
The Great Depression 2, 52, 59, 75, 97, 139, 188–9
Gunning, Tom 20, 42

Hawks, Howard 2, 10, 17, 34, 50, 73, 77, 78, 79, 80, 82, 201–4
Hepburn, Katharine 10, 11, 71, 77, 151, 203
Hitchcock, Alfred 72, 73, 90, 118, 119, 122, 126, 127, 174, 201–4
Hollywood
  ideology 11, 57, 94, 107, 150, 177–8, 179, 188–9, 194–5
  labor 179–180, 183, 194–5
  publicity 7–9, 10, 54, 56, 62, 64, 66, 74, 103, 138, 178, 184, 188–9
  studios' relationship with Production Code Administration 7, 76, 119–20, 126
  studio system 2, 7–9, 25, 64, 119–20, 125, 179, 206
  stars/stardom 3, 4, 5, 6, 7–9, 12, 13–15, 20, 25, 49–50, 54, 56–7, 59–60, 64, 66, 68, 80, 129, 141–2, 147–8, 174, 175, 188–9, 198–9

technology 77
  See also star couple; World War II
Hopkins, Miriam 55, 56, 67, 112, 114, 127, 179

Impersonation 89, 109, 172
In Name Only (1939) 156, 162–7, 173
Independent stardom
  gender 6, 9, 12, 136, 149–51, 179, 180–5, 194, 206
  legacy 206–7
  star couple 57, 136, 149–51, 204
  star persona 3, 6, 9, 11, 12, 50, 57, 91, 94, 136, 145, 149–51, 179, 180–5, 194, 204, 206
  See also Carman, Emily
Indiana 14, 61, 65, 116, 178, 189–90, 192–3

Jeffers McDonald, Tamar 71, 76, 200
Jenkins, Henry 90, 109, 111, 113

Keaton, Buster 26, 42
Keystone Film Company *see* Sennett, Mack
King, Barry 5, 89
King, Rob 25, 31, 36
Klevan, Andrew 156–7, 162

Labor 9, 11,12, 42, 179–80, 183, 189, 194–95, 200
La Cava, Gregory 2, 34, 54, 73, 75, 97, 98
Lang, Walter 50, 60, 68, 73, 88, 93
Legacy
  comedy 5–6, 71–2, 73, 134, 200–4, 205–7
  Lucy Bolton and Julie Lobalzo Wright *Lasting Screen Stars* 199–200
  performative labor 206–7
  See also posthumous stardom
Life magazine 1, 20, 34, 54, 104, 193
Love Before Breakfast (1936) 68, 73, 88–96, 106, 109, 115, 157
Loy, Myrna 53, 112, 114, 147, 152
Lubitsch, Ernst 59, 73, 127, 128, 133–4, 201

INDEX

March, Fredric 63, 106, 107, 109
Masculinity
  female comedy 113
  screwball comedy 76
  star persona 10, 14, 15, 31, 39–40, 115, 134, 179, 184
  See also Gable, Clark; physical comedy; Pollard, Daphne
Marriage
  domesticity 134, 144–6, 150
  ideology 136, 144, 148–50
  to Clark Gable 2–3, 11, 58, 68, 104, 118, 126, 134, 144, 149, 150, 155, 167, 198, 200, 204–5
  to William Powell 2, 3, 4, 56–9, 64–5, 67, 68, 98, 144
  See also star couple
Matchmaking Mamma (1929) 14, 44–7
Matzen, Robert 4, 6, 18, 19, 55, 60, 66, 103, 192
Mayer, Louis B. 192, 194
McDonald, Paul 5
Melodrama
  conventions 157–8, 162–3, 168–9, 174
  star persona 10, 49, 118, 126, 155–6, 166, 198, 206
  See also genre; performance
Methodology
  single-star 5, 6
  textual analysis 6, 14, 20–1, 47, 73–4, 156
Metro-Goldwyn Mayer (MGM) 96, 139, 140, 143, 148, 151, 166, 185, 190, 191
MGM *see* Metro-Goldwyn Mayer
Modernity
  automatism 34, 42–3
  gender 25, 32, 36, 77, 115
  stardom 58, 66, 115, 142, 144, 179, 181
  technology 31, 48
Mr. and Mrs. Smith (1941) 72, 73, 118–27, 174, 179, 183, 201, 203–4
Mulvey, Laura 23
  See also gaze
Munsterberg, Hugo 162

My Man Godfrey (1936) 2, 34, 68, 71, 72, 73, 75, 97–105, 107, 109, 157, 158, 181, 198

Naremore, James 84–5, 90, 124
New Deal 2, 12, 177, 188
  See also The Great Depression; Roosevelt, Franklin Delano
New York Times 72, 96, 105, 112, 133, 165
Nochimson, Martha 148, 151–2
No Man of Her Own (1932) 137, 138, 151
Nothing Sacred (1937) 2, 73, 105–17, 167, 181

Olsin Lent, Tina 76, 201
Orchid Lady 10, 59–60, 62, 172

Paramount Pictures 10, 49, 50, 51, 55–56, 58, 59, 60, 62, 63, 64, 67, 68–9, 80, 96, 102, 105, 137, 138, 198
Party girl 66–7, 80, 91, 103, 137, 141, 145, 147, 149, 199, 206
Pathé 16, 19, 48, 49, 51, 54, 55
Patriarchy 3, 38–9, 43, 86, 92, 147, 149–50, 152, 178, 185, 195
Patriotism 178, 189, 190, 193–5, 198, 204, 206
  See also war bonds; World War II
PCA *see* Production Code Administration
Performance
  body 26, 28, 31, 34, 37–40, 41–3, 48, 82, 83–6, 91–2, 93, 100, 101, 107–11, 121, 123–5, 128–32, 156, 163, 164, 173
  crying 99–100, 168–9
  eyes 99–100, 123, 168–9, 172–3
  face 89–91, 95–6, 156, 157–8, 163, 164, 169, 173
  gesture 26, 46, 86, 90, 120, 124, 131–2, 156, 157
  glamour 62–4
  methodology 1, 5, 6, 11, 21, 71–4
  voice 83–6, 97–98, 100, 101, 124–5, 131, 156, 157–8, 164

vocal pitch/tonality 98, 124–5, 158, 168, 172
See also gender; physical comedy
Personification 89–90
Peters, Elizabeth (Bess) 15, 16–17, 18, 140, 190, 191
Peters, Jane Alice 1, 5, 14, 56
Physical comedy
  abuse/violence 81, 83, 85–86, 89–90, 91, 95–6, 106–12, 115,
  female body 10–11, 25–7, 32, 42–3, 48, 81, 85–6, 90, 106–11, 112–15
  femininity 10–11, 15, 25–7, 38–40, 48, 72, 90, 106, 188–9
  gender 15, 38–40, 48, 72–4, 90, 92–4, 106–7, 112–15, 179, 181
  slapstick comedy 14, 19, 25–7, 28, 34, 38, 50–4
  screwball comedy 2, 10–11, 50–4, 72–8, 106, 118, 129, 134, 163, 174, 179, 181, 197, 199
  star persona 10–11, 15, 32, 38, 42–3, 48, 49, 50–4, 72, 95, 105, 106–7, 115–16, 127, 134, 145, 156, 171, 179, 181, 188–9, 197
Plane crash 178, 191–3
Pollard, Daphne 23–4, 26, 28, 30, 32, 33, 37, 38, 39–40, 44
Posthumous stardom 10, 71, 134, 149, 178, 193–4, 199
Powell, William
  film roles 56, 97, 98, 99, 114
  marriage 2, 3, 4, 56–8, 64, 65, 67, 68, 98, 144
  star persona 54, 56–7, 58–9
Production Code Administration (PCA)
  censorship 52, 76, 108, 111–12, 119, 126
  fan magazines 7
  innuendo 120, 121, 126
  morality 52, 76, 111–12, 119–21, 125, 126, 138
  physical comedy 52, 76, 108, 111–12
  screwball comedy 52, 76, 78, 119–20, 126
Proto-feminism 177–179, 184, 185, 187, 206

See also Progressive
Progressive
  feminist politics 2–3, 6, 11, 12, 106, 178–9, 184, 195
  taxes 188–9
  See also New Deal
Publicity
  publicity materials 17, 18, 19, 48, 49, 65, 95, 100, 102, 104, 105, 106, 115, 137, 148, 152, 181–4, 199
  studio publicity departments 5, 7, 9, 10, 11, 27, 36, 49, 54, 55–6, 68, 100, 103, 116, 140–2, 143, 144–5, 147, 165, 171, 174, 181, 192, 199
  See also fan magazine

Roosevelt, Franklin Delano 2, 12, 177, 188, 190, 193, 195
  See also New Deal
RKO Pictures (RKO) 118, 162, 165, 171, 174, 180
Run, Girl, Run (1928) 14, 28–32, 33, 34, 36, 37, 43, 48

Screwball comedy
  canon 6, 10–11, 71, 97
  genre conventions 2, 52, 74–8, 119–20
  origins 52, 53–4, 74–8
  "Queen of Screwball Comedy" 34, 71, 136, 145, 166, 206
  "Screwball Girl" 1, 12, 207
  screwball heroine 79, 80, 86, 111–13, 197
  star persona 1, 2, 4, 5–6, 9, 10, 12, 13, 20, 49, 50, 53, 71–4, 88, 96, 97, 103–4, 105, 118, 134, 140, 141, 145, 148, 154, 155, 156, 161, 171, 174, 178, 181, 197, 198, 199, 200–4, 206
  transgressive 73–74, 90, 106–16, 134, 178, 181, 187
  See also physical comedy
Sennett Girl Comedies 19, 20, 24, 28, 33, 37, 44, 45, 47
  See also Bathing Beauties; Sennett, Mack

Sennett, Mack 9, 10, 17, 20, 21, 22, 25, 26, 27, 36, 42, 46, 49, 51, 52
Selznick, David. O 105–6, 111, 167
Selznick International Pictures 116, 156, 161, 180
Sex
 innuendo 40, 52, 75–6, 77, 101, 107–8, 109, 111, 120, 121, 125, 126, 204
 sex appeal and pleasure 14, 23, 26, 31, 32, 33, 37, 39, 59, 90, 96, 106, 112, 115, 118–19, 128, 129–30, 131, 144, 152–3
Shearer, Norma 185
Silent era/film 6, 10, 13, 14, 15, 20–1, 40, 42, 45, 47, 52, 59, 77–8, 79, 207
 See also slapstick comedy
Slapstick comedy 5, 9–10, 13, 17, 20, 21, 22, 25, 26, 27, 28, 30, 32, 33, 34, 38, 39, 43, 47–8, 49–51, 52–4, 56, 73, 75–6, 79, 90–1, 174, 197–8
Smith's Pony (1927) 14, 19, 21–3, 26, 27, 43
Spectacle
 female comedy 25, 34, 43, 48, 111, 114
 physical comedy 31, 43
 technology 31, 45, 46
 See also gaze
Stanwyck, Barbara 59, 111, 112, 114, 124
Star couple
 with Clark Gable 2, 118, 134, 135–6, 137, 139, 140, 142, 144–6, 147–8, 150–1, 152–4
 "Mrs. Clark Gable" 149–50, 151, 153, 154
 with William Powell 2, 56–9, 68
 See also domesticity; marriage; Nochimson, Martha
Stardom
 economics 134, 148, 179–183, 189, 195

symbiosis 5, 68, 91, 128, 174, 200
 See also impersonation; labor; legacy; personification
Star persona
 American 2, 61–2, 92–4, 136, 147–8, 149, 182–3, 206
 construction and representation 2, 4, 58, 139–40, 142, 144, 147–8, 175, 179, 206
 See also beauty; gender; legacy
The Swim Princess (1928) 14, 40–3, 48
Swindell, Larry 4, 16, 18, 20, 27, 41, 54, 59–60, 63, 81, 192

Taxes 187, 188–9
 See also Progressive
Technicolor 24, 25, 33, 36, 44, 45, 46, 106
Transgressions
 gender 31, 37, 39, 92, 94–5, 114, 185, 187–8
 See also screwball comedy
Twentieth Century (1934) 2, 17, 34, 49, 51, 68, 73, 78–88, 89, 91, 96, 109, 157, 158, 198, 201–3

Unruly 21, 113–14

Variety 17, 72, 78, 88, 96, 116, 118, 133, 161, 165, 171, 174, 186

War bonds
 Indiana tour 178, 190, 192–5
 World War I 190
Williams, Linda 155, 157, 158
Winkler, Otto 190–1
Womanhood 31, 65, 94, 149, 206
Wood, Robin 201
World War II (1939–1945)
 Hollywood's war effort 127, 189–90
 Office of War Information (OWI) 127, 195
 Pearl Harbor 127, 178

Young, Loretta 138